CONSTITUTI
ADMINISTRAT

Private Law Tutor Publishing

Foreword

Thank you for buying this book. The problem that I encountered when studying law is: knowing everything. There is so much to read and so little time to do it. If you skip some material, or a case you are none the wiser. So throughout my years teaching law I have devised a system and I am going to share this with you.

You may have encountered different methods or formulas to help when advising a client in a mock scenario. One of example is the *IRAC* method or another is *Celo*. These are well documented and you can read about these. I never used them, because I had a method in my head that worked. It was not until I started teaching that I spoke about it. I call my method the **"Fact Law Sandwich"**. Let me explain. If you are asked to advise a party as to their legal rights this is how you present it:

FACTS
GENERAL PRINCIPLE
LAW
APPLY TO FACTS

In **Fact**: simply state what you have been told, this why you can never be accused of not considering the facts. In **General principle**: you simply state what the general rule of the relevant issue is. You express it as if you are speaking to a child who has no knowledge of law. In **Law**: you state "using the authority of.....and you go on to state which statute or case helps prove your point. Lastly in **Apply to Facts**: you apply the reasoning of the case to your factual scenario. Your advice will sound and look structured and professional. The reason it is called the "Fact Law Sandwich", is because the advice contains two outer layers of facts that sandwich the principle and law in the middle.

This book is written to provide the student with a good knowledge of the most important cases on their study. It is written in a way to facilitate the Fact Law Sandwich method. I provide the general principle, the name of the case with full citation, the facts, the Ratio (the thing the lecturers say you always need to use), and application i.e. how the case should be applied. No other book provides this information at your fingertips. I hope you enjoy using it.

CONSTITUTIONAL LAW

Private Law Tutor Publishing

Welcome/Introduction/Overview

This book provides you with basic information as a basis for you to form your own critical opinions on this area of law. Once you have mastered the basics, you will be inspired to question Constitutional framework principles in your essays and apply them in mock client advisory scenarios. Again, for your convenience, we have published a book that specifically provides you with examples of how to answer such questions and how to apply your knowledge as effectively as possible to help you get the best possible marks.

This aid is a fully-fledged source of basic information, which tries to give the student comprehensive understanding for this module. However, it is recommended that you compliment it with the further reading suggestions provided at the end of each topic, as well as read the cases themselves for more in-depth information. This book provides an analysis of the basic principles of modern Constitutional law. The following is a summary of the Book content:

- An introduction to the Law of the Con & Add;
- The legal relationships between the organs of state;
- What are the sources of the Constitutional framework of the UK;
- Law making;

The aim of this Book is to:

- Provide an introduction to anyone studying or interested in studying Law to the key principles and concepts that exist in the UK Con & Add.
- To provide a framework to consider the UK Constitutional and its law within the context of examinations.
- Provide a detailed learning resource in order for legal written examination skills to be developed.
- Facilitate the development of written and critical thinking skills.
- Promote the practice of problem solving skills.

- To establish a platform for students to gain a solid understanding of the basic principles and concepts of Constitutional Law, this can then be expanded upon through confident independent learning.

Through this Book, students will be able to demonstrate the ability to:
- Demonstrate an awareness of the core principles of Con & Add.
- Critically assess challenging mock factual scenarios and be able to pick out legal issues in the various areas of Con & Add.
- Apply their knowledge when writing a formal assessment.
- Present a reasoned argument and make a judgment on competing viewpoints.
- Make use of technical legalistic vocabulary in the appropriate manner.
- Be responsible for their learning process and work in an adaptable and flexible way.

Studying Constitutional & Administrative law

Constitutional Law is one of the seven core subjects that the Law Society and the Bar Council deem essential in a qualifying law degree. Therefore, it is vital that a student successfully pass this subject to become a lawyer. Additionally, a knowledge and understanding of Constitutional Law is needed in order to study other law subjects such as Politics, Administrative law, Immigration Law and international Law. The primary method by which your understanding of the law of Constitutional Law will develop is by understanding how to solve problem questions. You will also be given essay questions in your examinations. The methods by which these types of question should be approached are somewhat different.

Tackling Problems and Essay Questions

There are various ways of approaching problem and essay questions. We have provided students with an in-depth analysis with suggested questions and answers at the end of each chapter.

Chapter 1 - Introduction to Constitutional Law

Introduction

Law is generally divided into two different segments: public law and private law. While public law regulates relationships between the state and private individuals, private law generally regulates legal relationships between private persons. Public law is comprised of constitutional law which regulates the functioning of the state and administrative law which governs the relationships between the state and private individuals.

The distinction between private and public law

As stated above, private law is *in fine* a branch of the law that is concerned with the relationship that individuals have with one another. It should be noted that the notion of private persons encompasses both individuals and legal persons that are private entities (companies, associations etc.).

Private law will apply, for example, when an individual agrees to purchase a car and forms a legally binding contract with another person. Private law also regulates defamatory cases where for example, an individual sues a neighbour for making slanderous accusations about his past.

It is also worth noting that private persons can have legal relations of private law transactions with public persons (in this context and for the present purposes, the term public persons refers to the state in general including the government, local authorities etc.). For example; a private legal person, such as a company, can have private legal transactions with local authorities for the purposes of providing public services. Similarly, an individual may sue a public person in the law of negligence for having acted carelessly and caused harm.

However, these legal relationships, given that they involve the state, will generally imply a public law dimension. Accordingly, special rules will be applied to the state in order to not treat as an ordinary private individual defendant. In this connection, it is important to note that the line between public and private law may sometime be difficult to draw given that there is no absolute distinction. In this regard, Lord Wilberforce in **Davy v Spelthorne Borough Council** (1984) 1ac 262, commented: "the expressions "private law" and "public law" are convenient expressions for descriptive purposes. In this country they must be used with caution."

Public law subsumes constitutional and administrative law. It is the branch of law that focuses on the power of the state as well as its structure and organization. It deals with the location of state powers, how they are exercised and controlled and how it could impact on individuals. One of the questions raised by public law is to determine how the institutions relate between them and in relation to individuals.

At this stage, it is important to note that criminal law, although it has a public law dimension, has historically been taught separately. Indeed, the public law dimension comes from the fact that the society as a whole also suffers from an offense. Hence, public authorities are entitled to punish authors of criminal acts. Therefore, it is not wrong to say that the broad term of public law embraces criminal law, although it is usually taught in a different module.

The distinction between constitutional and administrative law

Although constitutional and administrative law form part of the generic term of public law, a distinction between them should be drawn. Constitutional law relates to the rules enshrined by a constitution. A precise definition of the term constitution will be given in the following chapters. However, for the present purposes, a constitution is a set of fundamental rules regulating the powers of the state and determining the relations between its institutions and individuals.

Constitutional law concerns various aspects of the structure and organization of the state such as the recognition of the principal institutions of the state (parliament, government and the courts) but it also confers their to these institutions specific roles and functions, determines their nature and the extent of their powers.
In addition to this, constitutional law sets procedures and mechanisms to oversee, regulate and check the powers conferred to the different institutions. This is usually done by the way the constitution organizes the way of how the main institutions relate to one another.

The constitution generally enshrines the fundamental rights of the individual of the state and how these rights can be judicially protected from infringements of the state.

In contrast with constitutional law, administrative law is generally concerned with the law relating to the administration/government. The government and its administration are invested with extensive prerogatives to provide services such as education and to adopt regulations to implement its political program. Administrative law therefore ensures that the administration is strictly acting within the limits of its mandate.

This branch of the law deals with different control mechanisms that can be judicial (for example the judicial review) or political (for example parliamentary control with ombudsman). Although a clear-cut distinction between administrative and constitutional law is impossible to draw, it should be noted that where constitutional law concerns the main structure and organisation of the state, administrative law relates rather to the concrete exercise of the governmental powers. For the purposes of clarity of the analysis, constitutional law and administrative law will be studied separately in the next chapters.

Recent developments in constitutional and administrative law

The general election victory by the conservative party, led by Margaret Thatcher in 1979 was a contextual starting point for many of the recent developments of the UK constitutional and administrative law. Margaret thatcher used the methodology of 'new public management' (NPM), an approach which rejected traditional bureaucratic methods and structures in favour of market-based and business-like regimes of public service.

Since then, the different administrations have been driven by the perceived need for greater efficiency and accountability of public action. For years the division between the public and private sectors in the UK had been clear-cut. Traditionally, the national provision of communications, power and utilities, the health service, and public transport were provided by public bodies, namely local authorities steered by government departments. However, the quest for greater efficiency brought dramatic changes in the nature and the structure of the state. This phenomenon, called privatisation of the public sphere, took two forms.

The first evolution de-nationalised many of the above-mentioned public prerogatives and encourage the state to buy a stake in the new competing private enterprises by buying shares. As a consequence, a great number of companies started competing for the consumer's business in the provision of energy, telecommunications, and transport. But what were the constitutional implications? Loveland puts it: *"in privatising former public services, the government effectively abolishes ministerial responsibility for matters which may have a significant impact on citizens' lives and welfare. If we regard the constitution as being concerned essentially with structuring both the substance*

[1] Ian Loveland, Constitutional Law, Administrative Law and Human Rights, (4th edn, Oxford University Press, 2006) pp. 24-5

10

and the processes of the relationship between a country's government and its citizens, it seems that a major part of the constitution has undergone substantial reform... "[1].

The second form of privatisation was through contracting-out to private providers specific services which were traditionally provided by public entities. For instance, the provision by private companies of 'outsourced' services from office-management to staff recruitment; waste-collection to social care; catering, cleaning and laundry provision for schools, hospitals and prisons. Through contractual arrangements to private companies the responsibility logically shifted although a number of problems relating to ultimate responsibility for the discharge of those functions and commensurate dimensions of accountability remained.

In 1988, the cabinet office efficiency unit published a report entitled "improving management in government: the next steps". The fundamental idea behind the program presented in this report was to improve the accountability of the government and clearly define responsibility of public bodies.

Historically, the constitutional convention of ministerial responsibility meant that government ministers were, in principle and in most cases in reality, accountable for everything done in the name of their department. In serious cases where something had gone badly wrong, this notion of ministerial responsibility could result in ministerial resignations or removal from that particular office.

The 2005 Act also brought about a major change to the UK's court structure. Historically, the House of Lords had both a legislative and a judicial capacity. To accentuate the separation between legislature and judiciary, however, the constitutional reform act provided for the House of Lords in its judicial capacity to become the new Supreme Court of the United Kingdom, and this change came into effect in October 2009.

One of the other main debates concerns the fundamental constitutional doctrine – that of parliamentary sovereignty, which is the core characteristic of UK's constitutional identity. The question of the UK parliamentary sovereignty raises another issue of devolution of executive and legislative powers to different parts of the United Kingdom. This question is particularly pertinent with regard to Scotland, following the referendum on Scottish independence in 2014 and the debates following the Brexit; but it also affects wales and Northern Ireland.

The mandate and missions of the administration of the state requires the government, local authorities or courts to use special public prerogatives which enables local authorities', for example to purchase property compulsorily or courts to impose imprisonment. These powers are, of course, granted to public authorities almost exclusively by means of statutes which – at least in theory – delineate the extent and scope of those powers.

Judicial review is often seen as the major way in which the legality of administrative action is controlled. This is an approach which stresses the part played by the law in the control of administrative activities, and is underpinned by the doctrine of *ultra vires* which imposes on public bodies the obligation to lawfully act within the limits of the powers given to it.

Historically, the massive expansion of the administrative state over the last hundred years, with the state taking on responsibility for education, health provision, energy, social services and housing; logically imposed on public bodies to operate within the bounds of legality. Consequently, administrative law is defined as the legal framework through which public bodies may deliver better, in other words more transparent and fair, public services.

Those in favour of these ideas are followers of the green-light theory. Taggart explained it: "green light theorists looked to the truly representative legislature to advance the causes of workers, women, minorities and the disadvantaged. For them, the role of law was to facilitate the provision of programmes of public services. Parliament was trusted to deliver socially desirable results". In this respect, the functions of administrative law are to facilitate and to regulate of public bodies.

In the 1990s has emerged a new function to administrative law which we may term a 'rights-based' approach. The achievement of this phenomenon has resulted on the incorporation of the European convention on human rights into English law through the human rights act 1998. This approach stresses the need not for a reactive verdict on the legality or otherwise of administrative action, but rather on the proactive development of standards of legality designed to protect human rights and prevent abuse of power. Like red-light theory, this view sees a central role for the judiciary in analysing the impact of governmental actions on rights.

Summary

•   Law is generally divided into two different segments: public law and private law.

•   While public law regulates relationships between the State and private individuals, private Law generally regulates legal relationships between private persons.

•   Although constitutional and administrative law form part of the generic term of public law, a distinction between them should be drawn.

•   Constitutional law concerns various aspects of the structure and organization of the state such as the recognition of the principal institutions of the state (Parliament, Government and the courts) but it also confers their to these institutions specific roles and functions, determines their nature and the extent of their powers.

• Although a clear-cut distinction between administrative and constitutional law is impossible to draw, it should be noted that where constitutional law concerns the main structure and organisation of the state, administrative law relates rather to the concrete exercise of the governmental powers.

• In 1979, the use of the methodology of 'new public management' (NPM) by Margaret Thatcher consequently led to a privatisation of the public sphere which changed the structure and organization of the administration.

• In 1988, the Cabinet Office Efficiency Unit published a report entitled "Improving Management in Government: the Next Steps" in order to improve the accountability of the government and clearly define responsibility of public bodies.

• In the same view, judicial review was introduced and the House of Lords became the Supreme Court of the UK.

• In the late 1990's, administrative law took a new turn with an "right-based" approach underlining the proactive development of standards of legality designed to protect human rights and prevent abuse of power.

Chapter 2 – The characteristics of a constitution

The idea of a constitution

All organisations – whether a sports club or a state – have a set of rules which serve as a constitution. Every society requires fundamental rules in order to function and to ensure order. However, before considering the importance for a state to have a constitution, it is crucial to define what a state is. Even though defining the notion of statehood, in its modern sense, is one of the most controversial issues of international relations, there is a definition, almost universally shared by the international community, coming from international law.

The Montevideo Convention on Rights and Duties of States 1933, art 1 defines a state as follows:

"The State as a person of international law should possess the following qualifications:
(a) a permanent population;
(b) a defined territory;
(c) government; and
(d) capacity to enter into relations with other states".

In international law, the concept of state recognition has been presented for a long as being a precondition of statehood. However, this issue seems to have been recently solved by modern international law which excludes this factor from the constitutive elements of statehood, as stated in the Montevideo convention. The idea of constitution comes from the historical evolution from the modern State and the Rule of Law: even the government is subjected to certain rules determining what he can or cannot do. These rules are meant to ensure the continuity of the state and its order.

In an attempt to define a constitution, Bradley and Ewing have noted that in a narrow sense, a constitution can be described as:
"(...) a document having a special legal status which sets out the framework and principal functions of the organs of government within the state and declares the principles or rules by which those organs must operate".
But there are other perspectives on what a constitution is about. A social scientific perspective would tend to view the state as those elements in society which, taken together, represent the central

source of political, military and economic power; and the constitution of a state is the formal expression at any given time of the allocation of this power as between individuals and groups.

As a conclusion and for the purposes of this chapter, we may conclude that a constitution is a set of supreme rules and principles regulating the organisation and structure of a state, which the governing institution should adhere to. Generally, these rules will be gathered in a written document entitled "Constitution" as being more or less supreme for each state. However, for some states, for instance the United Kingdom, these rules are located other than in a specific constitutional document.

The contents of a constitution

The exact contents of constitutions will vary from state to state. However, there are always common features present in almost every constitution. For example, as an introduction, a preamble will be found in many states constitutions. These preambles are usually symbolic and set the main values ideology of the rest of the text. For instance, the preamble to the United Nations Charter, which serves as a constitution for the organisation although it is not a constitution in the nationalist sense, is illustrative of the ideology and the spirit of the text: "We, the peoples of the united nations". In this respect, preambles of constitutions tend to be declaratory in nature but they generally identify the people as the constituent or the sovereign power from which the moral authority of the constitution derives.

A constitution will primarily establish the different institutions of the state and set out their different roles, powers and functions. Traditionally, the constitution will establish the legislative, the executive and the judiciary that are the three main powers of the state, divided by function. The law-making institution passes legislation. From state to state, the legislative will be called Parliament, Congress or Assembly. The government is the main institution responsible for complying with the obligations of the state towards its population and making policy decisions. The executive power is generally headed by the Prime Minister but it can also be headed by the President or a cabinet of ministers.
The judicial institution dictates and interprets the law. The courts

are usually part of a judicial system which is hierarchal and headed by the Supreme Court or a Constitutional Court. In some judicial systems, such as France, civil and administrative courts are separated and placed under a different hierarchy according to their functions.

The constitution may also confer specific powers to certain institutions. For example, the constitution may provide, by a specific provision of its text, that the President has the power to sign Treaties on the behalf of the state. A constitution will also determine the constitutional relationship between the different institutions that it establishes. For instance, the constitution will generally set out that the Parliament approves by a consulting vote the budget of the executive. This principle, which is inherent to any democracy, refers to the check and balances as it is generally called under US constitutional law. For example in the UK, the constitution establishes the relationship between the Queen and the Parliament in the context of the passage of legislation. Even though the Parliament adopts legislation the Queen is still required to grant Royal Assent to legislation.

Accordingly, a major theme of constitutional law and the study of the level of democracy in a state is how the state institutions work together, and most importantly, how these institutions check and balance one another. As stated above, a constitution will also deal with how the individual relates to the state. Democratic constitutions will do so by conferring fundamental rights to the individual. The enshrinement of these rights in the constitution will impose obligations on the state such as the protection of the life of an individual from murder for example. In this respect, the constitution will accord a special protection for individual's rights from infringement by the state. However, this list of rights will also contain the justifications to restrictions on individuals' rights.

Therefore a constitution will also set what powers the state can exert over the individual by regulating for instance in what circumstances an individual can be arrested or detained. To some extent, this can be seen as being a condition part of the social contract signed between the individual and its state. In a democracy, having such a bill of rights in the constitution will legitimate the public powers of the state institutions. One of the most famous declarations of fundamental rights is the French Declaration of Human and Citizens' Rights (1789), which has been interpreted by the French Constitutional Court as being part of the constitutional bloc.

Finally the constitution will generally contain the methods and procedures to be amended. Given that law is an evolutionary science, constitution have to be capable of being adapted and improved especially when they have been in force for decades or centuries. For example, amendments to the constitution of the United States can be made provided that two-thirds of both the Congress and three-quarters of the state legislatures approve such changes. The French fifth constitution (1958), in its article 89 adds a supplementary condition of popular consultation. This is because the people are considered as being the constituent, having the power to adopt and reform the constitution. As opposed to the theory of national sovereignty, this approach is generally referred to as popular sovereignty.

The purposes of a constitution

The *rationale* of having a constitution can be explained by several reasons. First of all, as any other organisation, a society needs rules to ensure stability. History, and particularly the middle age, has shown that the lack of regulations resulted on the instability of permanent military conflicts. In this regard, constitutionalism has been a factor of progress for modern societies.

In this respect, a constitution ensures that the state achieves its primary purpose and objectives. For instance, the third and fourth French constitutions have resulted on institutional blockages that prevented the executive from governing the country and the legislative power from adopting laws. This lack of stability inspired the fifth constitution (1958) that reaffirmed the legitimacy and stability of state institutions and particularly the executive.

A constitution also legitimates the state in its actions to maintain public order. The constitution will contain provisions about which institution is able to declare war in case of external attack but also which measures the state can take to efficiently tackle a civil war. Another function of a constitution will also be to ensure that institutions have certain legitimacy and act with consent of the people. Thomas Paine famously stated: *"A constitution is not the act of a government, but of a people constituting a government, and a government without a constitution is a power without right"*.

In our modern democracies the legitimacy of a constitution will be enacted through popular consultation. As noted above, according to the popular sovereignty theory, the sovereign is the people. For example, Article 6 section 1 of the Irish constitution specifically underlines this idea: *"All powers of government, legislative, executive, and judicial, derive, under God, from the people, whose right is to designate the rulers of the state"*. Therefore, once the sovereign, the people, has been granting official assent, the state institutions enjoy the public prerogatives required to govern the people. A safeguard to engage the responsibility of the state when exercising such powerful prerogatives is to enshrine, in the constitution, a bill of rights preventing the exercise of such powers to interfere with individuals' rights.

A constitution may also serve draw a clear line under an authoritarian past enshrining the values and principles of a new democracy. Needless to quote the numerous historical examples, a constitution may often be adopted after a revolution a drastic change of regime. The role a constitution is not only to distribute public powers amongst the state institutions but also to draw the limits of these powers and the mechanisms to check that they are not misused or abused at the expenses of the individuals.

Finally, a constitution is also a text that gathers the core values of a society and binds its individuals between them. These values keep the individuals of a society united and enable them to progress together towards common objectives. They will vary from state to state and can be for example the public good, the welfare of the population, the promotion of democratic values or the protection of human rights. For instance, the Brazilian constitution, under its Article 3, provides that one of the objective of the state is to eradicate poverty.

Religious states usually confer a special attachment to a religion. Generally, where a specific religion is predominant, this predominance will be enshrined in the constitution. For example, this is the case of the catholic states conferring a particular role to the Church. However, a constitution can also be used to unify different groups or religions or to recognize the rights of certain minorities. For example, the Moroccan Constitution (2011) in its preamble recognizes the Muslim and Jewish cultural identity of its citizens.

The classification of constitutions

Written and unwritten constitutions

A written constitution is traditionally seen as one formulated of one or several written documents. The USA provides a classic example of such a purely formal constitution. Similarly, the Indian constitution is made of one written document that contains 400 articles.

However, other constitutions, such as the French constitution, are comprised of multiple written documents (Déclaration of the Rights of Man and of the Citizen of 1789, Preamble of the 1946 constitution, the 1958 constitution, etc.). For some commentators, such as FF Ridley: *"There is no British Constitution"*. In this view, a single entrenched written document is the defining characteristic of constitutional states. The UK, in contrast, does not have a "traditional" written constitution. Its constitution has evolved over many centuries, and as a result cannot be found in any single, or even a small group of documents. For traditional constitutionalists, such as de Tocqueville, writing in the first half of the 19th century, the UK's lack of a written constitution left him to remark that in England: "there is no constitution". However, in line with definitions cited earlier, the UK can certainly be seen as a constitutional state. In addition to this, most of the constitutionalists agree to admit today that the UK has a constitution, although it is not a traditional written constitution. The UK constitution has a body of rules, both written and unwritten, which allocate the functions of the state. This is one of the primary functions of a constitution. Sir Ivor Jennings put it: *"If a constitution means a written document, then obviously Great Britain has no constitution ... But the document itself merely sets out the rules determining the creation and operation of governmental institutions, and obviously Great Britain has such institutions and such rules. The phrase 'British constitution' is used to describe those rules."* Therefore, it can be said that the UK has a *de facto* constitution.

Theorists use the distinction between those constitutions that are codified in one or several documents (as in the USA), and those that are uncodified and found from a number of legal sources (as in the UK).Nevertheless, the distinction between written and unwritten is not absolute since it has recently been admitted that other unwritten sources feed a constitution, even in states that have a written constitution. For example, jurisprudence of the national supreme courts interprets the constitution and sets principles that are constitutional. Moreover, written provisions are necessarily supplemented by political practices and conventions that have been developed throughout the state's constitutional history.

Rigid and flexible constitutions

Historically, a distinction has also arisen based on the process of amending constitutions. Accordingly, a rigid constitution is one where constitutional law can only be amended through a special constitutional procedure. These constitutions require several constitutional obstacles to be overcome as safeguards of the continuity of the state. This is because according to the traditional hierarchy of norms, constitutional law has a higher status than all other forms of national law.

Generally, rigid constitutions are contained in one written document. However, there are exceptions to this trend and the constitution of Singapore provides an example: it is written but flexible. The US Constitution is a very good example of a rigid constitution. In order to make a constitutional amendment; a proposal firstly has to be adopted by both houses in Congress (the legislature) with a two-thirds majority. The proposal then has to be ratified by three-quarters of the states.

On the other hand, a "flexible" constitution is one where constitutional laws can be amended by regular legislative laws. For instance, in the UK, Parliament is the supreme law-making body and it can pass, amend, or repeal any law with a simple majority. The Human Rights Act 1998, which is recognized as having constitutional value, for example, could be amended or even repealed entirely in exactly the same way as any other Act of Parliament. Accordingly, no special mechanisms are necessary to change important constitutional laws in the UK. The traditional legislative law-making process in the UK implies the consent of both the House of Commons and the House of Lords together with the Royal Assent. This can be explained by the central place of parliamentary supremacy (or sovereignty) in the UK. However, having a flexible constitution does not mean that Parliament, or other bodies entitled to do so, can amend the constitution without any limits. Because of the major importance of the constitution in every state, there are some legal and political constraints on what Parliament can and cannot do.

Unitary and federal constitutions

These classifications have to do with the structure of the state and the devolution of powers or sovereignty from the central to the local level. A unitary constitution has the majority of its legal and executive power vested in the central organs of the state. In the UK, most power is centrally controlled in Westminster and Whitehall. However, some power is devolved to regional bodies, for example local authorities ("councils"), to the London Assembly and most notably (since 1998) through the devolved Parliament in Scotland and the Assemblies in Northern Ireland and Wales.

The devolved nations of the UK have significant but limited jurisdiction in certain areas: their power is given by an Act of the Westminster Parliament (for example, the Scotland Act 1998 and the Government of Wales Act 1998), and the power to repeal those Acts remains with the Westminster Parliament. Therefore, these institutions remain subordinate, in the legal sense, to the supremacy of Westminster Parliament. This phenomenon is referred to by specialists as the decentralization of the power in unitary states and is also illustrated for example, in Spanish or French constitutional history.

In short, even if a unitary constitution recognizes and delegate power to decentralized institutions, they do not have express constitutional protection and do not formally exist as separate entities from the central state, unlike the state/provincial/legislatures in a federal constitution.

Conversely, in a federal constitution, power is divided between federal government and states or regional authorities. This model is generally established in a constitutional document, for example the German and US Constitutions. These constitutions establish the legal recognition of local states as separated entities, remaining inter-connected by the federation.

Some powers, like state security and foreign policy, are likely to be reserved to central government, but the regional authorities (such as the states in the USA or the German *"Bundesländer"*) have considerable powers to legislate on and administer their own affairs. For this reason, where the competence to legislate in a specific area belongs to regional states, you will find, within the same federation, different legislations from one state to another. For instance, in the US, since the power to adopt legislation on death penalty remains a state prerogative, some of them have prohibited death penalty and others are still practicing it.

Separated and fused powers

According to the theory of the separation of powers, one of the principles of constitutionalism is that power should be divided and dispersed in order to prevent abuse of power by those in control. This approach fosters checks and balances between the different bodies of the state.

The US Constitution is a clear example of a separated constitution; power is clearly dispersed between Congress, the Judiciary (Supreme Court), and the President. Each body has its own functions though it exercises some control or check over the other two. At the other end of the extreme would be an autocratic or totalitarian regime where power is vested in one body or one individual: this type of constitution is said to be fused. Thus, a separated constitution is an indicator of the democratic nature of a state.

Monarchical and Republican constitutions

A monarchical constitution provides that the head of state is a monarch. Most of the modern states in this category have adopted "constitutional monarchies" in which the monarch plays a largely symbolic role with only very limited powers, for example the UK, Spain, the Netherlands and Sweden.

In the UK, Queen Elizabeth II is still nowadays the head of state and all government acts are passed in the name of the Crown. She has a large amount of theoretical legal power but little practical power given that constitutional practices have led to political limits of her powers. Indeed, the Executive, on the Crown's behalf, exercises a large amount of the legal "prerogative" power of the Crown.

On the other hand, a republican constitution is one in which the head of state is usually democratically elected, and is most often known as a President. The degree of power that such leaders have depends on the constitution itself.

In some countries, the President will have very significant political power, as for instance in France and the USA. In other states, though, the President's role will be largely symbolic and ceremonial, such as in Germany or in the Republic of Ireland. In those countries, the Prime Minister or the Chancellor will be, *de facto*, the head of the executive.

The basic principles of constitutionalism

The main objective of constitutionalism is to ensure that governments act constitutionally. In other words, each institution of the state has to act in accordance with the rules and principles enshrined in the constitution. This is related to the Rule of Law which is of a crucial importance in the modern state where governance is bound by a legal system allocating and limiting powers.

As stated above, the function of a constitution is not only to describe the powers of governing institutions but also to set out control mechanisms and checks in the constitution. The rationale behind constitutionalism is linked to the separation of powers; the objective is to prevent abuse of power by state institution. To some extent, constitutionalism is a safeguard against the excesses of totalitarianism and authoritarianism. For instance, the executive cannot decide to monopolise legislative and judiciary functions by force just because it finds it necessary.

According to the modern notion of constitutionalism, acting constitutionally also entails to respect for the basic human rights of individuals. In this sense, the fact that the executive of the state is bound by the obligation to act constitutionally, prevents him, at least legally, to commit violations of individuals' rights. For instance, in the UK constitution, constitutionalism implies that the use of public power is controlled in accordance with the following principles:

- Basic rights of the individual are enshrined and safeguarded
- Public power is separated amongst the different state institutions
- When exercising public power, state institutions should act strictly within their legal prerogatives and limits
- An independent and impartial court system should review the constitutional use of public power
- The Kingdom should adhere to the basic principles and values of democracy

Chapter 3 – The nature and sources of the British Constitution

The debates on the existence of the British Constitution

The question at stake is to determine whether the UK has a constitution according to the theory of constitutionalism. At this stage, it is noteworthy to precise that the United Kingdom is not a traditional state in international law since it is composed of four countries: England, Scotland, Wales and Northern Ireland. In addition to this, the UK has three different legal jurisdictions: England and Wales as a single jurisdiction, Scotland and Northern Ireland.

The starting point from all the debates around the existence of a British constitution is that the UK has no formal written document entitled "the British Constitution". Accordingly, for some commentators, such as FF Ridley: *"There is no British Constitution"*. In this view, a single entrenched written document is the defining characteristic of constitutional states. The UK, in contrast, does not have a "traditional" written constitution. Its constitution has evolved over many centuries, and as a result cannot be found in any single, or even a small group of documents. For traditional constitutionalists, such as de Tocqueville, writing in the first half of the 19th century, the UK's lack of a written constitution left him to remark that in England: "there is no constitution".

However, in line with definitions cited earlier, the UK can certainly be seen as a constitutional state. In addition to this, most of the constitutionalists agree to admit today that the UK has a constitution, although it is not a traditional written constitution. The UK constitution has a body of rules, both written and unwritten, which allocate the functions of the state. This is one of the primary functions of a constitution. Sir Ivor Jennings put it: *"If a constitution means a written document, then obviously Great Britain has no constitution ... But the document itself merely sets out the rules determining the creation and operation of governmental institutions, and obviously Great Britain has such institutions and such rules. The phrase 'British constitution' is used to describe those rules."* Therefore, it can be said that the UK has a *de facto* constitution.

There are several factors which indicate, in practice that the UK has a constitution. First of all, if the UK had no constitution, the state would not function with a government, Parliament, or police force and the state would not be organized and ordered. Secondly, many other sources of UK law make reference to the constitution (see for example the Constitutional Reform Act 2005). Finally, there are many examples of governmental or parliamentary bodies, throughout the UK constitutional history, that have been in charge of matters related to the UK constitution (see, *inter alia*, The Department for Constitutional Affairs, the Political and Constitutional Reform Committee of the House of Lords).

The nature of the British Constitution

Although the UK constitution is traditionally classified as being unwritten, it is comprised of many constitutional rules that are located in a variety of sources such as acts of Parliament, case-law and binding political practices. Accordingly, instead of talking about an unwritten British constitution, some commentators prefer to refer to the British Constitution as to an uncodified Constitution as the constitutional rules have not been brought together in one single authoritative document or code.

This distinction is particularly important since many of the constitutional rules are written down and can be found in documentary form. For instance, the constitutional principle that parliamentary legislation can be enacted without the consent of the upper chamber is set out in the Parliament Act of 1911 and 1949. Therefore, many of the constitutional rules will be located in acts of Parliament and can be presented as written sources. The main danger for the continuity of the UK Constitution, however, is that theoretically these rules could be amended at any time by another regular act of Parliament.

Indeed, it has to be admitted that the UK uncodified constitution is less easy to identify and pinpoint compared to other national constitutions that are codified in one single document. In contradiction with the principles of constitutionalism, even in the

UK, academics might disagree over some of the constitution's sources and over what is, or is not, part of the Constitution.

As Barber puts it: *"Britain is one a very few states which lack a written constitution, but this bare accident of history does not provide an argument for us to adopt one. Britain's constitution has, by and large, been a success. It has produced stable government and - in terms of democracy, transparency, human rights and the provision of social welfare – it compares reasonably favourably with many other constitutions".*

One of the reasons why the UK has no formal written constitution is related to its history. As stated in Chapter 2, constitutions are generally drafted to enshrine a clear break with the past, which is usually caused by a political upheaval, a struggle for independence or a revolution. The institute for public Policy Research issued a report stating that there are very few examples, worldwide, of constitutions that have been patiently and measuredly drafted but rather that most of them are the consequences of major political or historical events. In short, the United Kingdom has never been colonised or invaded except a short period of time (1649 – 1660 with Oliver Cromwell). In addition to this, the UK Constitution has been functioning by a particularly impressing tool for governmental and institutional stability throughout Great Britain's history.

The key features of the British constitutions

The key features of the British constitution have been identified by the House of Lords Select Committee on the constitution. Composed of the main constitutional principles and rules governing the state, they were referred to by the Select Committee as to *"the five tenets of the British Constitution":*

- Parliamentary sovereignty
- The rule of law and the protection of individuals
- Responsible government
- The Union of the United Kingdom
- Membership of the Commonwealth and other international institutions

These five tenets will be studied throughout the different chapters of this book. These tenets are not new: the basic principles that they underline – the rule of law, check and balances between the different powers, territorial integrity of the state, international cooperation – are commonly protected by constitutionalism internationally in other constitutions.

Parliamentary sovereignty theoretically refers to the Queen in Parliament has being able to pass any law without restrictions. Historically, there has no constitutional limitation on the powers of Parliament to pass laws. This is, once again, something specific to the British constitution since other constitutions have legal limitations to the exercise of parliamentary powers within the framework of the codified constitution (see the US and the French constitutions). However, we will see that the developments of international law and especially the integration to the European Union have challenged this traditional principle given that another Parliament was indirectly capable of passing laws for the United Kingdom. Parliamentary sovereignty is often presented as a cornerstone of the British constitution and will be studied in details in Chapter 6.

Another particularity of the British constitution is that it does not recognize any hierarchy between the different laws according to their sources. Traditionally, constitutionalism protects higher laws from ordinary laws. This principle comes from Kelsen's theory of the pyramid of norms, which implies that fundamental laws should have higher legal status. The main distinction is generally made between constitutional and non-constitutional laws in order to protect the sustainability or continuity of the constitution and make it prevail over ordinary laws. This is not the case in the UK since its constitution does not draw a clear-cut distinction between these two types of law. As a result, constitutional law, could theatrically, be amended or repealed by ordinary acts of Parliament. However, as stated earlier, if this is legally possible, political safeguards ensure that it would be very difficult to achieve in practice. However, recent developments in the courts case-law have shown a desire to distinguish between two status of laws. As Laws LJ concluded in **Thoburn v Sunderland Council (2002)** EWHC 195: "We should recognize a hierarchy of Acts of Parliament: as it were "ordinary" statutes and "constitutional" statutes. The two categories must be distinguished on a principled basis".

The British Constitution also promotes territorial integrity of the United Kingdom through a unitary constitution. This safeguard is particularly important in a state that is comprised of historically different countries. However, the United Kingdom is not a federal state, as opposed to Germany or the US, but remains unitary given that the power is centrally focused in Westminster Parliament. Indeed, the UK Parliament, located in Westminster, has the legal power to pass any legislation applicable to the entire Kingdom.

However, the British constitution recognizes several layers of decentralised government which are mainly: The Scottish Parliament, The National Assembly of Wales, the London Assembly, The Northern Ireland Assembly and local authorities. These legal entities are nevertheless created by the Westminster Parliament, which remains the only sovereign and could abolish them by any Acts of Parliament. This fact therefore draws the unitary identity of the United Kingdom given that the local authorities are not constitutionally recognized and protected, as it would be the case in a federal constitution. The fact that local layers of decentralised government could be abolished by ordinary laws is one of the several illustrations of the flexibility of the British constitution.

The flexibility of a constitution is generally assessed by looking at the procedure to amend it. As stated above, any Acts of Parliament can amend or repeal existing constitutional laws that are usually themselves acts of Parliament. In other words, in the legal and theoretical perspective, the British constitution can be amended relatively easily. This broad constitutional flexibility on of the main characteristics of the British constitution compared to other constitutions, which traditionally have entrenched constitutional provisions that cannot be amended or that can be amended under very strict requirements. The following examples are acts of Parliament considered as having constitutional value:

- The Constitutional Reform Act 2005, under its section 18, creates the Supreme Court, independent from the legislature, to replace the Appellate Committee of the House of Lords, which was part of the UK Parliament. The legal status of state institutions are traditionally enshrined in codified constitution, whereas it is done through a simple act of Parliament in the UK.

- The Human Rights Act 1998 confers positive human rights on individuals. For instance, in the UK or France, the bill of rights is codified in the document of the constitution.
- The Constitutional Reform and Governance Act 2010 places, *inter alia*, the Civil Service in a statutory footing.
- The Government of Wales Act 1998 created the National Assembly of Wales.
- The House of Lords Act 1999 amended the composition of the House of Lords by removing the majority of hereditary peers.

Recent constitutional history of the United Kingdom has led to a significant number of constitutional reforms which illustrated the particular flexibility of the British constitution. It should be noted that these constitutional reforms were adopted without the need of special majorities in either House or any support from the people through referendums.

The British state remains a kingdom. In other words, the head of the United Kingdom is the monarch, although the role of the Queen in the British constitution is mainly ceremonial and symbolic. The United Kingdom is a modern democracy that could compared to Spain, in which the monarch has prerogatives that are constitutionally limited in a state where the powers are dispersed amongst different institutions.

However, the Queen of the United Kingdom still has considerable powers such as dispensing the prerogative of mercy (although it is a power which is commonly vested in head of states, even in republics), appointing the justices of the Supreme Court and life peers to the House of Lords. It should be noted that these powers are exercised by the monarch in compliance with constitutional convention. In other words the Queen acts on the political advices of her ministers. For instance, even though the Queen remains officially entitled to appoint ministers, she does so following the instructions of the Prime Minister. Accordingly, although the several powers presented above are still formally vested in the Queen, they are in effect practically exercised by her government ministers.

The United Kingdom, considering the crucial role of its Parliament, is strong representative democracy whereby the composition of the legislature is elected by the people through free national elections. However, the House of Lords remains highly criticized in this regard given that not all members of this chamber are democratically elected. The UK Parliament is a bicameral legislature composed of two houses: the House of Lords and the House of Commons. This is common in Parliamentary regimes. For instance, the French Republic also has a bicameral legislature comprised of the national assembly and the senate. In terms of the constitutionalism, bicameral legislatures disperse the legislative powers between to competing sources of powers, in line with the theory of the separation of powers. Nevertheless, it should be noted that, in practice, the two chambers will usually not have equal powers.

The British constitution confers a crucial importance to the independence and impartiality of the judiciary from both the executive and the legislature in order to prevent political pressure.
However, the British constitution confers a limited role to UK courts, compared to traditional constitutionalism. In most of the states, the judiciary is able to strike down legislation by declaring it unconstitutional. For instance, in the US the Supreme Court can declare and invalidate Acts of Congress and the Constitutional Court has similar powers in France. What is internationally known as the judicial review of legislation does not exist in the UK. Historically, the British constitution has been denying the power of squashing down Acts of Parliament to the judiciary.

The UK has a parliamentary executive, which is drawn from the legislature in a state where powers are not clearly separated. To some extent, the executive and the legislature are fused. This is different from presidential regimes for example in the US where the President is constitutionally separate from the legislature.

The sources of the UK Constitution

The British constitution has multiple sources and its particular nature and characteristics make it difficult in locating those. The sources of the UK constitution can be divided into two categories. On the one hand, the traditional legal sources encompass acts of Parliament, courts case-law and international law. On the other hand, the particularity of the UK constitution is that it is comprised of non-legal but politically binding rules that are known as constitutional conventions.

The difficulties with the sources of the British constitution

As stated above, the fact that the UK does not have a codified constitution renders makes it difficult to identify what is a constitutional issue. The first challenge is then to identify constitutional and non-constitutional laws. In this regard, as Hazell formulated it: *"There is no clear classification of what is a constitutional Bill or what is not, and with our unwritten constitution it is impossible to devise one"*.

In addition to this, the fact that there is no special procedure for enacting constitutional laws, constitutional laws are Acts of Parliament with no special requirements regarding majorities, does not help identifying those of constitutional nature. There is no exhaustive list of statutes of constitutional nature as stated by the House of Lords Select Committee on the constitution in its First report of session 2001-2002: *"The constitution is uncodified and although it is in part written there is no single, accepted and agreed list of statutes which form part of the constitution which is indeed written down"*.

Accordingly, In order to identify a constitutional provision, one has to look at for example a statute on an Act by Act basis in order to determine if it contains a rule or principal of constitutional nature. For instance, the Scotland Act is obviously a constitutional statute given that it creates a major institution of the State (the Scottish Parliament) having the power to pass legislation. In contrast, the Aircraft and Shipbuilding Industries Bill 1976-77 is a non-constitutional statute mainly concerned with contract law between individuals. In view of clarifying the status of constitutional statutes, the House of Lords Select Committee on the Constitution has suggested a possible subdivision between bills of first class constitutional significance and Bills representing minor amendments to the Constitution. The rationale behind this initiative is to provide Bills of first class with more effective scrutiny. However, if Acts of Parliament such as the Human Rights Act 1998 or the Constitutional Reform Act 2005 clearly fall within the first category, it not sure than other Acts of Parliament can be classified with such certainty (see for example the Political Parties, Elections and Referendums Bills 2000).

The main difficulty in the UK lies in the fact that there is no Supreme or Constitutional Court being responsible to resolve issues of constitutional nature. As stated earlier, this judicial review of legislation and conflict of norms of constitutional nature is generally the reasonability of higher courts in the US, Ireland of France. In contrast, the UK enshrines its constitutional principles from case law of all courts, regardless of their civil or criminal jurisdictions.

General principle: A case dealing with law of trespass, although appearing at first to deal with a matter restricted to private law, may also raise constitutional issues.

Entick v Carrington (1765) 19 St Tr 1030
Facts: The King's messenger trespassed on the applicant's property. This case seemed to be, *prima facie*, a simple case of application of trespass law.
Ratio: The particular circumstances of the case had a constitutional resonance as it was concerned with protecting the individuals' rights from state restrictions.
Application: While identifying constitutional issues, one should not draw conclusions solely based on traditional distinctions between private and public law.

General principle: : A case dealing with defamation law, although appearing at first to deal with a matter restricted to private law, may also raise constitutional issues.

Derbyshire County Council v Times Newspapers Ltd and Others (1983) 1 All ER 1011

Facts: The plaintiff, a local authority, brought an action for damages for libel against the defendants in respect of two newspaper articles which had questioned the propriety of investments made for its superannuation fund.

Ratio: The particular circumstances of the case had a constitutional resonance since defamation law raised issues related to one of the tenants of the UK Constitution: the protection of individuals fundamentals rights (namely freedom of speech and the right to criticize state institutions).

Application: Cases including traditional application of private law might raise constitutional issues in cases involving human rights.

However, it should be noted that the UK High Court which is part of the administrative jurisdiction, ensures that public authorities strictly exercise their powers in accordance with the law, which necessarily implies issues of constitutional nature. This point will be discussed more in the chapters of this book dedicated to the study of judicial review.

Legal sources of constitutional law

Acts of Parliament are the primary source of constitutional law in the UK. Acts of Parliament are passed by the Queen in Parliament. The legislative procedure of passing laws implies an approval from both the House of Lords and the House of Commons which is validated by Royal Assent. Here is a non-exhaustive list of examples of statutes containing constitutional rules or principles:

- The Magna Carta 1215 (affirmed as a statute in 1297): limited the powers of the monarch and protected the individuals rights of "freemen" not to be imprisoned.
- The Parliament Act 1911 (as amended in 1949) sets out he constitutional relationship between the House of Lords and the House of Commons.
- The European Communities Act 1972 incorporates the UK's international obligations under the European

Communities (today the European Union) into ITS domestic law.

- The Government of Wales Act 1998 establishes a new state institution: The National Assembly of Wales.
- The Succession of the Crown Act 2013: amends the conditions for the succession to the throne by removing male and religious preference.
- A couple of rights conferred rights on the individuals. For example, the Sex discrimination Act 1975 or the Equality Act 2010.
- Other Acts of Parliament conferred the state with the prerogative to restrict individuals' rights in particular circumstances: for example the Perjury Act 1911 or the Prevention of Terrorism Act 2005.

Recently, the traditional approach of placing all Acts of Parliament on an equal footing has been questioned by Laws LJ in **Thoburn v Sunderland City**: *"We should recognize a hierarchy of Acts of Parliament: as it were "ordinary" statutes and "constitutional" statutes"*, he added that constitutional statues should embrace, *inter alia*, the Magna Carta, the Human Rights Act, the Union with Scotland Act, etc. He then argued that whereas ordinary statutes could be impliedly repealed by a later inconsistent Act, it is not the case for constitutional statutes. Is this a start for conferring constitutional acts a higher status? The question of implied repeal will be discussed more in details later.

Delegated legislation is also a legal source of the UK Constitution which is made by the executive on the basis of enabling Acts of Parliament. Also known as secondary legislation this power is usually conferred to a government minister. For instance, the Prime Minister used a delegated legislative power in adopting The Secretary of State for Constitutional Affairs Order 20003 (SI 2003/1887).

Although delegated legislation can be seen as contravening with the separation of powers, it is generally based on constitutional provisions which are necessary for governance in practice. In addition to this, local authorities and devolved institutions can also use their delegated legislative powers within the strict limits of their competences. This is the case for local authorities such as district councils but also devolved institutions such as the Scottish Parliament. The legal provisions adopted by the former are generally referred to as Acts, for example *The Scottish Parliamentary Standards Commissioner Act 2002*.

Royal prerogatives have been defined by Professor A.V. Dicey as *"the residue of discretionary or arbitrary authority, which at any given time is legally left in the hands of the Crown"*. In other words, they are powers recognised by the common law, which are theoretically vested in the Crown but exercised in practice by the government in power in its name. It comprises, *inter alia*, the privileges and immunities recognised at common law as belonging to the Crown, such as the prerogative of mercy, the prerogative relating to the signing of treaties or the declaration of war.

General principle: The Royal prerogatives of the Crown are limited by Common Law which is determined by the Courts.

The Case of Proclamations (1611) 12 Co Rep 74
Facts: The King, during the 17th century, intended to create a new criminal offense although he had no legal basis for this. In connection to this, the enactment of this new offence, illustrating its lack of lawfulness, was referred to as "proclamation".
Ratio: The Court declared that the King only enjoyed the prerogatives that the law of the land permitted him.
Application: The Royal prerogatives are not absolute but rather strictly limited by Common Law, which is dictated by the courts.

Relating to the issue of Common Law, it should be noted that many of the many principles of constitutional law have originated from the decisions of the courts in the ordinary course of litigation. This is generally known in UK law as judicial precedent. The following examples of cases illustrate this phenomenon.

General principle: The government must act within the limits set by the law and cannot trespass on any individual's property without a warrant.

Entick v Carrington (1765) 19 St Tr 1030

Facts: The King's messenger trespassed on the applicant's property which was suspected with seditious libel. The King's messenger broke into the applicant's home and seized his papers without any legal authority or warrant. The applicant sued them for trespass.

Ratio: The Courts upheld the applicant's argument and affirmed that the powers of the state were limited by the protection of individual's liberties which should be free from arbitrary state power.

Application: In order for the state to enter an individual's property, it must have a legal warrant otherwise this will be considered unlawful by the courts. This case is often seen as one of the landmark cases in establishing a tradition of civil liberties in English law.

General principle: A resolution from one of the legislative chambers cannot alter Acts of Parliament, which are necessarily passed through the traditional concurrence of the two legislative bodies and the Crown.

Stockdale v Hansard [1839] 9 Ad & El

Facts: In this case the plaintiff sued for libel in respect of the contents of an official parliamentary report. The defendant pleaded a House of Commons' resolution of 1839 to the effect that all such publications should be treated as absolutely privileged and so could not be used as evidence in court proceedings.

Ratio: The Court declared the resolution as having no legal effect and awarded damages to the plaintiff for libel. In his judgement, Lord Denham CJ explained that: "The House of Commons is not Parliament but only a co-ordinate and component part of the Parliament. That sovereign power can make and unmake the laws; but the concurrence of the three legislative estates is necessary; the resolution of any one of them cannot alter the law, or place anyone beyond its control."

Application: Even the three legislative estates of Parliament, which is the supreme sovereign, have to act in accordance with constitutional law, which implies that Acts of Parliament are passed through a formal procedure.

General principle: The courts can quash delegated legislation and make declarations of incompatibility as regards to provisions of Acts of Parliament.

A and Others v Secretary of State for the Home Department [2004] UKHL 56 (also known as the 'Belmarsh case')
Facts: This case concerned the detention of a number of suspected terrorists held in Belmarsh Prison under the Anti-Terrorism, Crime and Security Act 2001. Section 23 of the Anti-Terrorism, Crime and Security Act 2001 permitted detention of suspected international terrorists without charge or trial. This provision raised serious concerns about compliance with the European Convention of Human Rights, under article 5 which protects individuals from arbitrary detention.
Ratio: The House of Lords ruled that the derogation did not satisfy the criteria required: as a result, they quashed the derogation order which then allowed them to issue a declaration of incompatibility in respect of section 23 of the Anti-Terrorism, Crime and Security Act 2001.
Application: The courts have a power to scrutinize the actions of the legislative and executive in order to ensure that they act in compliance with the law.

Finally, European Union law became a source of constitutional law following the enactment of the European Communities Act 1972 ("ECA"). After the 2016 referendum on Brexit, the application of this source of UK constitutional law will certainly change once negotiation have been found, after the 2-year-period between the UK and the EU in order to find an agreement for the UK withdrawal of membership. Until then, the different sources of EU law still apply in the UK under the principle of direct applicability:

- Primarily legislation is comprised of the founding and fundamental treaties of the EU such as the Treaty of Rome (1957) and the Treaty of Lisbon (2009).
- Secondary legislation is composed of Regulations (directly applicable), Directives (binding on the achievement of an objective which requires an implementation by the Member States), Decisions (addressed to specific member states) and Case law of the Court of Justice of the

European Union (**R v Secretary for Transport, ex parte Factortame Ltd and Others (No 2)**).

It should be noted that the European Convention on Human Rights and interpretation subsequent interpretation by the European Court of Human Rights have a significant impact in UK law and is also one of its source. This part of international law is not affected by Brexit which only concerns the withdrawal from the European Union, a separate institution. The same considerations can be applied to any other international treaties which the UK has ratified.

Non-legal sources of constitutional law

The main non-legal sources of the UK constitution are constitutional conventions. This is a particularly notable feature of the UK constitution: many of its important features are regulated by convention alone rather than strict law. For instance, the Queen, under her legislative powers, has the legal right to refuse royal assent to bills presented to her by Parliament, which would prevent it to pass Acts of Parliament. By convention, however, the Queen does not refuse assent. The idea is that even though there is no strict law enshrining this institutional practice, political safeguards ensure that this convention is respected.

The issue of constitutional conventions has been one of the most controversial issues of constitutional law discussed in the academic community. Constitutional conventions are informal rules of political practice that are developed throughout institutional practices and history. However, conventions do not have a clear source in legislation or case law. On the one hand, Dicey, in its Introduction to the Study of the Law of the Constitution (1885), identified this set of rules consisting of: *"... conventions, understandings, habits or practices, which, though they may regulate the conduct of officials are not in reality laws at all since they are not enforced by the courts"*. On the other hand, Jennings argued a slightly different opinion, viewing conventions as actual binding rules of behaviour, albeit not legally enforceable. Marshall and Moodie, in Constitutional Conventions, too a similar approach: *"... rules of constitutional behaviour which are considered to be binding by and upon those who operate the constitution, but which are not enforced by the law courts ... nor by the presiding officers in the Houses of Parliament."* The Cabinet Manual, published in 2011 is a very useful source gathering many examples of constitutional conventions:

- The House of Lords should defer to the House of Commons. This is particularly the case when a bill promoting an election manifesto commitment is being proposed – this is known as the Salisbury Convention.
- All parliamentary committees should reflect each party's relative strength in the House of Commons.
- The monarch must act in accordance with the advice provided by her ministers.
- The Prime Minister chooses the Cabinet.
- After a vote of no confidence, the government should resign and advise dissolution of Parliament (leading to a general election).
- Judges must not be politically active.
- The UK Parliament should not legislate for an independent Commonwealth nation unless that state has requested and consented to it.

Recently, a new convention has arisen from the parliamentary vote on Syria in August 2013. It stipulates that the Commons should be consulted before the government embarks on significant foreign policy initiatives, involving the use of the armed forces, (otherwise than in an emergency). Constitutional conventions have different purposes. For Jennings, conventions "fill in the gaps" in the UK's Constitution. They constitute a flexible way of amending the UK constitution. Constitutional conventions regulate the institutional interaction of powers and ensure that the executive is held accountable. There is a significant case law on the recognition of constitutional conventions by the courts and their relation to law.

General principle: Although the courts cannot enforce conventions directly because of their non-legal nature, in certain situations, the courts will uphold enforceable legal

rights that govern the same matter in order to indirectly recognize the conventional "rule".

Carltona v Commissioner of Works [1943] 2 All ER 560

Facts: The main issue in this case was whether the Commissioner of Works had unfairly delegated his power to requisition property to a relatively minor official.

Ratio: The Court held that existing law supported the constitutional convention at stake. As Lord Greene MR concluded: *"The whole system of departmental organisation and administration is based on the view that ministers, being responsible to Parliament, will see that important duties are committed to experienced officials. If they do not do that, Parliament is the place where complaint must be made against them."*

Application: Even though constitutional conventions cannot be enforced as if it were ordinary provisions of law, courts recognize them as having a persuasive influence when identifying the law that will be applied to a certain legal issue.

General principle: Where there is a conflict between a constitutional convention and a statutory provision of law, the courts must enforce the law.

Madzimbamuto v Lardner-Burke [1969] 1 AC 645

Facts: In this case the Judicial Committee of the Privy Council had to decide whether the Southern Rhodesia Act 1965 should take priority over a constitutional convention. Although there is a convention requiring that Parliament should legislate for a Commonwealth country only with the consent of the country's government, the statutory provision at stake was in contradiction.

Ratio: The Privy Council held that the Southern Rhodesia Act 1965 should prevail even though it contradicted the spirit of the existing convention.

Application: In case of conflict of norms, statutory provisions will always prevail over constitutional conventions. This can be explained by the crucial role of Parliamentary sovereignty in the UK, conferring a major value to Acts of Parliament.

General principle: Constitutional conventions, even in situations where they have been acknowledged by statutory

provisions, do not legally bind the courts to enforce them.

R (Miller) v Secretary of State Exiting the EU [2017] UKSC 5

Facts: In this case, following the 2016 referendum on exiting the EU, the question was to know whether the government could, on its own authority, trigger Article 50 of the Lisbon Treaty (a clause of the treaty enabling Member States to withdraw from the EU). However, a constitutional convention, The Sewel Convention, referred to in s. 28(8) of the Scotland Act 1998, brought in through s. 2 of the Scotland Act 2016 imposed on the UK government to firstly seek the consent of the Scottish Parliament before Article 50 was triggered. The argument was that the statutory recognition given to the convention created a legal obligation on the UK government that was bound by the convention.

Ratio: The Supreme Court rejected this view, however, and found that s. 28(8) merely functioned as an acknowledgment of the convention; it did not create a new legal rule or obligation. In its judgement, Lord Neuberger commented as follows: "… by such provisions, the UK Parliament is not seeking to convert the Sewel Convention into a rule which can be interpreted, let alone enforced, by the courts; rather it is recognising the convention for what it is, namely a political convention, and is effectively declaring that it is a permanent feature of the relevant devolution settlement … In reaching this conclusion we do not underestimate the importance of constitutional convention some of which play a fundamental role in the operation of our constitution. The Sewel Convention has an important role in facilitating harmonious relationships between the UK Parliament and the devolved legislatures. But the policing of its scope and the manner of its operation does not lie within the constitutional remit of the judiciary, which is to protect the rule of law"

Application: It is crucial to remember the very nature of constitutional conventions, which is political. Even though conventions can influence courts when identifying the law to be applied, the main role of the judiciary remains to protect the rule of law.

In case of breach of one of these constitutional conventions, the consequences are likely to be political rather than legal. However, this does not mean that they are not followed at all. Most of them are, respected thanks to the political pressure that breaching such traditional and historic conventions would entail.

However, the standard or level of obedience depends on the degree of obligation imposed by any particular convention. Munro argues, for example, that the convention on Royal Assent of for Acts of Parliament imposes a very large degree of obligation and it is highly unlikely that it would ever be breached.

Another type of non-legal sources, customs, is a set of rules of conduct, recognized by the courts. For instance, custom of Parliament refers to the rules concerning the functions, procedures, privileges and immunities of Parliament. They preserve the existence of both the House of Lords and the House of Commons prerogatives and protect them from courts interference. Erskine May: Parliamentary Practice and Procedure is regarded as the authoritative text in this area.

Finally, academic writers are also considered as being a persuasive non legal source of law in the UK. This is another particularity of the UK constitution, which is would be unconceivable in civil law systems such as France. Academic writers, in the judgements of UK courts are regularly cited in order to support legal standards. Examples include Bagehot's The English Constitution, Dicey's An Introduction to the Study of the Law of the Constitution, Sir Ivor Jennings' Cabinet Government.

Summary

- The UK, in contrast, does not have a "traditional" written constitution. Its constitution has evolved over many centuries, and as a result cannot be found in any single, or even a small group of documents. However, in line with definitions cited earlier, the UK can certainly be seen as a constitutional state.

- Accordingly, instead of talking about an unwritten British constitution, some commentators prefer to refer to the British Constitution as to an uncodified Constitution as the constitutional rules have not been brought together in one single authoritative document or code.

- Composed of the main constitutional principles and rules governing the state, they were referred to by the Select Committee as to "the five tenets of the British Constitution": Parliamentary sovereignty, The rule of law and the protection of individuals, Responsible government, The Union of the United Kingdom, Membership of the Commonwealth and other international institutions

- The British state remains a kingdom. In other words, the head of the United Kingdom is the monarch, although the role of the Queen in the British constitution is mainly ceremonial and symbolic. Accordingly, although the several powers presented above are still formally vested in the Queen, they are in effect practically exercised by her government ministers.

- The UK Parliament is a bicameral legislature composed of two houses: the House of Lords and the House of Commons.

- The UK has a parliamentary executive, which is drawn from the legislature in a state where powers are not clearly separated.

- As stated above, the fact that the UK does not have a codified constitution renders makes it difficult to identify what is a constitutional issue. The first challenge is then to identify constitutional and non-constitutional laws.

- In addition to this, the fact that there is no special procedure for enacting constitutional laws, constitutional laws are Acts of Parliament with no special requirements regarding majorities, does not help identifying those of constitutional nature.

- The main difficulty in the UK lies in the fact that there is no Supreme or Constitutional Court being responsible to resolve issues of constitutional nature.

- The sources of the UK constitution can be divided into two categories. On the one hand, the traditional legal sources encompass acts of Parliament, courts case-law and international law. On the other hand, the particularity of the UK constitution is that it is comprised of non-legal but politically binding rules that are known as constitutional conventions.

Chapter 4 – The separation of powers

The theory of the separation of powers

It is widely acknowledged that the concentration of all types of state power into the same hands generally leads to authoritarian or totalitarian states. In other words, legal systems where powers are concentrated do not provide with the necessary safeguards preventing excesses and abuses of powers. In this respect, as Lord Acton puts it: *"Power tends to corrupt; absolute power corrupts absolutely"*. The separation of powers is rooted in ancient political theory, more than two thousand years ago, which identified three branches of the State. According to Aristotle: "The three are, first, the deliberative, which discusses everything of common importance; second, the officials; and third, the judicial element".

In the 18th century, Montesquieu, in his book *De L'Esprit des Lois* (1689-1755), argued that such a theory ensures that liberties are respected: *"When the legislative and executive powers are united in the same person, or in the same body of magistrates, there can be no liberty ... again, there is no liberty if the power of judging is not separated from the legislative and the executive. If it were joined with the legislative, the life and liberty of the subject would be exposed to arbitrary control; for the judge would then be the legislator."*

Accordingly, modern constitutionalism considers that a Constitution, in order to be efficient and well-arranged, has to embrace the separation of powers. Montesquieu even stated that: *"There would be an end to everything, if the same man, or the same body, whether of the nobles, or of the people, were to exercise those three powers, that of enacting laws, that of executing public affairs and that of trying crimes or individual causes. Any society in which the safeguarding of rights is not assured, and the separation of powers is not observed, has no constitution"*.

Traditionally, the constitution will establish the legislative, the executive and the judiciary that are the three main powers of the state, divided by function. The law-making institution passes legislation. Depending on the country, the legislature will be called

Parliament, Congress or Assembly. The governing institution makes policy decisions and is the main responsible for the obligations of the state towards its population. The executive power is generally headed by the Prime Minister but it can also be headed by the President or a cabinet of ministers. The judicial institution dictates and interprets the law. The courts are usually part of a judicial system which is hierarchal and headed by the Supreme Court or a Constitutional Court. In some judicial systems, such as France, civil and administrative courts are separated and placed under a different hierarchy according to their jurisdictions.

The separation of powers does not provide for an absolute and automatic isolation of powers but instead regulates the interaction between the institutions creating checks and balances. In this regard, an institution may well interfere with the constitutional functions of another. For instance, in states where there is a judicial review of the constitutionality of laws adopted by the legislature, the judiciary clearly interferes with the primary function of the Parliament which is to pass laws.

The US constitution provides with a comprehensive example of an institutional system which is regulated by checks and balances. The President can veto a proposed legislation which was successfully passed through Congress. However, Congress can overturn the presidential veto by gathering a majority of the two thirds in each House. Moreover, as an example of an interaction between the three institutions, the President has the power to propose a Supreme Court's Justice that will be appointed only if the Senate confirms the nomination.

In addition to this, one of the main objectives of the separation of powers is to safeguard the independence of the judiciary. In a democratic constitution, it is of paramount importance that the judiciary is independent, impartial and free from the pressure of the other institutions. The main risk is that the judiciary is influenced, under political pressure, by the executive with judges taking arbitrary decisions. Therefore, special rules have to protect the judiciary from executive's pressure.

The practical influence of the theory of the separation of powers on constitutionalism

It should be noted that the practical impact of the theory of the separation of powers on the conception of modern states is significant. For instance, the organization of states across the globe is almost universally designed in line with the three traditional institutions including the legislative, executive and judiciary. Although their appellation varies from different states, the vast majority of states are composed of a Parliament, a Government and a court system. However, the separation of powers remains an ideal which is differently applied in states. According to the political culture of the country, there are different perspectives on the degree to which the theory should be implemented.

One of the best examples of a strict approach of the separation of powers is illustrated in the US Constitution, which was written by the founding fathers and influenced by Montesquieu. US constitutionalism prohibits firmly to office holders to wield power belonging to another branch of the state. The Constitution of the United States of America (1787) provides:

"Article I, section 1: All legislative powers herein granted shall be vested in a Congress of the United States, which shall consist of a Senate and a House of Representatives.

Article II, section 1: The executive powers shall be vested in a President of the United States of America.

Article III, section 1: The judicial power of the United States, shall be vested in one Supreme Court, and in such inferior courts as the Congress may from time to time establish"

Similarly, the German Constitution makes a clear distinction between the three powers: *"Article 20(2): All state authority shall emanate from the people. It shall be exercised by the people through elections and voting and by specific organs of the legislature, the executive power and the judiciary."*

Elements of the British Constitution in contradiction with the separation of powers

As we have explored in earlier chapters, the UK constitution is uncodified and has evolved over centuries, with particular specificities that can be explained by its history. As a result, the British constitution does not follow a pure separation of powers with each branch of the state completely separated from each other in terms of functions and personnel. However, as Sir John Donaldson Mr stated: "*Although the United Kingdom has no written constitution, it is a constitutional convention of the highest importance that the legislature and the judiciary are separate and independent of one another*". The British Constitution does not follow a pure separation of powers to several aspects that will be detailed below. However, it must be remembered that there is a recent trend towards reforms in favour of a greater respect of the separation of powers.

The executive and overlaps with other powers

First of all, the parliamentary executive, which is one of the key features of the United Kingdom, is perhaps the strongest overlap of the legislature and the executive. By constitutional convention, the executive is drawn from the Parliament. There is a clear breach of the separation of powers in terms of personnel which enjoys both legislative and executive functions. Bagehot puts it: "*The efficient secret of the English Constitution may be described as the close union, the nearly complete fusion of the executive and legislative powers*".

This feature, particular to the British Constitution, would be unconceivable in states such as France or the US. In the US, given that the system is a presidential one, the President does not seat in Congress. Similarly, in France, article 23 of the Constitution states that membership of government is incompatible with that of Parliament. However, Ireland, which has a codified constitution also, has a parliamentary executive. One of the advantages of having a parliamentary executive is that the government is directly accountable to the Parliament. This scrutiny is possible on a daily basis in Parliament where written and oral questions are asked to the ministers but also through debates and select committees. This form of parliamentary executive is a clear breach of separation of powers to the extent that Parliament, which is the supreme law-making body, is mainly composed of ministers. In this respect, most of the bills enacted as Acts of Parliament are government-sponsored bills. Nevertheless, the British constitution is a parliamentary one, as opposed to a presidential system. In a parliamentary system, the legislature selects the political part of the executive branch, which is then ultimately dependent on the legislature for its position and power. For this reason, parliamentary systems are often seen to create a fusion of powers rather than a separation of powers.

Secondly, in the UK, the Monarch is formally involved with the functions of all three branches of the state. The Crown is part of Parliament and grants Royal Assent to Acts of Parliament. In principle, the Crown is even the supreme entity of Parliament because it has the final word over the two chambers. However, as stated earlier, constitutional conventions ensure that the Crown grants the assent in general except if her government ministers advised her not to do so. Moreover, the Queen's speech is delivered at the beginning of every new parliamentary session detailing the government's legislative program. The Monarch is also involved with the executive function given that the Crown is officially the Head of State as being part of the executive. The Queen appoints the Prime Ministers and the other ministers. However, once again, this power is strongly limited to its symbolic nature given that it is restricted by constitutional conventions. In addition to this, the Monarch is also technically the Commander-in-chief of the armed forces. Finally, although the Queen does not sit in courts as a judge, she is the source of all justice. Indeed, judicial appointments are made in the name of the Crown. Although there is a formal power of making these appointments for the Queen, constitutional convention ensures that she acts on ministerial advice. For instance, the judicial oath of allegiance sworn by judges is not to the Constitution but instead to the Crown.

In principle, the theory of the separation of powers provides that the executive should not enjoy legislative functions. Delegated legislation is a legal source of law which is made by the executive on the basis of enabling Acts of Parliament. Although it can be seen as contravening with the separation of powers, it is generally based on constitutional provisions which are necessary for governance in practice.
However, in its most controversial form, executive-framed legislation can be created as a result of what is known as "Henry

VIII clauses". These clauses, contained in some Acts of Parliament, authorise the executive to pass secondary legislation that amend or repeal provisions in the original primary legislation without further parliamentary scrutiny.

The Privy Council, which is part of the executive and central government, historically acted as the main advisory body to the monarch. His functions have been reduced with the development of the Cabinet. The Privy Council is composed of 600 members including The Prime Minister, Cabinet Ministers, the leader of the opposition, senior judges and other high rank officials. The main contradiction with the separation of powers lies in the fact that the Privy Council exercises judicial function through its Judicial Committee created by the Judicial Committee Act 1833. Historically, it was the final Court of Appeal for various Commonwealth countries. This Committee is mainly comprised of Supreme Court judges and some of its responsibilities have recently been passed to the Supreme Court.

Historically, another concern was expressed regarding the administrative tribunals that were effectively associated with the administration. Administrative tribunals are courts, supposedly independent from the executive according to the separation of powers, which resolve disputes between individuals and the state.
Finally, the Lord Chancellor is a typical example of the UK's violation of the theory of the separation of powers. His main functions included overlaps with the three main powers. The Lords Chancellor sits in the upper chamber of the House of Lords, he or she is the head of a major government's department as a Minister of the Crown and also sits in the UK higher courts (the Court of Appeal, the Appellate Committee of the House of Lords, The Privy Council Judicial Committee) .

The judiciary and overlaps with other powers

The British Constitution, which enshrines a common law system, places judges as *de facto* legislators. The constitutional role of the judiciary is to resolve legal dispute, interpreting Acts of Parliament, identify the common law and provide remedies.
Firstly, interpreting statutes, which is recognized as the constitutional responsibility of the judiciary, implies that the courts

have to ascertain the intention Parliament when it passes legislation. However, interpreting statutes is not a simple task given that words in statutory provisions may have a variety of meanings. Therefore, the courts have developed principles of statutory interpretation such as the literal rule which requires judges to intent to give words their ordinary meaning. The common law enables the courts to declare points of law when resolving legal disputes. The main advantage of common law is flexibility. In other words, law may better adapt to moral or social changes in a society.

Regarding the legislative function of the judiciary, Dicey stated, in the 20th century: "A large proportion of English law is in reality made by our judges, the adhesion by our judges to precedent, that is, their habit of deciding one case in accordance with the principle, or supposed principle, which governed a former case, leaves inevitably to the gradual formation by the courts of fixed rules for decision, which are in effect law". Lord Scarman put it: *"society has permitted the judges to formulate and develop law"*.

However, there is a fine dividing line between developing the law and making it. Developing law, in terms of identifying the scope of application on statutes within a jurisprudential framework, is not *per se* to the separation of powers. Even in Civil law systems such as France, the importance of the jurisprudence of higher courts is increasingly recognized as a source of law. Nevertheless, in common law systems, such as the UK, judges are often seen as legislators in the sense that they do not only develop law but they also make law.

General principle: The judiciary has residual power to enforce the supreme and fundamental purpose of the law where there is no clear statutory provision for an unprecedented conviction.

Shaw v DPP [1962] AC 220
Facts: In this case, a writer wanted to publish a "ladies directory" giving details of prostitutes and their services. Nevertheless, a conviction of "conspiracy to corrupt public morals" was upheld (even though there was no such statutory offence and such a conviction was unprecedented). The question of constitutionality

of the legislative *de facto* function of the judiciary arose.

Ratio: The House of Lords held that courts had: "residual power to enforce the supreme and fundamental purpose of the law, to conserve not only the safety and order but also the moral welfare of the state".

Application: This is a very far-reaching example of the interpretative role of courts where the line between interpreting and making law is blurry. *Shaw v DPP* a landmark case which fed many criticisms on judicial activism. See also **Gillick v West Norfolk Health Authority [1984]** 1 All ER 365 and **Airedale NHS Trust v Bland [1993]** AC 789.

It should be noted that the notion of judges as *de facto* lawmakers is not solely confined to the UK constitution. For instance, this is also the case in the United States (see the judicial decision *Marbury v Madison (1803) 1 Cranch 137*) and in the European Union where the Court of Justice of the European Union has developed fundamental principles that were not explicitly spelt out in the funding treaties (for example the principles of primacy and direct effect of EU law).

General principle: The legislature can always overturn a judicial decision by passing legislation to nullify it.

Burmah Oil Co Ltd. v Lord Advocate [1965] AC 75

Facts: In this case, the applicant claimed compensation to the Crown for an prejudice suffered as a result of the action of armed forces.

Ratio: The Court upheld the applicant's claim and ordered the government to pay compensation.

Application: In order to nullify the effect of this decision, Parliament passed the War Damage Act 1965. Adopted with retrospective effect, the act had the effect to deny entitlement to compensation.

Due to an extensive approach of the role of the judiciary in the courts' case law, UK courts are accused of excessive "judicial activism". In this regard, the recent case *R (Evans) v Attorney General* has prompted a particularly lively recent debate amongst constitutional lawyers on this issue. The critics of judicial activism have even been published by "Power exchange" with a collection of 50 cases which they see as examples of judicial overreach.

General principle: Even though the judiciary is able to extend existing laws and principles, creating new rights is an exclusive prerogative of Parliament.

Malone v Metropolitan Police Commissioner, [1979] Ch 344

Facts: The plaintiff claimed that intercepting his telephone conversations, on authority of a warrant by the Secretary of State for Home Affairs, was unlawful, and asked for an injunction against the Metropolitan Police Commissioner for monitoring his telephone. He argued that he had a right of privacy.

Ratio: The court refused to support the plaintiff's argument that he had a right to privacy which was not enshrined by any statutory provision. Sir Robert Megarry VC affirmed that "judges do legislate but only interstitially and cannot create new rights".

Application: In contrast with the case discussed above, where some have criticised the courts for judicial law-making in areas of significant public importance, the court here adopts a rather restrictive approach of the legislature's territory.

Parliament and overlaps with other powers

Parliament is responsible for regulating, controlling and disciplining its members. This can be related to a judicial function given that both Houses can exercise their own jurisdiction punishing the members that are disregarding their rules or committing contempt of Parliament. Ordinary courts exercise no jurisdiction over these matters. These parliamentary privileges are derived from the law and custom of Parliament.

Accordingly, the High Court of Parliament is composed of each House, therefore performing a judicial function. For instance, in 2003, the High Court temporarily suspended an MP for breaching Parliamentary rules. However, this notion of judicial function of the Parliament is not confined to the UK constitution. Such a prerogative also exists in the Republic of Ireland, under 15.10 of the Irish Constitution.

For centuries, the highest court in the UK was the Appellate Committee of the House of Lords. This arrangement was often quoted as the clearest example of a further overlap in the separation of powers model in the UK. Accordingly, the historical constitutional function of the House of Lords, which is the upper chamber of Parliament, through its Appellate Committee, was a judiciary one. The main criticism against this two-fold function of the House of Lords lied in the fact that the independence of the judiciary from the executive is one of the core principles of the separation of powers. Another influence that led to a change of the House of Lords' functions was the necessary compliance with article 6 of the European Convention on Human Rights which conferred individuals a right to a fair trial, including the obligation to have independent and impartial judges.

Although the above examples illustrate *prima facie* violations of the separation of powers, they are driven by practical considerations and remain protected by several constitutional conventions.

Elements of the British Constitution in accord with the separation of powers

First of all, it should be noted that the United Kingdom remains a state with three distinguishable institutions divided according to their functions: The Parliament acting as the legislator, the Government acting as the executive and a court system comprised of professional judges. In addition to this, the fact that the UK Parliament is a bicameral legislature and that the executive is divided into central and local government also show a particular attachment to the separation of powers. Moreover, there are numerous examples illustrating that the British Constitution has progressively embraced the theory of the separation of powers as one of its core governing principles.

General principle: Although the doctrine of separation of powers is not itself a legal rule, it is a constitutional principle that is employed by courts when considering the best interpretation of the law.

Duport Steels Ltd and Others v Sirs and Others [1980] 1 All ER 529
Facts: This case concerned a trade dispute between private companies and the Iron and Steel Trade Confederations in 1980.

The Court of Appeal interpreted very restrictively section 13 of the Trade Union Act to the extent that it conferred immunity in tort in respect of acts done by a person in contemplation of furtherance of a trade dispute.

Ratio: As Lord Diplock stated in its judgement: "It cannot be too strongly emphasised that the British Constitution though largely unwritten, is firmly based on the separation of powers".

Application: The interpretative function of judges with respect to statutory legislation is limited by the doctrine of the separation of powers, which is a constitutional principle.

The legislature and the judiciary

Historically, there has been no judicial review of parliamentary legislation in the UK. In the light of a pure conception of the separation of powers, it ensures that there is no interference between judicial and legislative functions. As stated earlier, in countries such as the US or Ireland, supreme courts can invalidate parliamentary legislation. Moreover, the *sub judice* resolution prohibits Parliament members to comment on pending cases before the courts. In addition to this, the Parliament plays no role in judicial appointment of judges, whereas it is the case in the US.

In 1997, a major reform of the UK constitutional system was initiated by the new Labour government. The most recent element of the reform programme was the Constitutional Reform Act 2005, which had a significant impact on the separation of powers between the legislature and the judiciary. One of the most important changes that have been introduced is the formal and institutional separation of the judiciary from the legislature through the creation of the Supreme Court.

The Supreme Court, which first sat in October 2009, is no longer connected in any way with the legislature. Therefore, the Constitutional Reform emphasised and strengthened the functional independence and impartiality of the judiciary. Finally, it should be noted that, even though judges enjoy a constitutional function of statutory interpretation, the interpretation is limited to giving effect to the strict intentions of Parliament.

General principle: The role of the courts in relation to statutory provisions is to give effect to the words that

Parliament has approved.

Duport Steels Ltd and Others v Sirs and Others [1980] 1 All ER 529

Facts: This case concerned a trade dispute between private companies and the Iron and Steel Trade Confederations in 1980. The Court of Appeal interpreted very restrictively section 13 of the Trade Union Act to the extent that it conferred immunity in tort in respect of acts done by a person in contemplation of furtherance of a trade dispute.

Ratio: The House of Lords reversed the Court of Appeal's decision considering that the statutory interpretation was going too far. As Lord Diplock stated in its judgement: "Where the meaning of the statutory words is plain and unambiguous it is not for the judges to invent fancied ambiguities as an excuse for failing to give effect to its plain meaning because they themselves consider that the consequences of doing so would be inexpedient, or even unjust or immoral".

Application: The interpretative function of judges with respect to statutory legislation is limited and should always give effect to Parliament's intentions. Judges cannot interpret statutory legislation remotely from the words of the text just because of ethical or moral considerations in a specific case. As Lord Scarman concluded this case: *"In their desire to do justice the court failed to do justice according to the law"*.

The judiciary and the executive

Judicial independence from the executive has been reaffirmed by the Constitutional Reform Act 2005, providing under its section 3 that ministers of the Crown are prohibited from having special access to the judiciary. An independent judiciary means *inter alia* that judges cannot be sued for their actions within the limits of their functions, even if they act mistakenly. This judicial privilege extends to the law of defamation. The rationale behind this rule is that judges are required to reach their decisions freely and independently.

General principle: Even if judges act maliciously, so long as they reasonably believe that they are acting within their jurisdiction, they cannot be sued for his/her actions in Court.

Sirros v Moore [1975] QB 118

Facts: The plaintiff, an alien visiting the UK, was fined, recommended for deportation for breach of Aliens Order 1953 and later imprisoned. The plaintiff claimed damages for assault and false imprisonment against the defendants – the circuit judge and the police officers. The question which arose in this case was whether judges were immune from proceedings against them in respect of acts which they mistakenly do?

Ratio: Despite acting mistakenly, a judge and police officers acting on his instruction are immune from liability if the acts complained of are carried out by the judge when he acts in his capacity of a judge and does so in good faith.

Application: The central element relating to the immunity of judges relies on their good faith and the fact that they reasonably believed that they were acting within the limits of their jurisdiction. This is a safeguard of the judiciary's independence ensuring that judges are free from arbitrary prosecutions when they act within the limits of their functions.

In addition to this, by constitutional convention, members of the executive refrain from criticising judicial decisions. Sir Ivor: *"commenting on judicial decisions seems to me to be completely unacceptable"*. In recent decades, the judiciary has played an increasing role in exercising a check on the executive by extensively using judicial review. The recent evolution of judicial review illustrates the importance of the separation of powers in the modern British Constitution. As regards the relation of the separation of powers and judicial review, Craig wrote that the concept of separation of powers: "operates as a source of judicial legitimacy, with the courts defending their role as the rightful interpreters of legislation, and of the legality of executive action".

General principle: The judiciary, as a guardian of the separation of powers, can strike down executive action as upholding the democratic will of parliament.

R v Secretary of State for Home Department ex p Fire Brigades Union [1995] 2 All ER 244

Facts: This case concerned the use of prerogative powers by the Home Secretary's to introduce a criminal injuries compensation scheme.

Ratio: The House of Lords ruled that the executive's actions at variance with an unimplemented statutory provision were inconsistent with the will of Parliament. As Lord Mustill stated: "It is a feature of the peculiarly British conception of the separation of powers that parliament, the executive and the courts have each their distinct and largely exclusive domain. Parliament has a legally unchallengeable right to make whatever laws it thinks right. The executive carries on the administration of the country in accordance with the powers conferred on it by law. The courts interpret the laws, and see that they are obeyed".

Application: In this type of cases, courts exercise their powers to make sure that constitutional provisions, including the separation of powers between the legislative and the executive, are respected.

The Constitutional Reform also amended the Lord Chancellor's role with respect to the judiciary given that he is no longer the Head of the judiciary in England and Wales, surrendered his powers of judicial appointment to the Judicial Appointments Commission and can no longer sit as a judge.

The executive and the legislature

According to Section 1 of the House of Commons Disqualification Act 1975, non-elected members of the executive (even civil servants, member of the armed forces or the police) are prohibited from sitting in the House of Commons. In addition to this, the limit of government ministers has been fixed to 95, preventing the executive from dominating the lower House.

Moreover, under the Constitutional Reform Act 2005, the role of the Lord Chancellor was reorganised to remove overlaps with the office's executive and legislative functions. In particular, the Lord Chancellor ceased to be the Speaker or President of the House of Lords in May 2006. Nowadays, the speaker of the House of Lords is elected from the lords and cannot be a Cabinet member.

Summary

- The separation of powers in a key concept in any democratic state.

- Traditionally, the constitution will establish the legislative, the executive and the judiciary that are the three main powers of the state, divided by function. The law-making institution passes legislation. The government institution makes policy decisions and is the main responsible for the obligations of the state towards its population. The judicial institution dictates and interprets the law.

- One of the core objectives of the separation of powers is to safeguard the independence of the judiciary. The main risk is that the judiciary is influenced by the executive, resulting in judges taking arbitrary decisions.

- It should be noted that the practical impact of the theory of the separation of powers on the conception of modern states is significant. However, the separation of powers remains an ideal which is differently applied in states.

- The British Constitution does not follow a pure separation of powers to several aspects:
  o The British Constitution enshrines a Parliamentary executive.
  o The executive can pass delegated legislation.
  o The Crown is formally involved in all three functions.
  o The Parliament exercises its own jurisdiction for cases involving its members with the High Court.
  o Judges historically performed legislative functions.

- Although the above examples illustrate *prima facie* violations of the separation of powers, they are driven by practical considerations and remain protected by several constitutional conventions.

- The UK Constitution is devised in accordance to the separation of powers on the following points:
  - There was historically no judicial review for courts on parliamentary legislation.
  - According to the *Sub Judice* resolution, Parliament members refrain from commenting on pending cases before the courts.
  - By constitutional convention, members of the executive do not criticize judicial decisions.
  - The Constitutional Reform Act 2005 removed the Law Lords from the House of Lords and created the Supreme Court of the United Kingdom as the unique highest court with greater independence from Parliament. The role of the Lord Chancellor was also significantly amended.

Chapter 5 – The Rule of law

An introduction to the Rule of law

The Rule of law imposes on rulers to respect and act in compliance with law. It protects citizens from arbitrary use of power, tyranny and authoritarianism. It nevertheless emphasizes the need of social order as opposed to anarchy and chaos. For instance, a state governed by the Rule of law provides its citizens with peaceful means to resolve disputes, through courts proceedings, instead of having to use violence. In this connection, the independence of the judiciary is of paramount importance in order to ensure that legal disputes are resolved fairly by independent and impartial judges. Such guarantees result in citizens having confidence in the administration of justice, which legitimizes the entire system.

The theory of the Rule of law was advocated by Aristotle in ancient Greece as a protection against tyranny. According to his words (translated by Warrington) in 350BC: *"It is better for the law to rule than one of the citizens...so even the guardians of the laws are obeying the laws"*. Thomas Fuller also famously stated, several centuries later: *"Be you ever so high, law is above you"*.

Throughout the history of the United Kingdom, the theory of the Rule of law has been quoted many times. For instance, it was referred to by John Adams, in the Constitution of the Commonwealth of Massachusetts (1780) as: "… a government of laws not of men" but also by Justice Blackburn (later first Lord of Appeal in Ordinary) 1866 for which: "It is contrary to the general rule of law, not only in this country, but in every other, to make a person judge in his own case"   and finally by Lord Steyn who considered in 1999 (The Constitutionalisation of Public Law) that *"The rule of law is a term of political philosophy or institutional morality. It conveys the idea of government not under men but under laws"*. Quite recently, Lord Bingham, in his book The Rule of law (Allen Lane 2010), issued a comprehensive definition of the concept: *"The core of the existing principle is that all persons and authorities within the state, whether public or private, should be bound by and entitled to the benefit of laws publicly made, taking effect in the future and publically administered in the court"*.

The different theories of the Rule of law

However, there are different conceptions and opinions on the concrete content of the theory of the Rule of law. The two broad schools of thought among writers on the rule of law are the formal and substantive approaches. The debate relies on the content of the notion of Rule of law, its meaning but also its scope. For the formal school of thought, the Rule of law implies that the law, in order to guide the behaviours of its subjects, has to comply with certain procedural requirements. For instance, the law should be clear enough to enable every citizen to understand how they should behave in any given circumstances. In law must be prospective and clear in order to ensure its clarity. It should be dictated by an independent judiciary with an equal access to the courts for all citizens. In other words, the formal approach of the Rule of law does not deal with the morality or legitimacy of law but rather ensure that the formal function of law is respected. The substantive approach of the Rule of law embraces the formal vision presented above but also touches upon the quality and content of law considering that a Rule of law society must accommodate respect for fundamental human rights and freedoms.

Historically, Dicey identified, in an Introduction to the Study of the Law of the Constitution (1885), three meanings for the Rule of law:

- The supremacy of law over arbitrary power: *"We mean in the first place, that no man is punishable or can be lawfully made to suffer in body or goods except for a distinct breach of law established before the ordinary courts of the land ... It means ... the absolute supremacy or predominance of regular law as opposed to the influence or arbitrary power, and excludes the existence or arbitrariness, of prerogative, or even of wide discretionary authority on the part of the government. Englishmen are ruled by the law, and by the law alone; a man may with us be punished for a breach of the law, but he can be punished for nothing else".*

- Equality before the law: *"We mean ... when we speak of the "rule of law" as a characteristic of our country, not only that with us no man is above the law, but (what is a different thing) that here every man, whatever be his rank or condition, is subject to the ordinary law of the realm and amenable to the jurisdiction of the ordinary tribunals".*

- The rights of individuals as fundamental principles of the British Constitution are determined through the courts: *"The general principles of the constitution (as for example the right to personal liberty, or the right of public meeting) are with us the result of judicial decisions determining the rights of private persons in particular cases brought before the courts; whereas under many foreign constitutions the security (such as it is) given to the rights of individuals results, or appears to result, from the general principles of the constitution".*

Dicey's theory is a good starting point to understand the core principles of the Rule of law. However, Lord Bingham worked on Dicey's theory to render it more actual and modern. During Sir David Williams Lecture at the University of Cambridge given in November 2006, Lord Bingham stated that *"all persons and authorities within the state...should be bound by and entitled to the benefits of laws publicly and prospectively promulgated and publicly administered in the courts."* He then defined eight conditions required in order to establish the rule of law:

- The law must be accessible and so far as possible intelligible, clear and predictable.
- Questions of legal right and liability should ordinarily be resolved by application of the law and not the exercise of discretion.
- Laws of the land should apply equally to all, save to the extent that objective differences justify differentiation.

- Law must afford adequate protection of fundamental human rights.
- Means must be provided for resolving, without prohibitive cost or inordinate delay, *bona fide* disputes which the parties themselves are unable to resolve.
- Ministers and public officers at all levels must exercise the powers conferred on them reasonably, in good faith, in the purposes for which the powers were conferred and without exceeding the limit of such powers.
- Adjudicative procedures provided by the state should be fair.
- The Rule of law requires compliance by the state with its obligations in international law: the law which deriving from treaty or international custom and practice governs the conduct of nations.

The international conceptions of the Rule of law

The paramount importance of the Rule of law in modern constitutionalism has been enshrined internationally by the Universal Declaration of Human Rights (1948) *"Powers exercised by politicians must have a legitimate foundation ... based on authority conferred by law"*. In January 1959, the International Commission of Jurists issued the Declaration of Delhi. It presented a broad and substantive view of the Rule of law which appears to go much further than merely procedural conceptions. The declaration stated that the purpose of all law should be respect for the *"supreme value of human personality"*, and that the *observance should entail certain prerequisites such as "the existence of a representative government, respect for basic types of human freedoms, and an independent judiciary"*. It should be noted that both the European Union (rticle 2 of the Lisbon Treaty 2009) and the Council of Europe (who protects democracy, human rights and the Rule of law) have embraced the Rule of law as one of their fundamental values.

General principle: The European Court of Human rights, when appreciating the justification of an interference to a

conditional right with its traditional test (prescribed by law, legitimate aim and necessary in a democratic society), employs a reasoning that clearly draws upon principles underpinning the rule of law.

Handyside v. the United Kingdom (1976) ECHR 5493/72

Facts: The applicant is a book publisher, who published a book called "The Little Red Schoolbook", intended for children aged 12-18 which contained information about sexual subjects, such as pornography, abortion and masturbation, and about illegal drug use. Copies of The Little Red Schoolbook were seized and ultimately destroyed by the British authorities pursuant to the Obscene Publication Acts. The applicant complained to the Court alleging a violation of his right to freedom of expression under Article 10 of the ECHR and right to peaceful enjoyment of his property under Article 1 of Protocol No. 1 to the Convention.

Ratio: The Court held that there was an interference in the applicant's freedom of expression which was prescribed by law, pursuing the legitimate aim of the protection of morals. However, it considered that the interference was necessary in a democratic society and therefore was justifiable. In conclusion the Court the Court found no violation of Article 10 of the Convention: "On the strength of the data before it, the Court thus reaches the conclusion that no breach of the requirements of Article 10 has been established in the circumstances of the present case".

Application: The reasoning of the test to determine whether an interference was justified is also applicable to other conditional rights enshrined by the Convention (Articles 8, 9 and 11).

The Rule of law in the British Constitution

The Rule of law in the UK has become a more significant and constitutionally important concept in recent years, as illustrated by direct reference to it as a "constitutional principle" in section 1 of the Constitutional Reform Act 2005. Interestingly, the Act did not define what "Rule of law" meant in the context of a concrete case, it was left to the courts to interpret it.

In this regard, the House of Lords, in **R (on the application of Corner House Research) v Director of the Serious Fraud**

Office [2008] EWHC 714, was confronted to a case raising the question of the meaning of the Rule of law. In this case, the Director of the Serious Fraud Office decided to discontinue investigations into bribery allegations regarding arms contracts with the government of Saudi Arabia after Saudi representatives publically threatened the Prime Minister. The Divisional Court reversed this decision in contradiction with the constitutional principle of the Rule of law. However, the Law Lords decided to reverse the decision of the Divisional Court, adopting another line of reasoning, therefore avoiding to answer such a complex question. However, some of the features of the theory of the Rule of law, in the British Constitution, are undisputedly reflected by the following key principles:

Legal justification for action

One of core principles of the British Rule of law implies a prevalence of law over arbitrary powers. As a result, those exercising power can only act on the basis of a legal provision, subjected to the will and limited to the terms provided for by Parliament, as a justification of their action.

General principle: State actions interfering with individual's rights do not only have to be prescribed by law but should also respect the legal requirements permitting such action.

Entick v Carrington (1765) 19 St Tr 1029

Facts: The plaintiff's house was entered by force, whereby his belongings (all documents, and papers) were seized under the warrant issued by the Minister of State (member of Privy Council, the Earl of Halifax). However, the warrant was a prerogative power, exercised by State minister, in the event of slandering the King's name.

Ratio: The Court held that common law does not recognise interests of state as a justification for allowing what would otherwise be an unlawful search. As Lord Camden CJ said: "Our law holds the property of every man so sacred, that no man can set his foot upon his neighbour's close without his leave; if he does, he is a trespasser, though he does no damage at all; if he will tread upon his neighbour's ground, he must justify it by law (...) we can safely say there is no law in this

country to justify the defendants in what they have done; if there was, it would destroy all the comforts of society; for papers are often the dearest property a man can have.' and 'with respect to the argument of State necessity, or a distinction that has been aimed at between state offences and others, the common law does not understand that kind of reasoning, nor do our books take notice of any such distinctions."

Application: State authorities cannot proceed to trespass on the basis of a warrant that was issued without respecting the legal conditions for issuing warrants.

General principle: The obligation of legal justification for state's action equally applies in situations of emergency.

Kelly v Faulkner [1973] NI 31
Facts: British soldiers proceeded to an arrest in times of emergency, without respecting the legal conditions for a valid arrest.
Ratio: The Northern Ireland Court of Appeal upheld that British soldiers dealing with the emergency were not exempted from the normal legal requirements for the execution of a valid arrest merely because of the security situation.
Application: The *rationale* behind this decision is that a flexible legal framework for military action can lead to arbitrariness with particularly serious consequences considering the broad powers of coercion of soldiers.

Laws must be sufficiently clear

Key principles of the Rule of law include the need for certainty and clarity in the law. The clarity of laws guarantees that individuals are able to regulate their conduct in accordance with the law.

In the context of the European Convention for Human Rights, this notion is referred to as "prescribed by law" which is a requirement for the justification of interferences in individuals' rights. In **The Sunday Times v United Kingdom (1979)** n°6538/74, the European Court of Human Rights affirmed that laws must fulfil certain criteria: "In the Court's opinion, the following are two of the requirements that flow from the expression "prescribed by law". Firstly, the law must be adequately accessible: the citizen must be able to have an indication that is adequate in the circumstances of the legal rules applicable to a given case. Secondly, a norm cannot be regarded as a "law" unless it is formulated with sufficient precision to enable the citizen to regulate his conduct: he must be able - if need be with appropriate advice - to foresee, to a degree that is reasonable in the circumstances, the consequences which a given action may entail" (§49).

General principle: Even though the Rule of law seems to prohibit retrospective laws, in the UK, the Parliament can always overturn a judicial decision by passing retrospective legislation to nullify it.

Burmah Oil Co Ltd. v Lord Advocate [1965] AC 75
Facts: In this case, the applicant claimed compensation to the Crown for a prejudice suffered as a result of the action of armed forces.
Ratio: The Court upheld the applicant's claim and ordered the government to pay compensation.
Application: In order to nullify the effect of this decision, Parliament passed the War Damage Act 1965. Adopted with retrospective effect, the act had the effect to deny entitlement to compensation.

The Rule of law particularly prohibits retrospective criminal laws, also referred to as *ex post facto* laws, under Article 7 of the ECHR. According to the legal maxim *nulla poeana sine lege* (no punishment without law), a person can only be convicted and sentenced under criminal legislation if the perpetrated act constituted an offense when it was committed.

There are mainly two exceptions to this rule. Firstly, Article 7 of the ECHR provides that: "'the trial and punishment of any person for any act or omission which, at the time when it was committed, was criminal according to the general principles of law recognised by civilised nations". For instance, this exception permitted the UK to adopt the War Crimes Act 1991, which empowers the UK courts to punish war crimes committed by persons who were not subject to British jurisdiction at the time when the crimes were committed. Secondly, the concept of retroactive criminal legislation *in mitius* - legal changes which may alleviate potential punishments – also permits to infringe the Rule of law principle which prohibits *ex post facto* laws.

Control over discretionary power

The theory of the Rule of law warns against discretionary powers of the executive in order to avoid an arbitrary form of government. Even in modern states, the executive is vested with multiple discretionary powers. However, the executive is still obliged to legally justify any official action under the requirements of formal legality.

General principle: The Rule of law prohibits abuses of public power by the executive.

R v Secretary of State for the Home Department, ex parte Fir Brigades Union [1995] 2 All ER 244

Facts: Parliament had passed the 1988 Act which provided for a new Criminal Injuries Compensation Scheme. Instead of implementing the Act, the Home Secretary drew up a non-statutory scheme for a tariff based system by using prerogative powers. The claimants, members of trade unions that would have recourse to the scheme (as workers who were susceptible to violent crime in their work), sought an order that the Act should be implemented or the non-statutory scheme declared unlawful.

Ratio: The House of Lords held that there was no power for the courts to compel the executive to bring the Act into effect given that the executive enjoyed express statutory discretion to implement it. The doctrine of legitimate expectation could not reasonably be extended to the public at large as opposed to particular individuals or bodies who are directly affected by the executive action under consideration. The Court recalls that ministers' intentions are not law, and the courts cannot proceed on the assumption that they will necessarily become law. That is a matter for Parliament to decide in due course. However, while the Secretary of State is under no legally enforceable duty to bring the main provisions of the Act into force, he must consider when it is appropriate for him to do so

and does not enjoy an absolute and unfettered discretion not to do so. Accordingly, the decision not to implement the provisions of the Act and that a tariff scheme would be implemented in its place, was unlawful. According to Lord Browne-Wilkinson: "The Secretary of State comes under a clear duty to keep under consideration from time to time the question whether or not to bring the section (and therefore the statutory scheme) into force".

Application: This case illustrates that the Rule of law is an argument put forward by the courts in order to limit the wide discretionary powers conferred on executive authorities.

General principle: In situations of emergency, for example in times of armed conflicts, courts are generally reluctant to interfere with the executive's discretionary powers.

Liversidge v Anderson [1942] AC 206

Facts: During the Second World War, the Home Secretary was empowered under 18B of the Defence Regulations (issued under the Emergency Powers (Defence) Act 1939) to imprison any person if he had "reasonable cause to believe" that such a suspect had hostile intentions. The plaintiff was detained under this provision without any trial. He sued the Home Secretary for false imprisonment claiming that the decision to imprison him was not based on an objective factual standard.

Ratio: The House of Lords upheld that of regulation 18B contained no objective requirement; as long as the Home Secretary honestly believed he had reasonable cause to believe that he had sufficient grounds to act. Thus the courts could not inquire into the grounds for the detention, as long as there was no evidence to suggest that the Home Secretary had acted other than in good faith.

Application: Courts are usually cautious in times of war or threats to national security and refrain from interfering with discretionary powers of the executive. This notion is generally referred to as "judicial deference". The rationale behind it is when there is a threat to national security, the executive needs free hands to effectively combat this threat.

General principle: The judicial authorities are reluctant to control discretionary powers of the executive when national

security is at stake and highly confidential information has therefore to be protected from disclosure.

R v Secretary of State for Home Affairs ex p Hosenball [1977] 3 All ER 452

Facts: This case concerned the deportation of an American journalist by the Home Secretary in the interest of national security under section 3 of the Immigration Act 1971. The appellant, Hosenball, claimed that his deportation would breach the rules of natural justice given that the Home Secretary had not disclosed the grounds on which he considered him to be a security risk.

Ratio: The Court of Appeal rejected the plaintiff's maintaining that principles of natural justice had to be applied differently in times of security threats. In addition to this, public policy required to not disclose the reasons for the deportation. As Lord Denning Mr concluded: "There is a conflict here between the interests of national security on the one hand and the freedom of the individual on the other. The balance between these two is not for a court of law. It is for the Home Secretary, he in the person entrusted by Parliament with the task. In some parts of the world National Security has on occasions been used as an excuse for all kinds of infringements of individual liberties. But not in England".

Application: This case should be read in conjunction with *Liversidge* as a more recent example of the "hand-off approach" of the courts in sensitive cases.

Equality before the Law

Equality before the law is a principle at the heart of the Rule of law and the administration of justice. In this regard, the quotation "All men are created equal" has first been used by the philosopher Thomas Jefferson in 1776, in the context of the American Revolution. The same notion was emphasized later in the UN Universal Declaration of Human Rights (1948), Article 1: "All human beings are born free and equal in dignity and rights".

The idea is that every citizen should be subjected to the same law and to the same courts without unjustified differences of treatment. Equality before the law requires above all that a person cannot be punished unless it is prescribed by the law. Another way of understanding this is that a legal system under the Rule of law should have processes which give people, regardless of their status, equal access to the rights they are entitled to under the law.

Equality before the law in the criminal trial process means that all citizens are entitled, regardless of their social status in society or the crime they are accused with, to the presumption of innocence and the opportunity to put their case before an independent and impartial court.

However, there are several long standing examples of inequality in before the law in the UK. Most of these inequalities are also recognized as justifiable exceptions to the principles of equality before the law in other legal systems. These include: the powers of the Queens, special powers of certain officials (for example, police and custom officers), immunities of superior judges from civil litigation for acts done in the course of their judicial functions, diplomatic immunities and parliamentary privileges (See **Stourton v Stourton [1963]** 1 All ER 606).

The Rule of law and other constitutional theories

The rule of law and Parliamentary sovereignty

Although the Rule of law certainly operates as a check on executive powers, it can also represent a check on the scope of parliamentary authority by limiting the power of the supreme sovereign body in order to protect minorities or individual rights.

Nonetheless, the relationship between the Rule of law and Parliamentary sovereignty remains complex considering the special role of Parliament in the UK.

General principle: In the absence of express language or necessary implication to the contrary, the courts presume that general words of statutory provisions were intended to be subject to the basic rights of the individual.

R v Secretary of State for the Home Department ex p Simms [2000] 2 AC 115

Facts: The plaintiff was found guilty of murder and kept on claiming his innocence in journalistic interviews. A blanket ban was imposed by the Home Secretary, under the Prison Rules, prohibiting journalists to use information gained during such interviews with prisoners.

Ratio: The Court found the blanket ban to be *ultra vires*. Lord Hoffmann, considering the principle of legality, observed that: "But the principle of legality means that Parliament must squarely confront what it is doing and accept the political cost. Fundamental rights cannot be overridden by general or ambiguous words. This is because there is too great a risk that the full implications of their unqualified meaning may have passed unnoticed in the democratic process. In the absence of express language or necessary implication to the contrary, the courts therefore presume that even the most general words were intended to be subject to the basic rights of the individual. In this way the courts in the United Kingdom, though acknowledging the sovereignty of Parliament, apply principles of constitutionality little different from those which exist in countries where the power of the legislature is expressly limited by a constitutional document".

Application: It seems that the UK Constitution attributes a paramount importance to Parliamentary sovereignty as to prevail, in some circumstances, over the interests protected by the Rule of law. However, under the principle of legality and the constitutionally recognized theory of the Rule of law, the courts may presume statutory provisions written in general terms to comply with human rights.

The Rule of law and the Separation of Powers

Traditionally, the constitution will establish the legislative, the executive and the judiciary that are the three main powers of the state, divided by function. The theory of separation of powers therefore protects individuals from arbitrary governmental actions and abuse of power. The doctrine of the separation of powers is closely related to the Rule of law. A legal system respecting the Rule of law as a fundamental principle also respects the principle of separation of powers. For instance, when the judiciary keeps the executive within the bounds of its lawful authority and also upholds the law as devised by Parliament, both principles are protected.

Summary

- The Rule of law imposes on rulers to respect and act in compliance with law. It protects citizens from arbitrary use of power, tyranny and authoritarianism. It nevertheless emphasizes the need of social order as opposed to anarchy and chaos.

- As Thomas Fuller famously stated, the rationale behind the Rule fo law is the following: "Be you ever so high, law is above you".

- For the formal school of thought, the Rule of law implies that the law, in order to guide the behaviours of its subjects, has to comply with certain procedural requirements such as clarity, accessibility and should povide all citizens with equality before it.

- The substantive approach of the Rule of law embraces the formal vision presented above but also touches upon the quality and content of law considering that a Rule of law society must accommodate respect for fundamental human rights and freedoms.

- It should be noted that both the European Union (article 2 of the Lisbon Treaty 2009) and the Council of Europe (who protects democracy, human rights and the Rule of law) have embraced the Rule of law as one of their fundamental values.

- The Rule of law in the UK has become a more significant and constitutionally important concept in recent years, as illustrated by direct reference to it as a "constitutional principle" in section 1 of the Constitutional Reform Act 2005.

- One of core principles of the British Rule of law implies a prevalence of law over arbitrary powers. As a result, those exercising power can only act on the basis of a legal provision, subjected to the will and limited to the terms provided for by Parliament, as a justification of their action.

- Key principles of the Rule of law include the need for certainty and clarity in the law. The clarity of laws guarantees that individuals are able to regulate their conduct in accordance with the law.

- The theory of the Rule of law also warns against discretionary powers of the executive in order to avoid an arbitrary form of government.

- Equality before the law is a principle at the heart of the rule of law and the administration of justice. The idea is that every citizen should be subjected to the same law and to the same courts without unjustified differences of treatment.

Chapter 6 – Parliamentary sovereignty

An introduction to Parliamentary sovereignty

Parliamentary sovereignty is the central element of the UK Constitution. It is not possible to understand the nature and mechanisms of the constitution without studying this principle. Its paramount importance is illustrated by Bogdanor: *"The British Constitution could thus be summed up in just eight words : what the Queen in Parliament enacts is law"*.

In many legal systems, the judiciary is able to strike down legislation by declaring it unconstitutional. For instance, in the US, the Supreme Court may declare and invalidate Acts of Congress and the Constitutional Court has similar powers in France. Similarly, Article 15.4 of the Irish Constitution states that the Oireachtas shall not enact legislation "which is in any respect repugnant" to the Constitution. This means that law-making institutions in the US, Ireland or France, do not have absolute powers to pass legislation given that they are constitutionally and legally constrained by their respective codified constitutions.

What is internationally known as the judicial review of legislation passed by Parliament does not exist in the UK. Historically, the British constitution has been denying the power of squashing down Acts of Parliament to the judiciary. It can be explained by the fact that, historically, the British Parliament has not been limited in its legislative powers by a higher set of laws enshrined in a written constitution.

In contrast, UK courts do review delegated legislation passed by the executive because it does not have the supreme legitimacy which stems from primary legislation passed by Parliament. Although Parliamentary sovereignty is an unusual feature of the UK Constitution, it is not the unique example. For instance, New Zealand also has an uncodified constitution with a sovereign Parliament constitutionally able to pass any law without judicial review.

The term "sovereignty" should not be understood in its international meaning which defines the independence and control of a state over a territory under international law. In order to avoid the confusion, academics often use the term "legislative supremacy" of Parliament. Professor Dicey's conception of the theory has been very influential. As he has put it: "The principle of Parliamentary Sovereignty means nothing more or less than this, namely Parliament thus defined has, under the English Constitution, the right to make or unmake any law whatsoever; and, further, that no person or body is recognised by the law of England as having a right to override or set aside the legislation of Parliament".

It should be noted that this chapter is concerned with legal sovereignty which analyses constitutionally the relationship between the courts and the Queen in Parliament which is able to pass law in any subject. In contrast, political sovereignty rests in the electorate and the responsibility of the elected representatives to face their electors. Accordingly, if Parliament is legally capable of passing any laws, such as statutory provisions infringing individual rights' for example, political sovereignty places an external restraint on Parliament.

The doctrine of the unlimited sovereignty of Parliament was a product of a long historical struggle between Parliament and the Crown, which culminated in the Glorious Revolution of 1688 and the subsequent Bill of Rights. This resulted in a significant degree of power being transferred from the Crown to Parliament.

Constitutional conventions arose and it has been accepted progressively that Parliament enacts legislation, with the formal assent of the Crown. Since then, the courts have held, in a long succession of cases, that Acts of Parliament are the supreme form of law in the UK. Parliamentary sovereignty is therefore a common law doctrine. As Wade has put in 1955: "Legislation owes its authority to the rule: the rule does not owe its authority to legislation. To say that Parliament can change the rule, merely because it can change any other rule, is to put the cart before the horse".

General principle: A legal provision is considered to be a valid Act of Parliament has passed both Houses of Parliament and received Royal Assent. Under the "enrolled Bill Rule", the courts will not assess the internal process given that this "parliamentary roll" is ascertained.

Edinburgh and Dalkeith Railway Co v Wauchope (1842) 8 Cl & f 710

Facts: The plaintiff claimed that a Private Act of Parliament should not be applied in his instance because standing orders from the House of Commons were not complied with during the internal passage of the Act. The orders required to consult individuals affected by the proposals, which has not been done.

Ratio: The Court rejected the plaintiff's arguments upholding the "enrolled Bill Rule". This rule was explained by Lord Campbell: "All that a court of justice can look to is the Parliamentary roll; they see that an Act has passed both Houses of Parliament, and that it has received the Royal Assent, and no court of justice can inquire into the manner in which it was introduced into Parliament, what was done previously to its being introduced, or what passed in Parliament during the various stages of its progress through boss Houses of Parliament".

Application: The courts cannot look at the internal passage of a Bill in Parliament, as this would inevitably infringe parliamentary privilege which enables Parliament, under the Constitution, to be the only master of its own proceedings.

The Queen in Parliament legally can pass any law

This principle is the essence of UK Parliamentary sovereignty. It also includes the possibility for the Queen in Parliament to repeal or amend any existing legislation. Dicey's theory is *"Parliament has the right to make any law whatsoever"*. Although it appears that no legal limitations restrain the scope of this parliamentary prerogative, as stated earlier, there are clearly political limits on what Parliament can do.

General principle: Parliament can pass legislation amending some aspects of the British Constitution and courts cannot

overturn such laws.

Ex parte Canon Selwyn (1872) 36 JP 54

Facts: The validity of the Irish Church Act 1869 was challenged by a priest on the grounds that it disestablished his church in Ireland in contradiction with the Act of Union with Ireland (1800). It should be noted that the Act of Union with Ireland is considered to be of constitutional nature.

Ratio: The Court rejected this claim, as Cockburn CJ explained: "There is no judicial body in this country by which the validity of an Act of Parliament could be questioned. An Act of Legislature is superior in authority to any court of law. We have only to administer the law as we find it, and no court could pronounce judgment as to the validity of an Act of Parliament".

Application: This case makes it clear that no institution can question the validity of an Act of Parliament, regardless of its content.

General principle: Even in case of conflict between statutory provisions and international law, when the provision was clear and unambiguous, the courts will make Parliament's intentions prevail.

Cheney v Conn [1968] 1WLR 242

FActs: The Plaintiff was assessed for tax under Finance Act 1964. He challenged the assessment on the ground that part of the assessment was allegedly allocated to the development of nuclear weapons which was, according to him, in contradiction with international law.

Ratio: The High Court refused to invalidate the tax assessment and challenge the statutory provision. Even in case of conflict between statutory provisions and international law, when the provision was clear and unambiguous, the courts will make Parliament's intentions prevail. According to Ungoed-Thomas J *: "What the statute itself enacts cannot be unlawful, because what the statue says and provides is itself the law, and the highest form of law that is known to this country. It is the law which prevails over every other form of law, and it is not for the court to say that a Parliamentary enactment, the highest law in this country, is illegal".*

Application: Courts constantly held that they do not have the constitutional power to review or challenge Acts of Parliament and that the judicial function is limited to interpreting legislation in order to ascertain the intention of Parliament. Parliamentary sovereignty is rooted in this traditional common law principle.

General principle: Parliament's prerogatives are not restrained by geographical limitations. In theory, Parliament can legislate for territory beyond the jurisdiction of the UK.

Mortensen v Peters (1906) 14 SLT 227
Facts: The captain of a Norwegian ship was convicted for fishing in the Moray Firth contrary to the Herring Fisheries (Scotland) Act 1889. The Act restricted fishing beyond the three-mile territorial limit recognised by international law.
Ratio: The Court upheld the provisions of the Herring Fisheries (Scotland) Act 1889 regardless to the fact that it infringed international law of the sea. According to the Lord Justice-General: *"For us an Act of Parliament duly passed by Lords and Commons and assented by the King, is supreme, and we are bound to give effect to its terms".*
Application: Parliament is the supreme law-making body in the UK and enjoys large powers to legislate that are, in theory, not restricted by geographical limitations.

Nobody may question the validity of an enactment of Parliament
According to the Diceyan theory of law : "No person or body is recognized by the law of England as having a right to override or set aside the legislation of Parliament". This is the the negative side of Parliamentary sovereignty and the corollary principle of the first principle that the Crown in Parliament can pass any law.
The rule that nobody may question the validity of an enactment of Parliament is implicitly directed to courts which are traditionally able to do so, under judicial review of legislation, in many other legal systems.

General principle: The court's constitutional responsibility is simply to interpret and apply Parliament's will.

R v Jordan (1967) Crim LR 483

Facts: Jordan, the plaintiff, was convicted and sentenced for an offense committed under the Race Relation Act 1965. He claimed that the Act should be declared null and void by the Court because it infringed his freedom of expression.

Ratio: The High Court dismissed the plaintiff's claimed and upheld that courts do not have the power to question the validity of legislation passed by Parliament.

Application: This solution is well established in common law. For instance, it was similarly stated in **Duport Steels Ltd and others v Sirs and others (1980)** 1 All ER 529 by Lord Scarman: "The judge must not deny the statute. Unpalatable statute law may not be disregarded or rejected, merely because it is unpalatable".

General principle: Courts cannot question the validity of private Acts of Parliament, even when they were allegedly passed under fraud.

British Railways Board v Pickin (1974) AC 765

Facts: An Act of 1836 provided that the lands on a railway line, if it was to be abandoned, should vest in the owners of the adjoining lands. An Act of 1968 repealed the first Act and stipulated that such land would now vest in the British Railways Board. Both provisions were private Acts. The plaintiff owned an adjoining land and argued that the Board misled Parliament by a false recital in the preamble of the 1968 Act. The Court of Appeal upheld the plaintiff's arguments and considered that the 1968 Act should not be applied.

Ratio: The House of Lords dismissed the plaintiff's arguments, applied the 1968 Act and developed on the constitutional relationship between the courts and Parliament. The function of the courts was to apply Acts of Parliament. Courts cannot question the validity of legislation passed by Parliament, even for allegations of fraud. In the words of Lord Reid: "The idea that a Court is entitled to disregard a provision in an Act of Parliament on any ground must seem strange and startling to anyone with any knowledge of the history and law of our Constitution".

Application: Concerning the conception of Parliamentary sovereignty, it is worth noting that Lord Reid dismissed the plaintiff's claims that courts should be able to disregard Acts of Parliament when applying it would be contrary to "the law of God or natural justice" because he considered it obsolete after the 1688 Revolution and the consolidation of Parliamentary supremacy. This is clearly a repudiation of the ancient case law **Bonham (1610)** 8 Co Rep 114.

General principle: The House of Lords held that any future legislation passed in breach of section 2(1) of the Parliament Act 1911 (as amended in 1949) would not be considered by courts as a valid Act of Parliament, which would result on restricting Parliament's powers to adopt any legislation.

R (Jackson) v Attorney General [2005] UKHL 56
Facts: This case concerned the Hunting Act 2004, which was passed under the Parliament Act 1911 (as amended in 1949) allowing legislation to be adopted without the consent of the House of Lords. However, Section 2(1) of the Parliament Act (1911) expressly excludes the possibility to use these accelerated procedures for legislation extending "the life of Parliament".
Ratio: The majority of the House of Lords stated in this case that they would not recognise as a valid Act of Parliament, a legislation that would extend the maximum duration of Parliament beyond five years, therefore not complying with section 2(1) of the Parliament Act 1911 (as amended in 1949). In other words, any future legislation extending the life of Parliament, adopted by a Parliament only composed of the Monarch and the House of Commons, would be invalid as infringing section 2(1).
Application: It should be noted that the comments made in this case were *obiter*, therefore the precedential value of this case has to be mitigated. Turpin wrote: *"The comments made in Jackson were obiter and, moreover, they were uttered in the context of litigation concerning statutes passed without the consent of the House of Lords. It may be, for that reason, that they prove to be of little precedential value"*.

Parliament cannot be bound by its predecessors and bind its successors

According to Dicey: "Parliament has the right to unmake any law whatsoever". This rule relies on two interrelated corollary principles ; on the one hand Parliament in 2018 cannot bind its successors, it means that a legislature cannot restrict the laws that could be passed by Parliament in 2019. Conversely, on the other hand, Parliament in 2019 cannot be bound by its predecessor Parliament of 2018. In other word, academics have traditionally argued that Parliament cannot entrench legislation. The rationale behind this is that each legislature enjoys a similar Parliamentary sovereignty and full legislative power to pass any legislation that it chooses.

Express repeal

Express repeal entails that a later Act of Parliament expressly and explicitly repeals an earlier inconsistent Act or a part of it. Accordingly, even if an Act of Parliament states that it cannot be repealed, a later Act of Parliament can expressly repeal it. Express repeal is often used by Parliament to simplify legislation. For example the Sex Discrimination Act 1975, Race Relations Act 1976, and Disability Discrimination Act 1995 were all expressly repealed and replaced by the Equality Act 2010.

Implied repeal

The doctrine of implied repeal comes into operation when a later Act is inconsistent with an earlier Act on the same subject matter but does not expressly repeal it. The doctrine of implied repeal again follows from the principle that Parliament should not be able to bind its successors. However, two inconsistent Acts of Parliament on the same subject matter cannot stand together.

General principle: When two inconsistent Acts state two different rules on the same subject matter, the doctrine of implied repeal gives effect to the latest will of Parliament.

Vauxhall Estates v Liverpool Corporation [1932] 1 KB 133
Facts: The plaintiff claimed compensation for property that had been compulsorily purchased from them. Although the defendant argued that the level of compensation was to be assessed in compliance with the Housing Act 1925, the plaintiff considered that this had to be done under the Acquisition of Land Act 1919. The two Acts were inconsistent. The plaintiff expressly stipulated that its provisions were to prevail over any others passed or to be

passed.

Ratio: The Court held that it was bound to apply the terms of the later 1925 Act. It made the later will of Parliament prevail over an earlier Act. As Avory J stated: "Speaking for myself, I should certainly hold, until the contrary were decided, that no Act of Parliament can effectively provide that no future Act shall interfere with its provisions".

Application: As Avery J has put it in this case, the doctrine of implied repeal is rooted in the principle that Parliament should not be able to bind its successors.

General principle: It is impossible for Parliament to enact that in a subsequent statute dealing with the same subject matter there can be no implied repeal.

Ellen St Estates v Minister of Health [1934] 1 KB 590

Facts: The plaintiff claimed compensation for property that had been compulsorily purchased from them. Although the defendant argued that the level of compensation was to be assessed in compliance with the Housing Act 1925, the plaintiff considered that this had to be done under the Acquisition of Land Act 1919. The two Acts were inconsistent. Interestingly, in this case, the plaintiff argued that even though Parliament cannot bind its successors, it should be allowed to limit the right of its successors to repeal earlier legislation to express repeal and prohibit implied repeal.

Ratio: The Court of Appeal confirmed the Vauxhall decision and gave effect to the later will of Parliament (Housing Act 1925). Maugham LJ stated: *"The legislature cannot, according to our constitution, bind itself as to the force of subsequent legislation, and it is impossible for Parliament to enact that in a subsequent statute dealing with the same subject matter there can be no implied repeal. If in a subsequent Act Parliament chooses to make it plain that the earlier statute is being to some extent repealed, effect must be given to that intention just because it is the will of the Legislature".*

Application: In this case, common law made it clear that no distinction had to be drawn between implied or express repeals: in any cases Parliament cannot limit the right to future legislature to repeal earlier legislation.

The debate over legal entrenchment

Can Parliament limit its powers by binding its successors and restricting their power to legislate? Legal entrenchment would certainly infringe the principles of Parliamentary sovereignty, as it would restrict the powers of the future legislatures. However, a typical argument raised against this is that Parliamentary sovereignty is a common law rule that can be overridden by Parliament's will, given that a statute has a superior status. According to H Wade, *"What Salmond calls the "ultimate legal principle" is therefore a rule which is unique in being unchangeable by Parliament – it is changeable by revolution, not by legislation; it lies in the keeping of the courts, and no Act of Parliament can take it from them"*. Traditionally, academics have distinguished between two types of entrenchment: entrenchment in terms of subject-matter (substantive entrenchment) and entrenchment in terms of the manner and form of later legislation (formal entrenchment).

Substantive entrenchment

Some academics consider that Acts of Union between England, Scotland and Ireland were intended to represent a higher form of law and so should be seen as substantively entrenched therefore cannot be subsequently repealed. The two Acts of Union are: The Union with Scotland Act (1706) and The Union with Ireland Act (1800). The first Act united England and Wales with Scotland to form the Parliament of Great Britain and second integrated Ireland to form the Parliament of the United Kingdom.The theory behind the argument that Acts of Union are entrenched is that the UK Parliament was created by the English, Irish and Scottish parliaments and was therefore not sovereign at the origin. In the words of Professor J Mitchell, the new Parliament was "born unfree".

General principle: At first the theory that Acts of Union could limit Parliamentary sovereignty was not expressly rejected by the courts and left open for future decision.

McCormick v Lord Advocate [1953] SC 396

Facts: A Scottish nationalist challenged the designation of Queen Elisabeth the second and argued that she was the monarch of England but not of Scotland.

Ratio: The Court dissmissed the plaintiff's arguments on other grounds. However, Lord Cooper stated on the Acts of Union: "The principle of the unlimited sovereignty of parliament is a distinctively English principle which has no counterpart in Scottish Constitutional law (...) Considering that the Union legislation extinguished the parliaments of Scotland and England and replaced them by a new parliament, I have difficulty in seeing why it should have been supposed that the new parliament of Great Britain must inherit all the peculiar characteristics of the English parliament, as if all that happened in 1707 was that Scottish representatives were admitted to the Parliament of England. That is not what was done".

Application: In the judgement of Lord Cooper, one can see the pre-eminence of the theory that the Parliament of Great Britain was a product of the common will of the English and Scottish parliaments who were initially sovereign.

General principle: The Courts have never confirmed the entrenched nature of Acts of Union although they had opportunities to do so.

Gibson v Lord Advocate [1975] SLT 134

Facts: The Act of Union with Scotland contained the provision that alterations in private law must be "for the evident utility of the subjects in Scotland" (article XVIII). This case concerned the challenge of the European Communities Act with regard to common fisheries policy measures, because it gave access to Scottish waters. The plaintiff complained that this was a change in private law which was not for the "evident utility" of Scots.

Ratio: The court held that access to fisheries was not "private law" and therefore the measure could not be challenged. It refused to confirm the alleged entrenched nature of the Acts of Union.

Application: The cases **McCormick** and **Gibson** are both examples of the courts' reluctance to confirm that the Acts of Union can limit parliamentary sovereignty to the extent that these

Acts cannot be repealed. On the contrary, it should be noted that UK Parliament has subsequently altered many of the principles contained in both the Scottish and Irish Acts of Union.

The British Empire was gradually dismantled by grants of independence to the old colonies, namely from Canada and Australia. They became "Dominions" when their constitutions were established by UK Acts of Parliament but were effectively independent nations. As a constitutional convention, no Acts of Parliament can affect a Dominion without the request and consent of that Dominion (in recognition of their independent status). This was confirmed in the Statute of Westminster 1931 s. 4: "*No Act of parliament of the UK passed after the commencement of this Act shall extend, or be deemed to extend, to a Dominion as part of the law of that Dominion unless it is expressly declared in that Act that that Dominion has requested and consented to the enactment thereof.*" However, can we conclude that Parliament powers' to legislate for Dominions is limited by statutory legislation? The question is to know whether the 1931 Parliament bound its successors to adhere to the requirements of s. 4 of the Statute of Westminster, when passing subsequent legislation.

General principle: The Westminster Parliament, under its theoretical legal power as the sovereign body, remains able to pass laws affecting the UK's Dominions.

British Coal Corporation v The King [1935] AC 500
Facts: In this case, the main question was to determine whether the UK Parliament was able to legislate for Canada in breach of the Statute of Westminster, s. 4.
Ratio: In the words of Lord Sankey "It is doubtless true that the power of the Imperial [i.e. Westminster] Parliament to pass on its own initiative any legislation that it thought fit extending to Canada remains in theory unimpaired: indeed, the Imperial Parliament could as a matter of abstract law, repeal or disregard s 4 of the Statute (...) But that is theory and has no relation to realities".
Application: The grants of independence for Dominions have certainly imposed political constraints on the Westminster Parliament, but its theoretical legal power, as the soveregin body, to pass law affecting those new states remains unimpaired.

Formal entrenchment

This type of entrenchment refers to the procedure of making legislation. The question is to know whether Parliament can bind its successors on the manner and form of later legislation.

In theory, Parliament could pass law regulating the procedure of the enactement of later law. However, in principle, the validity of Acts of Parliament that would not respect the manner and form laid down in earlier legislation could not be challenged. This is because of the "enrolled bill rule" laid down in **Pickin v British Railways Board [1974]** AC 765. Academics have questioned this postulate, mainly with regard to the Human Rights Act or the European Communities Act.

General principle: The Privy Council upheld that the law amending the New South Wales Constitution had to comply with the manner and form lay down by an Act previously adopted.

Attorney-General for New South Wales v Trethowan, [1932] AC 526 (PC)

Facts: The Colonial Laws Validity Act (1865), which was an Act of the UK Parliament, enabled the New South Wales Legislature to pass laws amending the Constitution of that state. The Constitution Act (1902) was amended in 1929 and s. 7A was introduced, providing that no bill to abolish the Upper House in New South Wales could be passed unless it had been supported by a majority of voters in a referendum. In 1930, the New South Wales Government decided to repeal s. 7A and abolish the Upper House without consulting the people's will through a referundum. The Privy Council had to give their advice as to whether the proposed amendment was legal.

Ratio: The Privy Council confirmed that the Bills needed to comply with the "manner and form" as stipulated in s. 7A. Accordingly, the proposed amendment was not legal and needed the people's support before being lawfully presented.

Application: In this case the Privy Council confirmed that s. 7A of the Constitution Act 1902 (as amended in 1929) was formally entrenched.

General principle: The Supreme Court of South Africa declared null and void an Act passed in a manner and form which did not comply with the requirements of another Act previously adopted.

Harris v The Minister of the Interior (1952) (2) SA 428

Facts: The South Africa Act 1909, under its Section 152, laid down a special procedure to amend its Section 35 which concerned the denial of the right of registration for voting on the basis of colour. Section 152 required a majority of two-thirds of both Houses, sitting together, in order to amend Section 35. The Separate representation of Voters Act (1951), amending Section 35 of the South Africa Act 1909, was indeed passed with a majority of two-thirds in each house but not sitting together.

Ratio: The Supreme Court of South Africa held that the Separate representation of Voters Act (1951) was null and void. It upheld that, in order to be lawful, any amendment to Section 35 of the South Africa Act 1909 had to comply with Section 152 which required both houses to sit together.

Application: In this case, the Supreme Court of South Africa enforces a quite formal requirement of an entrenched Act compared to the substantive unsatisfied requirement in **Attorney-General for New South Wales**. The main requirements as to the manner and form for the amendment were satisfied, namely a majority of two-thirds in both Houses. However, they were not sitting together, infringing a formal entrenchment which was enforced by the Court.

General principle: The Privy Council affirmed a judgement of the Supreme Court of Ceylon holding that courts cannot enforce an Act which did not comply, in the process of law-making, with another entrenched Act.

The Bribery Commissioner v Pedrick Ranasinghe (1965) AC 172

Facts: Under Section 29 (4) of the Ceylon Constitution (Order in Council 1946), no Bill could be presented for Royal Assent without having been passed by at least two-thirds of the House of Representatives. This majority of the two-thirds had to be corroborated by the Speaker's certificate. The Bribery Amendment Act 1958, which indirectly altered the Constitution, did not seem to satisfy this requirement.

Ratio: The Privy Council held that the Bribery Amendment Act 1958 could not be enforced by courts against the plaintiff under provisions of the impugned Act because it did not comply with the manner and form set out in s. 29(4).

Application: In this case, the Privy Council confirmed the decision that an act was invalid and *ultra vires*, and therefore could not be enforced by courts, for not having complied with requirements as to the manner and form set out in a previous entrenched Act.

In conclusion, although the cases presented above demonstrate that the Legislature had to comply with the stipulated manner and form for later legislation, therefore recognizing the formal entrenched nature of these Acts, it should be noted that the concerned Acts were passed by parliaments from Commonwealth authorities and not from the UK Parliament. Some authors, such as Barnett, have argued that the same approach is not applicable to the UK Parliament, which enjoys a special sovereignty.

Modern developments and Parliamentary sovereignty

Parliamentary sovereignty and devolution

The UK Parliament passed a couple of devolution Acts in 1998 which delegated powers to the following regions: Scotland (Scotland Act), Wales (Government of Wales Act) and Northern Ireland (Northern Ireland Act). Under the Scotland Act 1998, the new Scottish Parliament is able to legislate for Scotland on a number of matters. However, with regard to Westminster's sovereignty, the Scotland Act 1998, at s. 28(7), specifically states that this does not affect the legal powers of the UK Parliament to legislate for Scotland when it considers it appropriate. Under section 28(7): "This section does not affect the power of the Parliament of the United Kingdom to make laws for Scotland".

More recently, two events have resulted on grants of greater devolution for Scotland. Firstly the 2014 Scottish referendum on whether Scotland should leave the UK (which was won by a 55% margin by those wishing to remain in the UK) and the establishment of the Smith Commission on devolution of the UK

Parliament. As a result, the Scotland Act 2016 has extended the matters on which the Scottish Parliament can legislate to areas including for example abortion law or equal opportunities. In legal theory, the UK Parliament remains fully capable of legislating for any regions for which it previously accepted to devolve prerogatives. In addition, the devolution Acts can be repealed or amended by any Act of the Westminster Parliament.

General principle: As Acts of the UK Parliament, Acts of the Scottish Parliament are not subjected to judicial review, unless they are not complying with the Rule of Law.

AXA General Insurance Ltd v Lord Advocate, [2011] UKSC 46
Facts: In this case, the UK Supreme Court had to define the relationship between the Scottish and the Westminster parliaments by determining if an Act of the former could be subjected to judiciacl review. Primary legislation is not subjected to judicial review in the UK, therefore, subjecting an Act of the Scottish Parliament to judicial review would have resulted in considering it as mere delegated legislation.
Ratio: Lord Hope and Lord Reid considered that judicial review of Acts of the Scottish Parliament was not appropriate as a source of primary legislation. However, they both agreed that such Acts that would be incompatible with the Rule of Law will not be enforced by the courts, recalling that: "the rule of law enforced by the courts is the ultimate controlling factor on which our constitution is based".
Application: In this case, by recognising Acts of the Scottish Parliament as a sort of primary legislation which is not subjected to judicial review, as any other Act of the UK Parliament, the Supreme Court admitted that the traditional approach on Parliamentary sovereignty has evolved along with the devolution process.

Parliamentary sovereignty and the Human Rights Act 1998

Although the practical effect of the Act on Parliamentary sovereignty has raised a number of important issues, it should be noted that the Act does not allow courts to invalidate Acts of Parliament that would be inconsistent with the European Convention for Human Rights (hereinafter "the Convention").

Therefore, the theoretical impact of the Human Rights (hereinafter HRA) Act on Parliamentary sovereignty has to be mitigated. In the words of Lord Steyn in **R v DPP ex p Kebilene and others (1999) 3 WLR 972**: "It is crystal clear that the carefully and subtly drafted Human Rights Act 1998preserves the principle of Parliamentary sovereignty".

However, the HRA, under section 4, enables the higher courts to issue declarations of incompatibility. The declarations, as such, do not invalidate the impugned legislation. Accordingly, it is not a legally binding declaration imposing to Parliament to repeal the legislation at stake but it certainly places political pressure on the Legislature to do so. In addition to declarations of incompatibility, the HRA 1998, s. 3(1) states: *"so far as it is possible to do so, primary legislation and subordinate legislation must be read and given effect in a way which is compatible with convention rights".* This is referred to as interpretation of legislation, where judges will read legislation in a way which is compatible with the rights enshrined by the Convention. The word "possible", at section 3 of the HRA 1998, is quite broad, and has given rise to intense debate.

General principle: The courts may use Section 3 of the HRA 1998 to interpret Acts of Parliament that seem to be incompatible with the Convention, to give them effect in a way which is compatible with convention rights.

R v A (Complainant's Sexual History) [2002] 1 AC 45
Facts: This case concerned the admissibility of evidence in a rape trial. The Youth Justice and Criminal Evidence Act 1999, s. 41, seemed incompatible with the Convention and the main question was to know whether it would be appropriate to use section 3 of the HRA in order give it an effect that would comply with convention rights.
Ratio: The House of Lords read the impugned legislation in a way which is compatible with convention rights. As Lord Steyn concluded: "After all it is realistic to proceed on the basis that the legislature would not if alerted to the problem have wished to deny the right to an accused to put forward a full and complete defence (...) It is therefore possible under section 3 to read section 41 '(...) as subject to the implied provision that evidence or questioning which is required to ensure a fair trial

under Article 6 of the Convention should not be treated as inadmissible". **Lord Hope added, in a concurring opinion, that section 3 had to be limited to interpretation only and did not give the judiciary the right to act as legislators, in accordance with Parliamentary sovereignty.**

Application: The House of Lords, in this case, have made use of their powers under section 3 of the HRA, which is an Act of Parliament. Accordingly, this judicial precedent seems to be in full compliance with the principle of Parliamentary sovereignty. However, this case and subsequent case law, have been heavily criticised and viewed as examples of judicial activism.

Parliamentary sovereignty and EU Law

The UK progressive compliance with EU Law supremacy was probably the most controversial incorporation in all 28 Member States. Partly because dualist states are generally not designed to integrate international orders implying any sort of supremacy but mainly because of its traditional Parliamentary sovereignty. However, the CJEU case-law on supremacy requires national Courts to suspend operations, declare as invalid and dis-apply Acts of Parliament that do not comply with higher norms of EU Law. This approach is completely opposed to the UK conception of the role of courts.

The United Kingdom being a dualist system allowed EC law to get an automatic incorporation through the European Communities Act 1972 (ECA). Section 2(1) of this act particularly conveyed how the UK limited its sovereign rights in favour of the EU. However section 2(4) limited the EU's sovereignty over domestic law by ensuring that all domestic enactments had effect only subject to directly applicable rules of community law. The ECA 1972 had two major consequences on the traditional UK system: overriding the usual presumption that any later enactment overruled prior law inconsistent with it and clearly terminates any effect of Acts of Parliament purporting to contradict EU Law.

In the early case of **E Coomes (Holdings) Ltd v Shields [1978] IRLR 263 CA**, Lord Denning stated that "By the 1972 Act, parliament enacted that we should abide by the principle as laid down by the European Court".

General principle: National courts confronted with statutory legislation incompatible with EU Law are required to do everything necessary to set aside the impugned law.

R (Factortame Ltd) v Secretary of State for Transport (Case C-213/89) 1990 ECR 1-2433

Facts: The case involved companies registered in the UK but mainly owned by Spanish nationals. The Merchant Shipping Act 1988 required a certain percentage of UK national ownership for the registration of a vessel. This provision expressly violated the "non-discrimination on nationality" principle of Article 12. The Divisional Court granted an interim relief suspending the operation of the impugned law. The House of Lords then made a reference to the ECJ arguing than nothing neither in the UK Constitution nor in EC Law permitted such interim. The question before the Court was the following one: does the incompatibility of an act of Parliament, enacted after accession to the Treaties and expressly introducing inconsistencies to EC Law, permits judges to suspend the legal effect of the domestic provision?

Ratio: The Court firmly recalled that no Act of Parliament, even enacted after the accession Treaties, that would be inconsistent with EU Law, can be enforced by the UK courts. In addition to this, national courts confronted with statutory legislation incompatible with EU Law are required to do everything necessary to set aside the impugned law.

Application: The UK constructive approach is overruled and the supremacy of EU Law is affirmed. There is now an external body competent to make laws affecting the United Kingdom, which are applied by the English Courts irrespective of the wishes of Parliament.

Authors such as Wade stated that the fact of setting aside an act of Parliament for an alleged incompatibility with a superior source meant that "something drastic had happened to the traditional doctrine of Parliamentary sovereignty". He claimed that this was revolutionary on the grounds that the Courts were no longer prepared to uphold absolute Parliamentary sovereignty.

In 2011, The European Union Act was passed by Parliament, by the coalition government that makes a number of statutory qualifications about the future relationship between the EU and the

UK. A very interesting provision related to the issue of supremacy can be found in section 18 of the Act. The latter subjects the UK membership to the continuing will of Parliament. Therefore, a simple Act of Parliament was all that was needed to withdraw from the EU treaties.

The recent events that led the UK to trigger article 50 TFEU support this last argument. Brexit has shown that the UK Parliament voluntarily transferred some powers to the Union and was entitled to take them back at any time.

Summary

- Parliamentary sovereignty is the central element of the UK Constitution; it is not possible to understand the nature and mechanisms of the constitution without studying this principle.

- What is internationally known as the judicial review of legislation passed by Parliament does not exist in the UK.

- The doctrine of the unlimited sovereignty of Parliament was a product of a long historical struggle between Parliament and the Crown, which culminated in the Glorious Revolution of 1688.

- The courts cannot look at the internal passage of a Bill in Parliament, as this would inevitably infringe parliamentary privilege which enables Parliament, under the Constitution, to be the only master of its own proceedings.

- The Queen in Parliament legally can pass any law. Although it appears that no legal limitations restrain the scope of this parliamentary prerogative, as stated earlier, there are clearly political limits on what Parliament can do.

- According to the Diceyan theory of law: "No person or body is recognized by the law of England as having a right to override or set aside the legislation of Parliament".

- According to Dicey: "Parliament has the right to unmake any law whatsoever".

- In legal theory, the UK Parliament remains fully capable of legislating for any regions for which it previously accepted to devolve prerogatives. In addition, the devolution Acts can be repealed or amended by any Act of the Westminster Parliament.

- Although the practical effect of the Human Rights Act (1998) on Parliamentary sovereignty has raised a number of important issues, it should be noted that the Act does not allow courts to invalidate Acts of Parliament that would be inconsistent with the European Convention for Human Rights.

- Brexit has shown that the UK Parliament voluntarily transferred some powers to the Union and was entitled to take them back at any time. The UK progressive compliance with EU Law supremacy was probably the most controversial incorporation in all 28 Member States.

Chapter 7 – The Crown and the Prerogative

The historical role of the Crown in the British Constitution

In the UK, the executive is composed of the Queen and her majesty's government. It should be noted that the United Kingdom has a constitutional monarchy with an unelected hereditary monarch as head of State. However, as stated earlier, in political practice, the Queen's role is a rather symbolic and ceremonial one. The British state remains a kingdom. In other words, the head of the United Kingdom is the monarch, although the role of the Queen in the British constitution is mainly ceremonial and symbolic. The United Kingdom is a modern democracy that could be compared to Spain, in which the monarch has prerogatives that are constitutionally limited in a state where the powers are dispersed amongst different institutions.

The government is referred to as her majesty's government because in legal theory, the monarch appoints and dismisses government ministers. Noteworthy, the Queen is also the Commander in chief of the armed forces, which, together with the various police forces, form the "executive in practical terms".
The term "royal prerogative" refers to those powers of the "Crown" that are recognised by the common law, as distinct from those conferred and exercised under statute. Generally, the "Crown" refers to the executive, which is composed of the Queen and her majesty's government. Indeed, the government acts on the behalf of the Queen, exercising prerogative powers in application of a strong constitutional convention that provides that although the Royal prerogative is still formally vested in the Queen, the executive exercises the monarch's powers.

The traditional definition of the Prerogative was formulated by Dicey: *"The residue of discretionary or arbitrary authority, which at any given time is legally left in the hands of the Crown (...) Every act which the executive government can lawfully do without the authority of an Act of Parliament is done in virtue of this prerogative"*. This definition has been approved in the famous case **Council for the Civil Service Unions v Minister for the Civil Service [1985]** AC 374 (commonly known as the "GCHQ" case).

However, as Sir William Blackstone added, the Prerogative should only include powers that are exclusively vested in the Crown: *"It can only be applied to those rights and capacities which the King enjoys alone, in contradiction to others and not to those which he enjoys in common with any of his subjects, for if once any prerogative of the Crown could be held in common with the subject, it would cease to be a prerogative any longer".*

Historically, courts have devised a distinction between absolute and ordinary powers of the Crown, the first being exercised almost entirely in a discretionary manner and the latter being exercised according to the established principles, practices and procedures. Absolute powers were referred to by academics as being the essence of the Prerogative. However, this distinction is no more used by the courts since the principles of the Rule of Law have been progressively embraced by the British Constitution.

Examples of prerogative powers

Most of the powers exercised by the executive are derived from statutes. However, the Crown also draws powers from common law. The conception of "residual power to act" is a common law principle which provides that public authorities can do everything that is not forbidden (see **Malone v Metropolitan Police Commissioner (1979) Ch 344**).

In addition to this, the Crown exercises the royal prerogative through her majesty's government. In this regard, the House of Commons Public Administration Select Committee, in 2004, identified the *"personal powers which remain in the Sovereign's hands"*. The following non-exhaustive examples of these powers are theoretically conferred by the Constitution to the Queen but the practical reality, under constitutional convention, is that the Queen acts on the advice of her government. For instance, the Queen appoints the Prime Minister and government ministers and grants the Royal Assent to Bills adopted by Parliament. The Royal prerogative also includes the power to declare war, to deploy armed forces both domestically and abroad and to ratify international treaties. The Queen may also create peers and the grant of other honours.

In addition to this, the power to issue and revoke passports and the prerogative of Mercy are both prerogative powers. The Home Secretary, on behalf of the Crown and under the prerogative of mercy, may pardon offences of a public nature. Government, exercising royal prerogative, recognises foreign states, their governments, heads of states and diplomatic envoys.

Until 2011, the prerogative to dissolve Parliament has conventionally been a power effectively exercised by the Prime Minister. The fixed-term Parliaments Act 2011 had the concrete effect of removing this prerogative power from the Crown. Now, elections are to be called on a pre-set date every five years rather than at any point during a government's five-year term. However, it is politically easy for government to convince Parliament, under s. 2(1) of the 2011 Act, to agree to its own dissolution (as Theresa May did in 2017). Historically, the Crown was also the administrator of justice and was referred to as the "fountain of justice". Today, the structure of the courts and their jurisdiction are mainly regulated by statute. However, some legal prerogatives remain vested in the Crown.

General principle: The Crown is not bound by statute except by express words or necessary implication.

Province of Bombay v Municipal Corporation of the City Bombay [1947] AC 58
Facts: The question in this case was to know whether or not the city of Bombay Municipal Act 1888 bound the Crown?
Ratio: The Privy Council held that the Crown was not bound by Sections 222(1) and 265 of the City of Bombay Municipal Act, 1888. In the words of Lord du Parcq: "If it is manifest from the very terms of the statute, that it was the intention of the legislature that the Crown should be bound, then the result is the same as if the Crown had been expressly named. It must then be inferred that the Crown, by assenting to the law, agreed to be bound by its provisions".
Application: This case should be understood as providing that the agreement of the Crown to be bound could be deduced where it was apparent from the terms of the statute that its main purpose

would be frustrated if the Crown was not bound.

General principle: The Crown is immune from income tax as long as no statute expressly binds it otherwise.

Lord Advocate v Dumbarton District Council [1989] 3 WLR 1346

Facts: The Ministry of Defence, in an attempt to improve the defence of borders at a nuclear submarine base, marked off a road that ran passed close to the base, however they did so without the permission of the local regional or district council, as required by statute. In this case, the question was whether or not the Ministry of Defence was immune from court orders on the grounds that their authority derived from the royal prerogative?

Ratio: The House of Lords overturned the courts' decisions and held that the Crown was not bound by statute. It reaffirmed that the Crown was either bound by statute or not and an analysis of other factors is unnecessary, rejecting the argument raised in first instance that a distinction should be made between the Crown acting inside or outside its rights.

Application: The decision in this case should however be contrasted with the findings of the High Court in the case **Australian case of Bropho v State of Western Australia [1990]** 64 ALJR 374.

The Crown is also protected by Crown immunities. In theory, the sovereign has personal immunity from prosecution or being sued for wrongful acts. However, this immunity from courts' jurisdiction is not absolute.

General principle: While reviewing acts of ministers of the Crown, in judicial review proceedings, courts can grant interim injunctions against ministers.

M v Home Office [1993] 3 All ER 537

Facts: A Zairian national sought asylum in the UK and his application was rejected. He contested this decision under judicial review and the Court accepted an undertaking from the Crown asserting that he will not be returned to Zaire until his case was heard once again. In breach of this undertaking, the plaintiff was deported.

Ratio: The House of Lords held that courts can grant interim injunctions prohibiting the Crown to deport an individual, regardless of the Crown's immunities. Lord Templeman wrote in this case: "My Lords, the argument that there is no power to enforce the law by injunction or contempt proceedings against a minister in his official capacity would, if upheld, establish the proposition that the executive obey the law as a matter of grace and not as a matter of necessity, a proposition which would reverse the result of the Civil War. For the reasons given by my noble and learned friend, Lord Woolf, and on principle, I am satisfied that injunctions and contempt proceedings may be brought against the minister in his official capacity and that in the present case the Home Office for which the Secretary of State was responsible was in contempt".

Application: This case overturned a previous position of English Law which provided that courts could not grant interim injunctions against ministers (see **Factortame Ltd v Secretary of State for Transport [1990]** 2 AC 85). It should be noted that the European Court of Justice took the opposite approach in the its decision **Factortame [1990]** ECR I-2433, which was later embraced by British courts in **M v Home Office [1993]** 3 All ER 537.

Scrutiny of the Prerogative

Historically, even though prerogative powers of the Crown were considered almost absolute in theory, they were still limited by law. This is because of the early incorporation in the British Constitution of the principles of the Rule of Law: "The King hath no prerogative but that which the law of the land allows him" (see the **Case of Proclamations (1611)** 12 Co Rep 74).

Constitutional powers of Parliament over the royal prerogative

Parliament, on several occasions, has limited and even abolished some of the Monarch's prerogative powers. Thus, Parliament can legislate to modify, abolish, or simply put on a statutory footing any particular prerogative power. It has done so, for example, by enacting the Bill of rights 1689.

General principle: Parliament can pass laws to supersede prerogative powers of the Crown. In such cases the Crown

cannot act under royal prerogative.

Attorney General v De Keyser's Royal Hotel Limited (1920) AC 508

Facts: In this case, a hotel was expropriated by the Crown to accommodate the Royal Flying Corps. The owner of the hotel sought compensation for occupation and use of his property (under the Defence Act 1842 which made provision for compensation) but the Government replied that because the expropriation was made under royal prerogative, no compensation could be claimed.

Ratio: The House of Lord held that the government occupation of the hotel was under the terms of the Defence Act 1842. Therefore, compensation had to be paid to the plaintiff. In other words, the House of Lord affirmed that the Crown cannot act under royal prerogative where the power in question was superseded by legislation. In the words of Lord Atkinson: "When a statute, expressing the will and intention of the King and of the three estates of the realm, is passed, it abridges the Royal prerogative while it is in force to this extent: that the Crown can only do the particular thing under and in accordance with the statutory provisions, and that its prerogative power to do that thing is in abeyance".

Application: In this case, the fact that Acts of Parliament prevail over royal prerogative underlines the relevance of Parliamentary sovereignty in constitutional relationships between state's institutions.

The possibility for Parliament to displace prerogative powers through legislation is an ultimate form of scrutiny of the executive which ensures that the latter is held accountable.

General principle: Once a statue substitutes prerogative powers in a given subject matter, the Crown has no right to amend the rules laid down by Parliament.

R (Alvi) v Secretary of State for the Home Department [2012] UKSC 33

Facts: In this case, the Home Secretary claimed to use prerogative powers to amend the rules governing immigration controls, which were regulated by Parliament that previously amended prerogative powers of the Crown by adopting The Immigration Act 1971. In particular, the Home Secretary wanted to modify the rules related to working permits for foreigners with specific skills and education.

Ratio: The Supreme Court unanimously dismissed the appeal of the Secretary of State. It upheld that everything which is in the nature of a rule as to the practice to be followed in the administration of the 1971 Act must be laid before Parliament. Accordingly, the Supreme Court rejected the argument of the Home Secretary claiming that it could, under Royal prerogative, create new rules on immigration controls that were not covered by the Act.

Application: In this case, the Supreme Court affirmed that once Parliament has taken the statutory control of a subject matter over Royal prerogative, the Crown cannot amend or regulate the matter anymore.

General principle: A statute may also impliedly suspend prerogative powers where Parliament seeks to regulate a matter previously falling under the prerogative, but does not expressly abolish the prerogative.

Laker Airways v Department of Trade [1977] QB 643

Facts: This case was related to the regulation of the transatlantic air route. The Bermuda Agreement of (1946) between the US and the UK provided that each party could designate air carriers in order to operate between the two countries. In order for a UK airline to operate, it also had to obtain a licence from the Civil Aviation Authority (CAA). The Secretary of State then issued new guidance for the CAA in order to limit the grants of licence and place British Airways in a position of Monopoly. This was not expressly provided for by the Civil Aviation Act 1971. The plaintiff, whose application for a licence was rejected, sought compensation by judicial review.

Ratio: The Court held that the Secretary of State's guidance was _ultra vires_. In other words, where statutory legislation also impliedly suspends prerogative powers, the statute should prevail. According to Lord Denning: "Seeing that these statutory means were available for stopping Skytrain if there was a proper case for it, the question is whether the Secretary of State can stop it by other means. Can he do it by withdrawing the designation? Can he do indirectly that which

he cannot do directly? Can he displace the statute by invoking a prerogative? If he could do this, it would mean by a side wind, Laker Airways Ltd would be deprived of the protection that statute affords them. There would be no hearing, no safeguard against injustice (...) To my mind such a procedure was never contemplated by the statute".

Application: **Laker Airways v Department of Trade [1977]** QB 643 illustrates that Parliament can limit and regulate prerogative powers and whenever a conflict of norms may arise, the statute should prevail in most of the cases.

General principle: In situations where both statutory legislation and royal prerogative regulate the same general subject matter, prerogative powers may still apply where it is exercised for the public good.

R v Secretary of State for the Home Department, ex parte Northumbria Police Authority [1988] 1 All ER 556

Facts: Following riots in the early 1980s, the Home Office, by adopting a circular (40/1986), increased police powers in situations of public disorder. This was adopted without the approval of the Chief Constable. Section 4(4) of the Police Act 1964 stated that "police authorities are to provide for the supply of equipment to their local forces", something that conflicted with the exercise of the prerogative.

Ratio: The Court dismissed the appeal, considering that the circular was adopted for the public good, in order to preserve peace. As summed up by Lord Justice Croom-Johnson: "A prerogative of keeping the peace within the realm existed in mediaeval times, probably since the Conquest and, particular statutory provision apart, that it has not been surrendered by the Crown in the process of giving its express or implied assent to the modern system of keeping the peace through the agency of independent police forces. I therefore conclude that, if the necessary power had not been available under section 41 of the 1964 Act, the terms and implementation of paragraph 4 of the Home Office circular would have been within the prerogative powers of the Crown".

Application: This case seems to create an exception to the De Keyser's principle. However, it was not significantly applied in later practice and was heavily criticized by the academic community.

General principle: The judiciary, as a guardian of the separation of powers, can strike down executive action in order to uphold the democratic will of Parliament.

R v Secretary of State for Home Department ex p Fire Brigades Union [1995] 2 All ER 244

Facts: This case concerned the use of prerogative powers by the Home Secretary's to introduce a criminal injuries compensation scheme.

Ratio: The House of Lords ruled that using prerogative power, while refusing to implement a statutory scheme which had been enacted in an Act of Parliament was unconstitutional because it infringed Parliament's will. As Lord Browne-Wilkinson stated: "'My Lords, it would be most surprising if, at the present day, prerogative powers could be validly exercised by the executive so as to frustrate the will of Parliament expressed in a statute and, to an extent, to pre-empt the decision of Parliament whether or not to continue with the statutory scheme even though the old scheme has been abandoned. It is not for the executive, as the Lord Advocate accepted, to state as it did in the White Paper that the provisions in the Act of 1988 "will accordingly be repealed when a suitable legislative opportunity occurs". It is for Parliament, not the executive, to repeal legislation. The constitutional history of this country is the history of the prerogative powers of the Crown being made subject to the overriding powers of the democratically elected legislature as the sovereign body. The prerogative powers of the Crown remain in existence to the extent that Parliament has not expressly or by implication extinguished them".

Application: In this type of cases, courts exercise their powers to make sure that constitutional provisions, including the separation of powers between the legislative and the executive, are respected.

General principle: In the context of Brexit and the significant constitutional changes that it implies, the Crown cannot trigger article 50 of the TFEU in use of prerogative powers, which was previously incorporated by Parliament when it enacted the ECA 1972, without parliamentary approval.

R (Miller) v Secretary of State for Exiting the European Union [2017] UKSC

Facts: In the context of Brexit, Theresa May announced her will, as the Prime Minister, to trigger Article 50 of the TFEU, without consulting Parliament. She argued that she could do so in use of her prerogative powers to make treaties. Government argued that the 1972 Parliament, by enacting the 1972 European Communities Act, only intended to give effect to EU Law in the UK as far as it would remain a member of the EU and that leaving the EU was a prerogative power of the Crown.

Ratio: The Supreme Court reiterated the High Court's approach considering that the 1972 Parliament cannot have intended that the rights brought by the UK's membership to the EU could be removed through the mere use of prerogative powers without parliamentary approval. The Court insisted in the significance of the constitutional changes that would trigger a withdrawal of the TFEU. As Lord Neuberger concluded: *"The main difficulty with the Secretary of State's argument is that it does not answer the objection based on the constitutional implications of withdrawal from the EU. As we have said, withdrawal is fundamentally different from variations in the content of EU law arising from further EU Treaties or legislation. A complete withdrawal represents a change which is different not just in degree but in kind from the abrogation of particular rights, duties or rules derived from EU law. It will constitute as significant a constitutional change as that which occurred when EU law was first incorporated in domestic law by the 1972 Act. And, if Notice is given, this change will occur irrespective of whether Parliament repeals the 1972 Act. It would be inconsistent with long-standing and fundamental principle for such a far-reaching change to the UK constitutional arrangements to be brought about by ministerial decision or ministerial action alone. All the more so when the source in question was brought into existence by Parliament through primary legislation, which gave that source an overriding supremacy in the hierarchy of domestic law sources".*

Application: This case consolidated the De Keyser principle which was certainly affected by the decision in **R v Secretary of State for the Home Department, ex parte Northumbria Police Authority [1988]** 1 All ER 556. The Supreme Court reaffirmed the major role of Parliament in controlling the exercise of the royal prerogative.

In addition to this, it is generally recognized that time does not run against the Crown at common law. However, Parliament can impose the observation of time limitations. For instance, the Crown Proceedings Act 1947 expressly requires the Crown to observe any statutory time limitations. Ministers of the Crown are also accountable to Parliament for their actions, which are namely scrutinized by Parliament's Select Committees. Moreover, Parliament also approves the Government's expenditure, which also impacts, to some extent, the use of prerogative powers.

Judicial control of the prerogative

The main default to scrutiny of the executive by Parliament is the lack of political independence of MPs who support their own party's administration. For this reason, the scrutiny of the executive by courts is crucial, given the political neutrality of judges.

Historically, the courts have been quite reluctant to intervene in the scrutiny of the executive, in accordance with the principle of separation of powers. The more the issue is political and the more it is likely that courts will avoid the question and defer it to Parliament. As stated by Lord Bingham: "The more purely political a question is, the more appropriate it will be for political resolution and the less likely it is to be an appropriate matter for judicial decision" (See **R (A & Others) v Secretary of State for the Home Department [2004]** UKHL 56).

General principle: It is impossible to create new prerogative powers of the Crown that did not exist before the advent of the parliamentary system in 1688.

BBC v Johns (Inspector of Taxes) (1965) 1 CH 32
Facts: The BBC argued that it was exempt from income tax, claiming to be a monopoly established by royal prerogative.
Ratio: The Court upheld that BBC was not exempt from paying income taxes since exemptions could only be granted by legislation. In addition to this, it was unconstitutional to create

new prerogative powers for the executive. Lord Diplock famously commented: "It is 350 years and a civil war too late for the Queen's courts to broaden the prerogative. The limits within which the executive government may impose obligations or restraints upon citizens of the United Kingdom without any statutory authority are now well settled and incapable of extension (...) Today, save in so far as the power is preserved by the Statute of Monopolies, or created by other statutes, the executive government has no constitutional right either itself to exercise through its agents or to confer upon other persons a monopoly of any form of activity".

Application: This case was the first case where the courts expressly and firmly intervened in scrutinizing the executive. It marked a turning point which resulted in subsequent case law with a similar approach adopted by the judiciary.

General principle: In certain subject matters identified by common law, courts can legally supervise the Crown use of the royal prerogative in the same way that they review the manner in which statutory powers are exercised.

Council of Civil Service Unions v Minister for the Civil Service (1985) 1 AC 374 (the GCHQ case)
Facts: The Prime Minister issued an instruction that civil servants would no longer be permitted to be members of trade unions without previously consulting civil servants already members of trade unions. Civil servants sought judicial review of the said instruction for breach of the duty to act fairly. The government justified the lack of consultation by national security considerations.

Ratio: The House of Lords upheld that the mere fact that the instruction was derived from royal prerogative does not justify immunity for government actions from the courts' jurisdiction. As Lord Roskill stated: "I am unable to see (...) that there is any logical reason why the fact that the source of the power is the prerogative and not statute should today deprive the citizen of that right of challenge to the manner of its exercise which he would possess were the source of the power statutory. In either case the act in question is the act of the executive". However, The House of Lords held that it was for the executive and not for the judiciary to decide whether or not consulting the civil servants because of national security considerations.

Application: In this case, the House of Lords expressly stated that the manner in which common law powers, as any other statutory powers, are exercised by the executive, were subject to supervision of the courts. In other words, by adopting this decision, the House of Lords removed any doubts about the fact that prerogative powers were covered by judicial review, resulting on a subsequent practice of control of the Crown's use of the prerogative by the courts.

General principle: The issuing and revocation of passports, which is determined by a minister of the Crown, is reviewable by the judiciary.

R v Secretary of State for Foreign and Commonwealth Affairs, ex parte Everett (1989) 1 QB 811

Facts: A British citizen applied for a new passport in Spain. His request was rejected under the Secretary of State's policy that passports were not issued for individuals against whom a warrant for arrest had been issued in the UK. He therefore sought judicial review of this refusal.

Ratio: The Court of Appeal recalled that the judicial review of prerogative powers depended on the subject-matter. Because the decision at stake affected an individual's rights, it should be subject to the supervision of the courts. According to Taylor LJ: *"The majority of their Lordships [in GCHQ] indicated that whether judicial review of the exercise of prerogative power is open depends upon the subject matter and in particular whether it is justiciable. At the top of the scale of executive functions under the prerogative are matters of high policy, of which examples were given by their Lordships; making treaties, making war, dissolving Parliament (...) Clearly those matters (...) are not justiciable. But the grant or refusal of a passport is in a quite different category. It is a matter of administrative decision, affecting the rights of individuals and their freedom to travel".* **However, the Court of Appeal concluded that in the present case, the plaintiff did not suffer any injustice and there was no suggestion that there were any special circumstances to justify an exception to the Secretary of State's policy.**

Application: In application of the GCHQ principle, the courts have jurisdiction under judicial review in cases concerning the use of prerogative powers by the Crown in foreign affairs.

General principle: The use of prerogative powers by the Crown in defence and mobilisation of armed forces is justiciable before the courts when, in practice, it affects individuals' rights.

R v Ministry of Defence, ex parte Smith [1996] QB 517

Facts: In this case, the question was to know whether the ban on homosexuals to serve in the armed forces could be reviewed by the courts.

Ratio: The Court of Appeal did not feel entitled to declare the ban unlawful. However, it declared the justiciability of the matter under judicial review. In the words of Sir Thomas Bingham MR: "The present cases do not affect the lives or liberty of those involved. But they do concern innate qualities of a very personal kind and the decisions of which the appellants complain have had a profound effect on their careers and prospects. The appellants' rights as human beings are very much in issue. It is now accepted that this issue is justiciable. This does not of course mean that the court is thrust into the position of the primary decision-maker. It is not the constitutional role of the court to regulate the conditions of service in the armed forces of the Crown, nor has it the expertise to do so. But it has the constitutional role and duty of ensuring that the rights of citizens are not abused by the unlawful exercise of executive power. While the court must properly defer to the expertise of responsible decision-makers, it must not shrink from its fundamental duty to "do right to all manner of people".

Application: In the present case, it should be noted that the ban was later lifted by the European Court of Human Rights in its decision **Smith and Grady v UK (2000)** 29 EHRR 493. However courts remain quite reluctant to review the use of prerogative powers by the Crown in issues related to defence or political decisions related to armed conflicts.

General principle: Courts can review the use of the Crown's prerogative of mercy when it was wrongfully exercised by the Home Secretary.

R v Secretary of State for the Home Department, ex parte Bentley (1994) QB 349

Facts: Derek Bentley was executed after having been convicted for a murder in 1953. His brother sought for posthumous conditional pardon to the Home Secretary but his request was rejected. Therefore he challenged this decision under judicial review.

Ratio: The Court did not make orders to the Home Secretary, given the sensitive political context, but recognized the matter justiciable and invited the Home Secretary to reconsider its decision. According to Watkins LJ: "As the argument before us developed, it became clear that the substance of the applicant's case was that the Home Secretary failed to recognise the fact that the prerogative of mercy is capable of being exercised in many different circumstances and over a wide range and therefore failed to consider the form of pardon which might be appropriate to meet the facts of the present case. Such a failure is, we think, reviewable". The Court also held that the use of prerogative powers was subject to judicial review only when the nature of their subject-matter was amenable to judicial adjudication. In other words, the courts will only review cases that do not require them to review questions of policy.

Application: In application of the GCHQ principle, the courts have jurisdiction, under judicial review, in cases concerning the use of the Crown's prerogative of mercy.

General Principle: It was unlawful for the Prime Minister to act unconstitutionally (who had lied to the Queen) under his power to advise the Queen to prorogue Parliament. This had the effect that the withdrawal deal in relation to Brexit could not be debated.

R (on the application of Miller) (Appellant) v The Prime Minister (Respondent) [2019] UKSC 41

Facts: This was two combined appeals, one from the High Court of England and Wales and the other from Scotland's Inner House of the Court of Session. The Scottish case was filed in response to concerns that Parliament could be prorogued in order to prevent further discussion in the run-up to exit day on October 31st. A memo was sent to the Prime Minister proposing that his

Parliamentary Private Secretary approach the Palace with a proposal for prorogation to begin between the 9th and 12th of September and a Queen's Speech on the 14th of October, to which the Prime Minister responded affirmatively. In the English case Prime Minister Boris Johonson formally ordered Her Majesty to prorogue Parliament between those dates on the 27th or 28th of August. An order was issued ordering Parliament to be prorogued between those dates. Mrs Miller (business women) started the proceedings as soon as the decision was made public, questioning its legality. The High Court of England and Wales dismissed Mrs Miller's appeal the matter was not justiciable. The Inner House of the Court of Session in Scotland declared that the issue was justiciable, that it was driven by the improper goal of stifling Parliamentary oversight of the government through debate, and that it, as well as any prorogation that followed it, were illegal, invalid, and of no consequence. This issue was appeal to the Supreme Court the issues in the case were: i) was the lawfulness of the Prime Minister's advice to the Queen justiciable; ii) what are the limits to the power to advise the Queen to prorogue Parliament; and iii) did this prorogation have the effect of frustrating or preventing the ability of Parliament to carry out its constitutional functions without reasonable justification. **Ratio: Baroness Hale gave the majority judgement as follows:**

1. **On the first question before the court, it was determined that the courts had authority to determine the existence and limits of a prerogative power. For decades, beginning in 1611, the courts have had supervisory authority over the legality of government actions. As a result, the legality of the Prime Minister's advice to the Queen was found to be justiciable.**

2. **The power to prorogue is restricted by constitutional rules with which it would otherwise clash, according to the ruling. A decision to prorogue (or urging the monarch to prorogue) would be unconstitutional if the prorogation has the effect of frustrating or blocking Parliament's ability to carry out its constitutional duties as a legislature and as the body responsible for supervising the executive without fair justification.**

3. It was determined that this was not a typical prorogation in the run-up to the Queen's Speech; it stopped Parliament from fulfilling its constitutional position between the end of the summer recess and the Brexit deadline on October 31st. It was reported that when the Houses were prorogued, neither could meet, pass legislation, or discuss government policy. The prorogation's extraordinary circumstances were also taken into account, as it occurred during a time of radical reform in the UK constitution, with the 31st October exit day. Parliament was found to have a right to a say on how the reform is implemented. In this case, the Court received no excuse for taking the prorogation decision. In light of this, the Court determined that the decision to urge Her Majesty to prorogue Parliament was illegal because it hampered or prevented Parliament from performing its constitutional duties without fair excuse.

Summary

- The term "royal prerogative" refers to those powers of the "Crown" that are recognised by the common law, as distinct from those conferred and exercised under statute.

- Generally, the "Crown" refers to the executive, which is composed of the Queen and her majesty's government.

- For instance, the Queen appoints the Prime Minister and government ministers and grants the Royal Assent to Bills adopted by Parliament. The Royal prerogative also includes the power to declare war, to deploy armed forces both domestically and abroad and to ratify international treaties. Government, exercising royal prerogative, also recognises foreign states, their governments, heads of states and diplomatic envoys.

- Historically, the Crown was also the administrator of justice and was referred to as the "fountain of justice". Today, the structure of the courts and their jurisdiction are mainly regulated by statute.

- In theory, the sovereign has personal immunity from prosecution or being sued for wrongful acts. However, this immunity from courts' jurisdiction is not absolute.

- Historically, even though prerogative powers of the Crown were considered almost absolute in theory, they were still limited by law.

- Parliament can legislate to modify, abolish, or simply put on a statutory footing any particular prerogative power. It has done so, for example, by enacting the Bill of rights 1689.

- The possibility for Parliament to displace prerogative powers through legislation is an ultimate form of scrutiny of the executive which ensures that the latter is held accountable.
- For instance, in a Brexit context and the significant constitutional changes that it implies, the Crown cannot trigger article 50 of the TFEU in use of prerogative powers, which was previously incorporated by Parliament when it enacted the ECA 1972, without parliamentary approval.

- The main default to scrutiny of the executive by Parliament is the lack of political independence of MPs who support their own party's administration. For this reason, the scrutiny of the executive by courts is crucial, given the political neutrality of judges.

- In certain subject matters identified by common law, courts can legally supervise the Crown use of the royal prerogative in the same way that they review the manner in which statutory powers are exercised.

Chapter 8 – Powers and accountability of the Executive

Introduction to the Executive in the UK

The central executive

In the UK, the executive is composed of the Queen and her majesty's government. It should be noted that the United Kingdom has a constitutional monarchy with an unelected hereditary monarch as head of State. However, as stated earlier, in political practice, the Queen's role is a rather symbolic and ceremonial one. The government is referred to as her majesty's government because in legal theory, the monarch appoints and dismisses government ministers. Noteworthy, the Queen is also the Commander in chief of the armed forces, which, together with the various police forces, form the "executive in practical terms".

Although the monarch is historically the head of State, the head of the government is the Prime Minister. The Queen, exercising her royal prerogative power, appoints the Prime Minister. By constitutional convention, the Prime Minister is drawn from the House of Commons, as being the leader of the party in Parliament. Therefore, the he is directly held accountable to the elected representatives of the people (hereinafter "MPs"). The Prime Minister has, *inter alia*, the following constitutional functions: he presides over the Cabinet, acts as a conduit between the monarch and the government and more importantly he co-ordinates the government policy. In theory, the Cabinet is the most important decision-making body as regards government's policy. The Cabinet is composed of the most senior ministers (head of government departments), and are generally known as Secretaries of State. Under the presidency of the Prime Minister, the Cabinet debates and collectively agrees on government policy. In recent decades, constitutional practice has led to an increase of the Prime Minister's leadership and domination over the Cabinet.

Administrative bodies

A range of administrative bodies, which are technically part of the executive, exist under the British Constitution. Those bodies include central government departments operating under the control of a government minister and OPERATED by civil servants. In addition to this, as part of the devolved settlements (the 1998's Acts of Parliament on Scotland, Wales and Northern Ireland) other executive bodies were created, such as the Scottish government, the Executive Committee for Northern Ireland and the Welsh Assembly Government. Administrative bodies also include local authorities. For instance, local councillors are elected by local residents but are still part of the broad concept of the executive.

The civil service

The civil service is a non-political but rather bureaucratic body supporting the government to implement its policy on a daily basis. The civil service is composed of civil servants of two types. Firstly, the lower-ranking civil servants, which form the vast majority of the Civil service, and implement government's policy on the field. Secondly, there are senior civil servants who are experts in their domains and advice ministers on policy matters.
Three constitutional principles govern the function of civil servants:

- Permanence: The civil service is permanent. In other words, it does not change personnel every time a new government is elected. The advantage of this principle is that it produces experienced civil servants that have worked under various governments.

- Political neutrality: This is the corollary principle of the principle of permanence. It is necessary for civil servants to be politically neutral if they are to serve different governments from various political parties. While lower-ranking civil servants are allowed to engage in political activity, those employed in higher grades are prevented from doing so at a national level.

- Anonymity: Civil servants act on the behalf of their department and not on their own name. The responsibility is already on the ministers who represent the department publically. This principle protects civil servants and provides the civil service with more flexibility to effectively assist government in implementing its policy.

The function and powers of the executive

Traditionally, the executive is the main institution responsible for complying with the obligations of the state towards its population and making policy decisions. One of the most important constitutional functions of the executive is to govern the State. This means that government formulates domestic public policy as debated in the Cabinet. Another crucial function of the executive in the implementation of its policy is to initiate legislative proposals to Parliament. Most of the Acts enacted by Parliament are introduced by executive's proposals. Government ministers pilot these Bills through Parliament. The executive is also in charge of implementing foreign policy such as programmes for development and cooperation in third countries or deployment of armed forces overseas in cases of conflicts or humanitarian crisis. Finally, the executive enforces the law mainly through its police and armed forces. In practical terms, the enforcement of the law ensures that Parliament's will is respected on a daily basis.

Most of the powers exercised by the executive are derived from statutes. The main statutory prerogative of the executive is the power to enact delegated legislation. Acts of Parliament may confer powers to the government or to a minister in particular to pass delegated legislation for a specific aim. For instance, Parliament may delegate to government the power to determine when primary legislation should be brought into force through delegated legislation (see, *inter alia*, Section 171 of the Criminal Justice Act 1988).

In addition to this, other statutory powers enable the executive to pass delegated legislation having the effect of amending primary legislation. This is known as Henry VIII clauses. For example Section 10 of the Human Rights Act authorises ministers to pass remedial orders in order for a provision of primary legislation to comply with the European Convention for Human Rights. The executive also draws powers from common law. The conception of "residual power to act" is a common law principle which provides that public authorities can do everything that is not forbidden (**Malone v Metropolitan Police Commissioner (1979) Ch 344**). Moreover, the executive indirectly exercises the royal prerogative through her majesty's government. In this regard, the House of Commons Public Administration Select Committee, in 2004, identified the "personal powers which remain in the Sovereign's hands".

The following non-exhaustive examples of these powers are theoretically conferred by the Constitution to the Queen but the practical reality, ensured by constitutional convention, is that the Queen acts on the advice of her government. For instance, the Queen appoints the Prime Minister and government ministers and grants the Royal Assent to Bills adopted by Parliament. The Royal prerogative also includes the power to declare war, to deploy armed forces both domestically and abroad and to ratify international treaties.

Scrutiny of the Executive by Parliament

Traditionally, in addition to legislative functions, the House of Commons has the crucial role of calling the executive to account for its policies and administration as well as for the personal behaviour of ministers. The House of Lords also plays a role by asking Parliamentary questions to the government.

Parliamentary questions

Parliamentary questions are often seen as a very important tool for Parliament to hold the executive accountable by providing more transparency to the public about the government's policies and actions. Questions can be asked in both Houses of Parliament. Noteworthy, out of 40,000 questions tabled each year, about 3,000 are put down for oral answer. Oral questions are asked to ministers at question time which is held approximately four times a week for one hour both in the House of Lords and in the House of Commons. However, due to the important number of oral questions asked, they are not answered orally, but replied to later in writing. Ministers are under an obligation to reply to these questions. As an exception, they can refuse to answer questions on certain subject matters such as national security. In addition to this, 30 minutes are dedicated every week in Parliament to oral questions directed to the Prime Minister. Urgent oral questions about matters of public importance can also be asked to ministers. This is known as private notice questions. Although these questions are considered as a priority in parliamentary work, they have to be transmitted first to the Speaker who has absolute discretion as to whether to allow the question. Finally, some questions that require detailed answers can be asked to ministers with the mention that the answer should be in written. There is no limit to the numbers of such questions tabled by MPs.

Debates

Debates take place between MPs and ministers on the floor of the House. Even though their concrete impact in terms of decision-making can be questioned, such debates certainly hold the executive accountable to the extent that it challenges its policies on a public forum. In particular, emergency debates are of significant importance to the scrutiny of the executive as they allow MPs to discuss specific and current issues. The most famous emergency debate took place in 2003 on the proposed war in Iraq.

Select and standing Committees

Standing Committees of the House of Commons are Committees of a temporal nature whereas Select Committees are rather permanent. Select Committees are appointed by the House of Commons for various tasks including scrutinizing the executive policies by departments, their expenditure or even their administration. They determine the subjects into which they will inquire and they have extensive powers to gather evidence, both written and oral. Their findings and recommendations are submitted to the House and published as reports. There are 40 Select Committees in the House of Commons and a couple of joint committees comprised of members of both houses. Their work has been increasingly covered by media recently. Therefore, they contribute to consequently raise awareness and influence the public opinion on sensitive issues. Recently, the increasing number of draft bills published by government for pre-legislative consideration in Parliament through the select committee system of both Houses has been an important phenomenon regarding the scrutiny of the executive. For instance, the Joint Committee on Human Rights considers draft bills at the pre-legislative stage and reports to both Houses on their compatibility with convention rights.

Constitutional powers of Parliament over the royal prerogative

Historically, Parliament has limited and even abolished some of the Monarch's prerogative powers. It has done so, for example, by enacting the Bill of rights 1689.

General principle: Parliament can pass laws to supersede prerogative powers of the Crown. In such cases the Crown cannot act under royal prerogative.

Attorney General v De Keyser's Royal Hotel Limited (1920) AC 508
Facts: In this case, a hotel was expropriated by the Crown to accommodate the Royal Flying Corps. The owner of the hotel sought compensation for occupation and use of his property (under the Defence Act 1842 which made provision for compensation) but the Government replied that because the expropriation was made under royal prerogative, no compensation could be claimed.
Ratio: The House of Lord held that the government occupation of the hotel was under the terms of the Defence Act 1842. Therefore, compensation had to be paid to the plaintiff. In other words, the House of Lord affirmed that the Crown cannot act under royal prerogative where the power in question was superseded by legislation.
Application: In this case, the fact that Acts of Parliament prevail over royal prerogative underlines the relevance of Parliamentary sovereignty in constitutional relationships between state's institutions.

In the words of Lord Brown Wilkinson in **R v Secretary of State for the Home Department, ex parte Fire brigades Union and others (1995)** 2 All ER 244: *"the royal prerogative powers continue in existence to the extent that Parliament has not expressly or by implication extinguished them"*. The possibility for Parliament to displace prerogative powers through legislation is an ultimate form of scrutiny of the executive which ensures that the latter is held accountable.

Scrutiny of the Executive by the judiciary

The main default to scrutiny of the executive by Parliament is the lack of political independence of MPs who support their own party's administration. For this reason, the scrutiny of the executive by the courts is particularly important, given the political neutrality of judges.

Historically, the courts have been quite reluctant to intervene in the scrutiny of the executive, in accordance with the principle of separation of powers. The more the issue is political and the more it is likely that the courts will avoid the question and defer it to Parliament. As stated by Lord Birgham: "The more purely political a question is, the more appropriate it will be for political resolution and the less likely it is to be an appropriate matter for judicial decision" (See **R (A & Others) v Secretary of State for the Home Department [2004]** UKHL 56).Since the 1960s, however, the courts have played an increased role in holding the executive to account, notably through the mechanism of judicial review and the use of powers conferred to the courts by Parliament by enacting the Human Rights Act 1998.

General principle: It is impossible to create new prerogative powers for the executive.
BBC v Johns (Inspector of Taxes) (1965) 1 CH 32

Facts: The BBC argued that it was exempt from income tax, claiming to be a monopoly established by royal prerogative.
Ratio: The Court upheld that BBC was not exempt from paying income taxes since exemptions could only be granted by legislation. In addition to this, it was unconstitutional to create new prerogative powers for the executive. Lord Diplock famously commented: "It is 350 years and a civil war too late for the Queen's courts to broaden the prerogative. The limits within which the executive government may impose obligations or restraints upon citizens of the United Kingdom without any statutory authority are now well settled and incapable of extension (...) Today, save in so far as the power is preserved

by the Statute of Monopolies, or created by other statutes, the executive government has no constitutional right either itself to exercise through its agents or to confer upon other persons a monopoly of any form of activity".

Application: This case was the first case where the courts expressly and firmly intervened in scrutinizing the executive. It marked a turning point which resulted in subsequent case law with a similar approach adopted by the judiciary.

General principle: Courts can legally supervise executive use of the royal prerogative in the same way that they review the manner in which statutory powers are exercised.

Council of Civil Service Unions v Minister for the Civil Service (1985) 1 AC 374 (the GCHQ case)

Facts: The Prime Minister issued an instruction that civil servants would no longer be permitted to be members of trade unions without previously consulting civil servants already members of trade unions. Civil servants sought judicial review of the said instruction for breach of the duty to act fairly. The government justified the lack of consultation by national security considerations.

Ratio: The House of Lords upheld that the mere fact that the instruction was derived from royal prerogative does not justify immunity for government actions from the courts' jurisdiction. However, it was for the executive and not for the judiciary to decide whether or not consulting the civil servants because of national security considerations.

Application: In this case, the House of Lords expressly stated that the manner in which common law powers, as any other statutory powers, are exercised by the executive, were subject to supervision of the courts.

General principle: The issuing and revocation of passports, which is determined by a government minister, is reviewable by the courts.

R v Secretary of State for Foreign and Commonwealth Affairs, ex parte Everett (1989) 1 QB 811

Facts: A British citizen applied for a new passport in Spain. His request was rejected under the Secretary of State's policy that passports were not issued for individuals against whom a warrant for arrest had been issued in the UK. He therefore sought judicial review of this refusal.

Ratio: The Court of Appeal recalled that the judicial review of prerogative powers depended on the subject-matter. Because the decision at stake affected an individual's rights, it should be subject to the supervision of the courts. However, in the present case, the plaintiff did not suffer any injustice and there was no suggestion that there were any special circumstances to justify an exception to the Secretary of State's policy.

Application: This case can be used as an example of scrutiny of the executive by the judiciary.

General principle: Decisions taken by the executive under the royal prerogative are subject to judicial review where the nature of the subject-matter does not require the Court to review questions of policy.

R v Secretary of State for the Home Department, ex parte Bentley (1994) QB 349

Facts: Derek Bentley was executed after having been convicted for a murder in 1953. His brother sought for posthumous conditional pardon to the Home Secretary but his request was rejected. Therefore he challenged this decision under judicial review.

Ratio: The Court held that the use of prerogative powers was subject to judicial review only when the nature of their subject-matter was amenable to judicial adjudication. In other words, the courts will only review cases that do not require them to review questions of policy.

Application: The **Bentley** case provided a significant precedent with regards the question to know whether or not prerogative powers are subject to judicial review on the basis of the nature of their subject-matter.

Conventional political practices as tools to hold the Executive accountable

The two key conventions, the so-called "twin conventions" are collective ministerial responsibility and individual ministerial responsibility. They are referred to in the Ministerial Code issued in December 2016.

Collective Ministerial Responsibility

The Ministerial Code refers to collective ministerial responsibility in the following terms: *"The principle of collective responsibility requires that Ministers should be able to express their views frankly in the expectation that they can argue freely in private while maintaining a united front when decisions have been reached. This in turn requires that the privacy of opinions expressed in Cabinet and Ministerial Committees, including in correspondence, should be maintained"*.

The rationale behind this convention is confidence: the government needs to present a united front in order to maintain public and parliamentary support. In order to remain in office, government must enjoy confidence from the House of Commons. Accordingly, the convention provides that ministers should collectively resign if they lose a vote on a specific "no-confidence" motion. Essentially, it is a vote that is triggered when MPs have lost faith in their leader. For instance, the government has recently been called into question, in late 2018 when Conservative MPs have triggered a vote of no confidence in Theresa May, the Prime Minister. Around 50 letters from Conservative MPs were received claiming that they no longer had faith in the prime minister to deliver the deal. On December 19th, London CNN wrote: "The British government will not allow lawmakers to vote on a symbolic motion of no confidence in Prime Minister Theresa May, forcing the opposition to decide whether it will now try to topple her entire administration". This recent examples clearly shows that a specific "no-confidence" motion is a crucial tool for the executive scrutiny by Parliament. The second principle governing collective ministerial responsibility is unanimity. It requires ministers to publically support decisions agreed, as if it was adopted unanimously as a government policy, or to resign. This rule applies even when the minister is not present during the discussion. However, when dealing with important decisions where the political disagreement might be of great magnitude, the Prime Minister may suspend the application of the unanimity rule and allow open dissenting opinions. This has been done recently during the 2016 EU referendum campaign. The third aspect of collective responsibility is confidentiality which prohibits ministers from disclosing confidential information which includes Cabinet papers and ministerial memoirs.

General principle: The duty not to disclose confidential information is not unlimited in time but rather laps as far as the public interest requires the publication to be restrained.

Attorney-General v Jonathan Cape, [1976] QB 752 ("the Crossman Diaries case")

Facts: The Attorney-General sought restraint on the publication of certain materials in the diary of a former cabinet minister, submitting that the protection from disclosure of Cabinet papers was based on collective responsibility. It should however be noted that the disclosure occurred after the end of the mandate.

Ratio: The Court rejected the Attorney-General's injunction. However, it acknowledged that confidentiality was a major principle because free discussion between ministers and the convention of collective ministerial responsibility may both be prejudiced by premature disclosure of the views of individual ministers. As regards timing of the disclosure, Lord Widgery CJ stated that: "There must, however, be a limit in time after which the confidential character of the information, and the duty of the court to restrain publication will lapse' and 'It may, of course, be intensely difficult in a particular case, to say at what point the material loses its confidential character, on the ground that publication will no longer undermine the doctrine of cabinet responsibility (…) The Attorney-General must show (a) that such publication would be a breach of confidence; (b) that the public interest requires that the publication be restrained; and (c) that there are no other facts of the public interest contradictory of and more compelling than that relied upon".

Application: This case clarified the extent of the duty of ministers not to disclose confidential information and restrained it in time until it is no longer required by public interest.

Individual Ministerial Responsibility

The first general principle to presented in the Ministerial Code

(2016) is the individual ministerial responsibility "Ministers have a duty to Parliament to account, and be held to account, for the policies, decisions and actions of their departments and agencies".

The idea is that ministers, individually, must accept responsibility due to errors or failures from their departments and resign in such situations. The use of this convention has rarely been observed in recent times. However, there is a trend for ministers who feel obliged to resign for their errors of judgement. The most famous illustration of practice of the convention of individual ministerial responsibility is the Crichel Down Affair. In 1938, Land in Devon was purchased compulsorily by the Ministry of Agriculture for use as a bombing range. The initial owner and neighbouring landowners were denied to buy it back later on. An inquiry found that civil servants of the Ministry of Agriculture had acted in bad faith. Accordingly, the Minister of Agriculture, Sir Thomas Dugdale, resigned. Following the Crichel Down Affair, Sir David Maxwell Fyfe, Home Secretary at the time, proposed a redefinition of the traditional convention. The criterion to determine whether the minister should protect their civil servants is personal knowledge. This argument has been confirmed by subsequent practice. For instance, the Northern Ireland Secretary, James Prior, did not resign in 1983 after the mass breakout of IRA prisoners as he argued that there was a failure of officials to properly implement policy. One of the significant consequences of the existence of such a convention for the scrutiny of the executive is that public opinion or the media might call officials to resign due to departmental problems with the implementation of policy. For instance, in 2006, the opposition called Charles Clarke to resign in relation to Home Office failures to track foreign nationals who had been released from prison. Although he did not resign at the time, he was later sacked by the former Prime Minister Tony Blair. Recently, there has been an increasing trend of resignations of ministers for personal errors or issues of personal morality or property. There are numerous examples, such as the resignations of Peter Mandelson (Secretary of State for Trade and Industry) and Geoffrey Robinson (the Paymaster General) over an undisclosed loan for a house purchase. Another example is the resignation of David Laws (Chief Secretary to the Treasury in 2010) following the disclosure of an inappropriate parliamentary expenses claim.

To conclude, rather than necessarily resigning for every failure, it is nowadays crucial for ministers to keep Parliament informed about departmental problems and errors. This is particularly true since the last two decades, notably following the lessons drawn in the Scott Report (published in 1996) into the "arms to Iraq affair".

Summary

- In the UK, the executive is composed of the Queen and her majesty's government. However, as stated earlier, in political practice, the Queen's role is a rather symbolic and ceremonial one.

- The Queen, exercising her royal prerogative power, appoints the Prime Minister. By constitutional convention, the Prime Minister is drawn from the House of Commons, as being the leader of the party in Parliament.

- The civil service is a non-political but rather bureaucratic body supporting the government to implement its policy on a daily basis.

- One of the most important constitutional functions of the executive is to govern the State. This means that government formulates domestic public policy as debated in the Cabinet.

- The executive enforces the law mainly through its police and armed forces. In practical terms, the enforcement of the law ensures that Parliament's will is respected on a daily basis.

- Standing Committees of the House of Commons are Committees of a temporal nature whereas Select Committees are rather permanent.

- There are 40 Select Committees in the House of Commons and a couple of joint committees comprised of members of both houses. Their work has been increasingly covered by media recently.

- The possibility for Parliament to displace prerogative powers through legislation is an ultimate form of scrutiny of the executive which ensures that the latter is held accountable.

- Historically, the courts have been quite reluctant to intervene in the scrutiny of the executive, in accordance with the principle of separation of powers. Since the 1960s, however, the courts have played an increased role in holding the executive to account.

- The two conventional political practices to hold the executive accountable, the so-called "twin conventions", are collective ministerial responsibility and individual ministerial responsibility.

Chapter 9 – The decentralisation of public powers

Introduction to the decentralisation of public powers

A unitary constitution has the majority of its legal and executive power vested in the central organs of the state. Conversely, in a federal constitution, power is divided between federal government and states or regional authorities. This model is generally established in a constitutional document, for example the German and US constitutions. A main difference between unitary and federal states remain: even if a unitary constitution recognizes and delegates power to decentralized institutions, these institutions do not have express constitutional protection and do not formally exist as separate entities from the central state, unlike the state/provincial/ legislatures in a federal constitution.

The United Kingdom is a unitary state where power is, in principle, centrally controlled in Westminster and Whitehall. However, some power has also been devolved to regional bodies, for example local authorities ("councils"), to the London Assembly and most notably (since 1998) through the devolved Parliament in Scotland and the Assemblies in Northern Ireland and Wales. In the words of Tony Blair: *"Local government is a vital part of our democracy. The vast majority of interactions between citizens and the state take place through local government. It provides leadership for local areas and communities; democratic accountability for a wide range of public services; and is the key to effective partnership working at local level"*.

The decentralisation of public powers implies a delegation of power to local authorities which are administrating governmental functions at a local level. The delegation is generally made by statute and limits strictly the power of local authorities in order to preserve the unitary nature of the nation. Devolution of power can be a solution to preserve the unitary nature of a nation composed of local and cultural particularities. According to the Scotland Office: "Unity is not uniformity". The different parts of the UK have different stories, distinctive cultures and differing aspirations. That is why the Government believes in devolution and decentralisation throughout the UK. In each part of the country that can and should take different forms" (Scotland's future in the UK, 2009). Here is an illustration of the central institutions and the powers devolved to other local authorities in the UK:

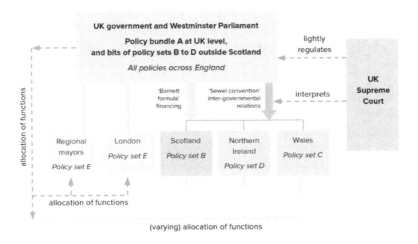

(varying) allocation of functions

Devolution and local government

A range of administrative bodies, which are technically part of the executive, exist under the British Constitution. Those bodies include central government departments operating under the control of a government minister and operated by civil servants. Administrative bodies also include local authorities. For instance, local councillors are elected by local residents but are still part of the broad concept of the executive. The role of local government is to implement central policy on a daily basis. Various functions have been historically attributed to local authorities.

First of all, local authorities provide services such as public housing. It also regulates the professions that require licenses (taxis, cinema, bars). Another mission of local government is to provide social services such as care for vulnerable people or education by providing and maintain schools. Finally, local government maintains public roads and street lightings and manages libraries and museums.

As indicated earlier, local government also has an administrative role of implementing in practice certain policies is of the central government. For example local government takes administrative decisions with respect to land planning. Local government has a discretionary power to adapt some of the services to local needs. For example a central policy will not be implemented equally in rural and city areas. In this regard, the Localism Act 2011 vested in local authorities a "general power of competence" which has been used innovatively.

Finally, local authorities have a legislative role to enact a form of secondary legislation also known as byelaws. It allows, for example, local authorities to reduce the speed limit in a specified area for legitimate reasons (such as the presence of a school nearby). However, this power to enact byelaws is not absolute. Its use is controlled by the requirement of ministerial approval and its reviewability by courts under judicial review. In order to finance all these services and missions, local authorities collect money through the council taxes.

The decentralisation of public powers has several advantages. Firstly, local power can serve as a sort of counter-power to central government and avoid abuses of power. As for the theory of the separation of powers, devolution ensures that power is not only focused in central institutions. There is also a practical dimension to the decentralisation of powers given that, practically speaking, all services cannot be provided from central government. Therefore, decentralising powers can be an efficient way of governing. In addition to this, as stated above, local governance also ensures that central policies are adapted to local needs. Moreover, local governance, with decision-making taken closer to the citizens, also promotes a participatory democracy whereby individuals can actively engage in governing. Accordingly, in modern states theories, devolution and local governance is considered to be a symbol of a healthy democracy where decisions are made as closely as possible to the citizens. The *rationale* behind devolution is similar to the EU Law principle of subsidiarity; decision-making should be dealt with at the most immediate (or local) level that is consistent with their resolution. Arguably, local governance can be more efficient and realistic because local authorities have a better knowledge of local needs.

In addition to this, local authorities are locally elected and therefore held directly accountable to local people. Accordingly, it draws a more realistic representation of local communities but also minorities since it is way easier to access such elected positions (for example local councillor) than it is for central positions as MPs or members of the government in Whitehall.

One of the main recent problems of local governance is that citizens seem to lack interest in voting for local elections, preferring to vote for national elections. The legitimacy of local authorities is thereby affected. Wilson and Game wrote: *"The one thing everyone thinks they know about local elections is that most people don't vote in them. In almost all countries, fewer voters turn out for what are sometimes termed "second-order" elections, for local councils and the European Parliament, but in England the local-national gap is currently between, say, 38% and 65%, whereas in Western Europe generally it is between about 65% and 80%"*. There are many reasons to explain this lack of interest, such as for example that people do not believe that their vote might have an impact, or rather that they prefer to vote for more "important" elections of the central government. The multiplication of governmental authorities can also become a problem for local governance where governmental action may lose visibility to citizens. It might also create political conflicts where central and local governments are not from the same political party. This can lead to institutional blockages (see the 1980s frictions with central conservative government and local labour authorities).

The scrutiny of local government

Democratic and institutional control

In terms of democratic control, local councillors are held directly accountable by the local electorate when they seek re-election. It should be noted that the procedures for local elections vary in the UK, depending on the regions. In addition to this, local authorities, as any other public bodies, according to the theory of the Rule of Law, have to comply with law when exercising their powers.

General principle: Decisions of local authorities are subject to judicial review by the courts. They must act fairly when their actions might aggrieve citizens.

Regina v Liverpool Corporation ex parte Liverpool Taxi Fleet Operators Association [1972] 2 QB 299
Facts: A local Council took the decision to increase the numbers of hackney cabs operating in the city, without consulting local trade unions and in breach of a previous undertaking that the numbers of hackney cabs would not be increased until the proposed legislation.
Ratio: The Court held that on account of this public representation, the applicants were "justifiably aggrieved" by the council's subsequent unfair conduct. As stated by Sir Gordon Willmer: "It seems to me that in these very special circumstances, having regard to the history of how this matter had been dealt with in the past, and having regard especially to the giving of the undertaking, the Applicants are justified in regarding themselves as "aggrieved" by what I can only describe as unfair treatment on the part of Liverpool Corporation".
Application: The first restriction to powers of local authorities is that they are bound by law. The courts, under judicial review, have historically conducted active scrutiny.

General principle: Local authorities can also be held to account on the basis of a breach of private law.

Infolines Public Network Ltd v Nottingham City Council [2009] EWCA Civ 708
Facts: A local highway authority decided to remove the telephone kiosks which were owned and operated by a private company.
Ratio: The Court upheld that the disposal constituted a wrongful interference with the company's goods. The local authority was therefore liable for any loss caused by that disposal. According to John Lambe: "The case serves as a cautionary tale for local authorities and others who seek to exercise emergency powers and the restrictive interpretation which is likely to be adopted and applied when those powers concern dealing with the potential deprivation of another's

property".

Application: Local authorities are subject to private law for their actions (including contract law and tort law).

General principle: When local authorities enact delegated legislation beyond their legal powers, they can be held accountable in the courts.

Arlidge v Mayor, Aldermen, and Councillors of the Metropolitan Borough of Islington [1909] 2 KB 127

Facts: A local council enacted a byelaw with respect of real estate property under the Public Health (London) Act 1891. As a consequence, a landlord had to commit a trespass to comply with the byelaw.

Ratio: The Court found that the byelaw was unreasonable and held the local authority liable for acting beyond its legal powers.

Application: As for the central executive, courts strictly control that local authorities act within the limits of their legal powers.

It should also be noted that local authorities will be held accountable by the Audit Commission which analyses their financial efficiency. In addition to this, the Ombudsman investigates maladministration of local authorities which result in injustice for individuals. A system of complaint enables every individual to communicate their case to the Commissioner for Local Administration. The Annual report of the Local Government Ombudsman indicated that it assisted more than 20 000 individuals in their endeavours to seek justice.

Control from central government

Local authorities govern their territories under the supervision of central government. Central government sets the legal and financial framework permitting local authorities to implement its policy. It should be noted that a significant proportion of the money received by local authorities is determined discretionarily by central government. Central government can also advice local authorities through circulars on how delegated powers should be exercised. As stated above, the legislative function of local authorities to pass byelaws is depending on ministerial approval from central government.

An important principle is that central government enjoys a "default power" to exercise decentralised power instead of local authorities or even to transfer it (see **R v Secreatry of State for the Environment, ex parte Norwich City Council** [1982] 1 QB 808).

In addition to this, it should be remembered that the UK is a unitary state with an unwritten constitution. Therefore, local authorities do not have a constitutional status, which would be the case for example in a federal state. Accordingly, in line with the theory of Parliamentary sovereignty, the UK Parliament remains fully capable of legislating for any regions for which it previously accepted to devolve prerogatives. In addition, the devolution Acts can be repealed or amended by any Act adopted by the Westminster Parliament.

Historically, central governments have been re-modelling the role and powers of local authorities for greater coherence with their policy, by pushing legislation through Parliament. This resulted, for example, to the adoption of the Local Government Planning and Land Act 1980, the Local Government Finance Act 1988, the local government Act 2000, the Local Government and Public Involvement in Health Act 2007 and the Localism Act 2011. Even though the consensual relationship between central and local government has been historically marked by cooperation, conflicts have arisen between the 1970s and the 1990s.

General principle: Courts can refuse to issue orders compelling local authorities to comply with the central government's will.

Secretary of State for education and science v Tameside Metropolitan Borough Council [1976] 3 WLR 641
Facts: In this case, a Labour Secretary of State for education and science (central government) sought an order to compel a Conservative council (local authority) to comply with a scheme approved by a previous Labour Council.
Ratio: The House of Lords rejected the central government's request.
Application: This case gave rise to important debates in the

academic sphere. As an illustration, Professor J. A. G. Griffith, discussing this case, remarked that: "I can see no justification for this judicial intervention and it sets a dangerous precedent for the future"

General principle: Courts are reluctant to review the budget allocated by central government to local authorities when it was previously approved by the House of Commons.

Nottinghamshire County Council v Secretary of State for the Environment [1986] 1 AC 240

Facts: Local authorities sought judicial review to challenge the budget allocated to them by central government that they considered unfairly low. They claimed unreasonableness and irrationality of the decision under judicial review.

Ratio: The House of Lords refused to intervene in public financial administration which had been previously approved by the House of Commons. It recalled that a low intensity of review is applied to cases involving issues depending essentially on political judgment. In the words of Lord Scarman: "To sum it up, the levels of public expenditure and the incidence and distribution of taxation are matters for Parliament, and, within Parliament, especially for the House of Commons . If a statute, as in this case, requires the House of Commons to approve a minister's decision before he can lawfully enforce it, and if the action proposed complies with the terms of the statute, it is not for the judges to say that the action has such unreasonable consequences that the guidance upon which the action is based and of which the House of Commons had notice was perverse and must be set aside. For that is a question of policy for the minister and the Commons, unless there has been bad faith or misconduct by the minister"

Application: As in many other instances, courts ae reluctant to intervene in questions of policies, especially when Parliament has previously approved the actions of the executive.

Decentralisation and compliance with the European Convention on Human Rights

Under Article 6 of the Human Rights Act, local authorities cannot act in a way which is incompatible with the European Convention for Human Rights. In other words, a decision or act of a local authority that violates a Convention's provision is unlawful.

General principle: Local authorities, while using devolved powers, cannot act in a way which is incompatible with the European Convention for Human Rights.

Starrs v Ruxton [2000] SLT 42

Facts: In this case, the use of delegated powers in the Scottish criminal proceedings raised issues as the lawfulness of Temporary Sheriffs. Such temporary trial judges were appointed by the Secretary of State on the advice of the Lord Advocate, himself also a member of the Executive. The question here for the Court was to determine whether the Lord Advocate has acted in a way which was incompatible with the rights of the accused under art 6(1) of the Convention to fair trial by "an independent and impartial tribunal" within the meaning of that article.

Ratio: The High Court of Justiciary held the appointment of Temporary Sheriffs to be inconsistent with the necessity to guarantee the independence of the judges in question. In the words of Lord Reed: "Conceptions of constitutional principles such as the independence of the judiciary, and of how those principles should be given effect in practice, change over time. Although the principle of judicial independence has found expression in similar language in Scotland and England since at least the late seventeenth century, conceptions of what it requires in substance – of what is necessary, or desirable, or feasible – have changed greatly since that time".

Application: Compliance with the European Convention is another efficient mechanism used by courts for the scrutiny of local governance. It should be noted that following this case, the Scottish Parliament abolished the office of Temporary Sheriffs (Judicial Appointment Act Scotland 2000).

General principle: Scottish criminal proceedings must fully comply with the right of a fair trial under Article 6 of the European Convention.

Alvin Lee Sinclair v Her Majesty's Advocate [2005] UKPC D2

Facts: In this case, the defendant complained that the prosecutor had failed to disclose all the witness statements taken, which revealed inconsistencies in their versions of events.

Ratio: The Privy Council held that the prosecution had a duty to disclose to the defence anything material including "any evidence which would tend to undermine the prosecution's case or to assist the case for the defence". The defendant had been denied an opportunity to cross examine a prosecution witness which resulted on an unfair trial. Lord Hope stated: "First, it is a fundamental aspect of the accused's right to a fair trial that there should be an adversarial procedure in which there is equality of arms between the prosecution and the defence. The phrase "equality of arms" brings to mind the rules of a mediaeval tournament – the idea that neither side may seek an unfair advantage by concealing weapons behind its back. But in this context the rules operate in one direction only. The prosecution has no Convention right which it can assert against the accused. Nor can it avoid the accused's Convention right by insisting that the duty does not arise unless the accused invokes it first. Secondly, the prosecution is under a duty to disclose to the defence all material evidence in its possession for or against the accused. For this purpose any evidence which would tend to undermine the prosecution's case or to assist the case for the defence is to be taken as material. Thirdly, the defence does not have an absolute right to the disclosure of all relevant evidence. There may be competing interests which it is in the public interest to protect. But decisions as to whether the withholding of relevant information is in the public interest, cannot be left exclusively to the Crown. There must be sufficient judicial safeguards in place to ensure that information is not withheld on the grounds of public interest unless this is strictly necessary".

Application: Local authorities, as well as any central governmental body, have to comply with the European Convention.

The devolution process with Scotland, Northern Ireland and Wales

As part of the devolved settlements (the 1998's Acts of Parliament on Scotland, Wales and Northern Ireland), new executive bodies were created, such as the Scottish government, the Executive Committee for Northern Ireland and the Welsh Assembly Government. The table below gives an overview of the main powers given to the Northern Irish and Welsh assemblies, as well as the Scottish Parliament:

Scotland	Wales	Northern Ireland
Agriculture, Crown Estate, forestry and fishing	Agriculture, forestry and fishing	Agriculture
Education and training	Education	Education
Environment	Environment	Environment and planning
Health and social work	Health and social welfare	Health and social services
Housing	Housing	Enterprise, trade and investment
Justice, policing and courts*	Local government	Local government
Local government	Fire and rescue services	Justice and policing
Fire service	Economic development	Control over air passenger duty and corporation tax (from 2017)
Economic development and tourism	Highways and transport	Transport
Internal transport	Control over stamp duty and landfill tax	Pensions and child support
The ability to change and top up benefits such as Universal Credit, Tax Credits and Child Benefit	Welsh language	Culture and sport
Limited power over local taxes, the basic rate of tax and landfill tax		
Right to receive half of the VAT raised in Scotland		

These devolved institutions can pass delegated legislation, within the limits of their competences, as laid down by the UK Parliament.

Scottish devolution

Historically, under the Union with Scotland Act 1706, Scotland and England had separate parliaments. In 1997, the election of the Labour government marked a political will to place devolution back on the political agenda. A white paper, issued in July 1997, stated: "The Government that the people of Scotland should have a greater say over their own affairs. With their agreement we will change the way Scotland is governed by legislating to create a Scottish Parliament with devolved powers within the United Kingdom". The UK Parliament passed a couple of devolution Acts in 1998 which delegated po wers to three regions, including Scotland (Scotland Act 1998).Under the Scotland Act 1998, the new Scottish Parliament is empowered to legislate for Scotland on a number of matters. However, with regard to Westminster's sovereignty, the Scotland Act 1998, at s. 28(7), specifically states that this does not affect the legal powers of the UK Parliament to legislate for Scotland when it considers it appropriate. Under section 28(7): "This section does not affect the power of the Parliament of the United Kingdom to make laws for Scotland".

More recently, two events have resulted on grants of greater devolution for Scotland: firstly the 2014 Scottish referendum on whether Scotland should leave the UK (which was won by a 55% margin by those wishing to remain in the UK) and secondly the establishement of the Smith Commission on devolution of the UK Parliament. As a result, the Scotland Act 2016 has extended the matters on which the Scottish Parliament can legislate to areas including for example abortion or equal opportunities. In legal theory, the UK Parliament remains fully capable of legislating for any regions for which it previously accepted to devolve prerogatives. In addition, the devolution Acts can be repealed or amended by any Act of the Westminster Parliament.

The Northern Irish devolution

The devolved institutions in Northern Ireland were established under the Northern Ireland Act 1998, with several institutional reforms having taken place since then. Northern Ireland ministers are designated by the Northern Ireland Assembly (hereinafter "the Assembly") in proportion to parties' representation using the d'Hondt formula. The Executive is headed by a First Minister and a deputy First Minister who must act jointly. The Executive is composed of ten other ministers appointed following a similar process. Each minister heads a department with responsibility for specific areas of policy. The Justice Minister is also a member of the Executive, but is elected by the Assembly following a cross-community vote rather than by d'Hondt. The Northern Ireland devolution settlement gives legislative control over certain matters (known as "transferred matters") to the Assembly. These transferred matters are mainly in the economic and social fields. Matters of national importance are known as "excepted matters" and the Assembly does not have competence to legislate on these (see Schedule 2 of the Northern Ireland Act 1998). Issues such as broadcasting and genetic research are known as "reserved matters". It originally included policing and criminal justice but those matters were devolved and therefore moved into the transferred field on 12 April 2010 (see Schedule 3 of the Northern Ireland Act). As a matter of principle, anything that is not explicitly reserved to the UK Parliament in Schedules 2 or 3 of the Northern Ireland Act is deemed to be devolved to the Assembly without requiring consent from Westminster.

Welsh devolution

Historically, Wales has been closely connected to England, as illustrated by the 1536 Union Act. Therefore, the historical relationship between those two countries is different than the one between Scotland and England, for example. The National Assembly for Wales was established, under the devolution Act 1998, following the affirmative devolution referendum in September 1997. Schedule 7A to the Government of Wales Act 2006 defines the scope of the Assembly's legislative competence to make Assembly Acts. The Government of Wales Act (GoWA) 2006 implemented the separation of the Welsh government and the National Assembly in order to improve scrutiny of public powers in line with the theory of the separation of powers. Later, the Wales Act 2014 devolved fiscal powers to the National Assembly, followed by the Wales Act 2017 which delegated areas such as elections, transport, energy, and protection of the environment. The Welsh Assembly Government is composed of ministers who are members of and accountable to the National Assembly. For instance, Welsh ministers have delegated powers to adopt subordinate legislation.

Summary

- The United Kingdom is a unitary state where power is, in principle, centrally controlled in Westminster and Whitehall. However, some power has also been devolved to regional bodies.

- Administrative bodies, which are technically part of the executive, include central government departments and local authorities.

- The role of local government is to implement central policy on a daily basis. Various functions have been historically attributed to local authorities.

- Local government has a discretionary power to adapt some of the services to local needs. For example a central policy will not be implemented equally in rural and city areas.

- Finally, local authorities have a legislative role to enact a form of secondary legislation also known as byelaws. Its use is controlled by the requirement of ministerial approval and its reviewability by courts under judicial review.

- Local power can serve as a sort of counter-power to central government and avoid abuses of power, it ensures that central policies are adapted to local needs and promotes a participatory democracy whereby individuals can actively engage in governing.

- The rationale behind devolution is similar to the EU Law principle of subsidiarity; decision-making should be dealt with at the most immediate (or local) level that is consistent with their resolution.

- Local authorities, as any other public bodies, according to the theory of the Rule of Law, have to comply with law when exercising their powers.

- It should also be noted that local authorities will be held accountable by the Audit Commission which analyses their financial efficiency. In addition to this, the Ombudsman investigates maladministration of local authorities which result in injustice for individuals.

- Central government sets the legal and financial framework permitting local authorities to implement its policy. Central government can also advice local authorities through circulars on how delegated powers should be exercised.

- Under Article 6 of the Human Rights Act, local authorities cannot act in a way which is incompatible with the European Convention for Human Rights. In other words, a decision or act of a local authority that violates a Convention's provision is unlawful.
- As part of the devolved settlements (the 1998's Acts of Parliament on Scotland, Wales and Northern Ireland) new executive bodies were created, such as the Scottish government, the Executive Committee for Northern Ireland and the Welsh Assembly Government.

Chapter 10 – The European Convention on Human Rights

Human Rights and the adoption of the European Convention

The concept of human rights relies on the postulate that individuals have rights simply because they are human beings. One of the fundamental principles of human rights is equality; human rights are vested in all individuals regardless of their race, ethnicity, religion, gender, sexual orientation or nor matter whether they are disabled or abled.

Human rights have developed through history along the principles of natural law, which comes from the period of Enlightenment. Authors like John Locke, Thomas Paine, Jean-Jacques Rousseau argued at the time that a body of superior principles and values should be complied with by any other laws. The American Constitution and its Bill of rights (1787) and the French Declaration of the Rights of Man and the Citizen (1789) had major influences in the legal codification of human rights theories.

Later on, in 1945, the United Nations were created by the international community in order to ensure peaceful settlement of conflicts. In 1948, the Universal Declaration of Human Rights was adopted by the UN General Assembly. Although originally considered in international law as a soft law, it is nowadays undisputed that it has the effect of customary international law.

At the European level, the Council of Europe was created in 1949 with three main objectives: the protection of Human Rights, Democracy and the Rule of Law. The Council of Europe has to be distinguished from the European Union. It is an inter-governmental organization composed of 47 Member States, often referred to as the "broad Europe". For instance, Turkey and Russia are also members of the Council of Europe.

In 1950, the Member States of the Council of Europe adopted, according to the Council of Europe's mandate given that one of its main objective is the protection of human rights, the Convention for the Protection of Human Rights and Fundamental Freedoms (hereinafter "the Convention"). The Convention is an international treaty which protects, *inter alia*, the right to life (Article 2), the prohibition of torture (Article 3), the prohibition of slavery (article 4), liberty and security of the person (Article 5), the right to a fair trial (Article 6), the right to private life (Article 8), freedom of thought, conscience and religion (Article 9) and freedom of expression (Article 10).

As of today, the Convention has 16 protocols. The latest entered into force in August 2018. In this regards, Protocol No. 16 to the Convention allows the highest courts and tribunals of a State Party to request the Court to give advisory opinions on questions of principle relating to the interpretation or application of the rights and freedoms defined in the Convention or the protocols thereto.

The status of the European Convention and its legal force

The Convention, for the purposes of public international law, is a bilateral Treaty. Article 46 of the Convention and subsequent practice: all final judgments (Chamber and Grand Chamber) are binding on the respondent States. After a judgement is issued, the concerned contracting State has to comply with it by paying any just satisfaction ordered by the Court or/and by taking the necessary steps to amend the impugned domestic law which is not compatible with the Convention. For instance, following the European Court's judgement in the case **Malone v. UK, no 8691/79, 02/08/1984**, ECHR which found a violation of Article 8 (right to private life) concerning telephone tapping, the British Parliament adopted the Interception of Communication Acts 1985, in order to comply with the Court's judgement.

The Committee of Ministers supervises the enforcement of judgments. It not only ensures that damages awarded by the Court are paid, but it also assists the State in question in trying to find suitable measures in order to comply with all other demands made by the Court. Should a Member State refuse to implement a judgment, the Committee of Ministers can apply multilateral peer-pressure or bilateral pressure from neighbouring States. It can also threaten the Member State in question with the publication of a list, containing all its pending cases before the Court, or – as a last resort – with the exclusion from the Council of Europe.

Derogations, reservations and denunciations

According to Article 15 of the Convention, temporary derogations are allowed in times of public emergency, under the following conditions: *"1. In time of war or other public emergency threatening the life of the nation any High Contracting Party may take measures derogating from its obligations under this Convention to the extent strictly required by the exigencies of the situation, provided that such measures are not inconsistent with its other obligations under international law".*

However, the second paragraph of Article 15 prohibits derogations to rights as protected by Article 2 (except regarding deaths resulting from lawful acts of war), 3, 4(1) and 7. These rights are often referred to as "absolute rights" as opposed to "conditional rights" that can be derogated from. This concept of absolute rights is also applicable to the rights that do not allow for interferences. Conversely, conditional rights, such as Article 8,9,10 and 11 allow interferences if they can be justified (prescribed by law, protecting a legitimate aim and necessary in a democratic society).

General principle: The natural and customary meaning of "public emergency threatening the life of the nation" is clear and refers to an exceptional situation of crisis or emergency which affects the whole population and constitutes a threat to the organised life of the community of which the State is composed.

Lawless v. Ireland (No. 3), no 332/57, 01/07/1961, ECHR
Facts: In this case, the applicant, a member of the organization IRA, had been detained for a period of five months without trial under the Offences against the State (Amendment) Act 1940. He claimed that his detention constituted a violation of Article 5. Ireland however previously informed the Council of Europe, under Article 15 of the Convention, that it might take measures interfering with some of the rights protected by the Convention.
Ratio: The Court acknowledged the difficulties faced by States in protecting their populations from terrorist violence, which constitutes, in itself, a grave threat to human rights. Accordingly, it concluded that the measures taken in derogation from obligations under the Convention were

"strictly required by the exigencies of the situation".

Application: The Court interpreted the notion of public emergency quite flexibly in order to enable State to protect citizens from terrorism.

In addition to this, under Article 15 § 3, any High Contracting Party availing itself of this right of derogation shall keep the Secretary General of the Council of Europe fully informed of the measures which it has taken and the reasons therefore. It shall also inform the Secretary General of the Council of Europe when such measures have ceased to operate and the provisions of the Convention are again being fully executed. The primary purpose of informing the Secretary General is that the derogation becomes public and the measures taken by the State are covered by public scrutiny. Reservations to the Convention are also possible under Article 57. In other words, any State, when signing or ratifying the Convention can subject its accession to a condition or limit the scope of one of the provisions of the Convention. However, Article 57 prohibits general reservations which would defeat the object and purpose of the Convention (**Loizidou v Turkey, no 15318/89, 23/03/1995**, ECHR).

As regards withdrawal, according to Article 58(1) of the Convention: *"A High Contracting Party may denounce the present Convention only after the expiry of five years from the date on which it became a party to it and after six months' notice contained in a notification addressed to the Secretary General of the Council of Europe, who shall inform the other High Contracting Parties".* In other words, the Court has still jurisdiction to review pending cases against a State that denounces the Convention but also on cases lodged up to 6 months after the denunciation. In practice, only Greece denounced the Convention in 1970 after a military coup but ratified the Convention once again in 1974. In a Brexit context, the same question was debated for the UK. However, although withdrawing from the European Convention is legally possible for the UK, and even easier in practice than exiting the EU, it seems that it is not yet on the political agenda.

Proceedings before the European Court of Human Rights

The European Court of Human Rights (hereinafter "the Court") is located in Strasbourg, France. It is composed of 47 judges, each one of them representing one of the Member States. The Judges are appointed by the Parliamentary Assembly of the Council of Europe (PACE), which selects one judge out of a list of three proposed by the concerned Member State. If the PACE does not find any suitable candidate in the list, it can refuse the list and ask the Member State to present a new one. The Court is composed of a Chamber who takes judgements that can be referred to the Grand Chamber by a panel of judges upon the request of one of the parties. This is a sort of appeal given that the Grand Chamber's judgement prevails over the Chamber's judgement. Since the entry into force of Protocol 14 in 2010, the Court can issue single-judge decisions to declare applications inadmissible. The Court initiated new working methods to tackle the massive backlog of clearly inadmissible cases. In 2011 over 100,000 of such applications were pending. As of today, the total of pending applications is approximately 60 000.

Jurisdiction

Under Article 1 of the Convention: "The High Contracting Parties shall secure to everyone within their jurisdiction the rights and freedoms defined in Section I of this Convention". Here the term "everyone" should be emphasised. It means that there is no requirement regarding citizenship to claim that applicants have been victims of human rights violations by the any responding State. In addition to this, the contracting parties' obligation to secure the Convention's rights applies to every human being, regardless their residence status in the concerned Member States. Therefore, a State cannot pretend that the Court does not have jurisdiction over alleged violations of the rights of undocumented migrants, for example.

The term "jurisdiction" in Article 1 of the Convention refers to the traditional concept of territorial jurisdiction, which encompasses the combination of the European territories of 'the contracting parties but also the overseas' territories. For instance, the Court has jurisdiction for alleged violations committed in Martinique (French overseas region). In addition to the traditional concept of territorial jurisdiction, the Court, in specific circumstances, also has extra-territorial jurisdiction. In those cases, the Member States will be held responsible for acts that have occurred outside the geographical jurisdiction of a contracting State. These could include matters arising from the activities of State agents abroad, for instance, or when a Member State has effective control of the relevant territory abroad as a consequence of military occupation, or because the government of that territory had consented or acquiesced to the exercise of its powers. The Convention allows individual complaints (under Article 34 of the Convention) but also inter-States complaints (Article 33 of the Convention) to be lodged to the European Court of Human Rights for a review of potential violation of human rights as provided for by the Convention.

General principle: The European Court of Human Rights can review both individual and inter-States complaints.

Ireland v. The United Kingdom, no 5310/71, 18/01/1978, ECHR
Facts: The Irish government brought an inter-State complaint against the United Kingdom for alleged violations of Article 3 of the Convention (prohibition of torture, inhuman and degrading treatment) of the rights of suspected terrorists by British soldiers in Northern Ireland.
Ratio: The Court held that the authorities' use of the five techniques of interrogation in 1971 constituted a practice of inhuman and degrading treatment, in breach of Article 3, and that the said use of the five techniques did not constitute a practice of torture within the meaning of this Article.
Application: Although a vast majority of the applications to the Court are lodged by individuals, inter-States complaints can also be reviewed by the Strasbourg Court under Article 33 of the Convention. It should be noted that the Court recently received a request for revision of this judgement for new facts, which was dismissed on 20/03/2018.

Admissibility

The Court, before examining the merits of a case, will first look at its admissibility. Admissibility criteria are listed in Article 34 and 35 of the Convention. These rules are aimed at filtering out helpless claims or claims presented in bad faith and helps reducing the backlog of applications by processing cases more rapidly. Most of the criteria are formal or procedural. Accordingly, we will only discuss those of greater significance.

First of all, the Court will only review applications lodged by applicants who claim to be "victims" of a breach of the Convention. According to Article 34 of the Convention, individual applications can be lodged by "any person, non-governmental organisation or group of individuals claiming to be a victim of a violation" of their rights by one or several Member States. The term "person", in line with its traditional legal signification, covers both individuals and legal persons such as companies, trade unions or political parties.

Applicants must demonstrate that they have been directly affected by State action or inaction in order to be a "victim" for the purposes of admissibility of their applications. However, the Court may accept indirect victims such as relatives of a deceased person with claims related to Article 2, for example.

General principle: In very exceptional circumstances, a non-governmental organisation that was in contact with the direct victim might have standing to lodge an application on behalf of a deceased mental patient without relatives.
Centre for Legal Resources on behalf of Valentin Campeanu v. Romania [GC], no 47848/08, 17/07/2014, ECHR
Facts: The application was lodged by a non-governmental organisation, the Centre for Legal Resources (CLR), on behalf of a young Roma man, Mr Câmpeanu, who died in 2004 at the age of 18 because of the alleged medical negligence of a hospital.
Ratio: The Court dismissed the Government's preliminary objection that the CLR had no standing to lodge the application. It accepted that the CLR could not be regarded as a victim of the alleged Convention violations as Mr Câmpeanu was indisputably the direct victim while the CLR had not demonstrated a sufficiently "close link" with him or established a "personal interest" in pursuing the complaints before the Court to be considered an indirect victim. However, in the exceptional circumstances of the case and bearing in mind the serious nature of the allegations, it had to have been open to the CLR to act as Mr Câmpeanu's representative.

Application: In this case the Court conceded that in exceptional circumstances resulting on the death of a direct victim of a breach of the Convention, persons related to the deceased could have standing to lodge an application on his/her behalf where declaring such application inadmissible would result on a flagrant injustice.

Another admissibility criterion is that applications have to be lodged within six months after the final domestic decision. The 6-month-rule is closely related to the main admissibility criterion that requires applicants to exhaust all domestic remedies before lodging an application to the Court. One of the main exceptions to this rule requires the applicant to demonstrate that the said remedy was not effective in the sense that it did not present reasonable prospects of success in order to redress the breach of the Convention.

In addition to this, since 2010 and the entry into force of Protocol 14, the Court can declare applications inadmissible if the applicant has not demonstrated that he or she suffered a significant disadvantage. This rule will be applied, for example, if the financial loss suffered by the applicant is modest.

It should be noted that the Court increasingly made use of the manifestly ill-founded ground to reject cases that did not disclose *prima facie* violations. Mainly invoked in single-judge decisions, this ground of inadmissibility is located between admissibility and the review of the merits of a case. The doctrine qualifies this use as abusive and dangerous for the administration of justice. In this regard, it should be noted that more than 90% of the applications are declared inadmissible by the Court.

Key jurisprudential principles developed by the European Court to examine the merits of applications

The notion of positive obligations

The idea of traditional negative obligations under the Convention is that a State should refrain from actively interfering with an individual's rights. In a concrete example, the negative obligations of contracting States under Article 3 means that they should refrain from torturing or subjecting individuals to ill treatments.

It should be noted that the defendant, before the Strasbourg Court will always be a Member State. However, the State can still be condemned by the Court for failure to act, for example, in a case implying infringements of individual's rights by private actors. This is the theory of positive obligations: Member States are held responsible for their inactivity in protecting from or investigating into human rights violations committed by private actors. In Article 3 example, a Member State would be in breach of its positive obligations if it is demonstrated that it failed to protect the individual's right to not be subjected to torture or ill-treatments.

Historically, positive obligations have been developed by the Strasbourg Court as regards the violations often referred to as the "most serious", namely violations of rights under Articles 2 and 3. On the one hand, "positive obligations to protect" require Member State to protect individuals from interferences with their rights under Article 2 and 3. This include that Member States are required to enact laws in their domestic legal systems that prohibit, deter, and punish individuals who commit such violations.

General principle: Positive obligations regarding Article 2 may require Member States to take preventative measures to protect an individual whose life is at risk from the criminal acts of another private individual.

Osman v United Kingdom, no 23452/94, 28/10/1998, ECHR
Facts: This case concerned the obsession of a teacher for one of his students. After having moved to another school, the family of the kid reported vandalism at their home and declared having seen the teacher walking around the house. Several signs of possible implication of the teacher in such acts were communicated to the police. The kid was later killed by the teacher. The family of the kid argued that the UK failed to take preventative measures to protect the kid and therefore breached its obligation under Article 2 of the Convention.
Ratio: The Court Stated that a contracting State is under positive obligation to take preventative measures to protect life if it is: "established (...) that the authorities knew or ought to have known at the time of the existence of a real and immediate risk to the life of an identified individual or individuals from the criminal acts of a third party and that

they failed to take measures within the scope of their powers which, judged reasonably, might have been expected to avoid that risk". However, the Court clearly restricted this obligation to what could reasonably be expected from Member States: "For the Court, and bearing in mind the difficulties involved in policing modern societies, the unpredictability of human conduct and the operational choices which must be made in terms of priorities and resources, such an obligation must be interpreted in a way which does not impose an impossible or disproportionate burden on the authorities. Accordingly, not every claimed risk to life can entail for the authorities a Convention requirement to take operational measures to prevent that risk from materialising".
Application: The positive obligation to take preventative measures to protect life is part of the substantial obligations of States to protect the lives of individuals.

On the other hand, positive obligations of a procedural nature include, *inter alia*, the duty for States to investigate deaths that may have occurred in breach of the Convention (**Mccann and Others v. The United Kingdom, no 18984/91, 27/09/1995,** ECHR).

Prescribed by law

The Strasbourg Court appreciates the justification of interference to a conditional right using its traditional test (prescribed by law, pursuing a legitimate aim and necessary in a democratic society). In accordance with key principles of the Rule of law, the prescription by law should present a minimum standard of certainty and clarity. The clarity of laws guarantees that individuals are able to regulate their conduct in accordance with the law. In the context of the European Convention for Human Rights, this notion is referred to as "prescribed by law" which is a requirement for the justification of interferences in individuals' rights.

General principle: The expression "prescribed by law", covering both statutes and unwritten provisions, ensures that a legal provision allowing for an interference on individuals' rights must be adequately accessible to citizens and formulated

with sufficient precision to enable the citizen to regulate his conduct.

The Sunday Times v. The United Kingdom n°6538/74, 26/04/1979, ECHR

Facts: The applicant, a British newspaper, published an article on titled the Thalidomide, a drug taken by pregnant women allegedly causing birth defects to new-borns, and criticizing English law for failing to tackle this issue. In this article, a footnote announced another article to be published later on the same topic. In November 17, 1972, the Divisional Court of the Queen's Bench granted an injunction in order to restrain the publication of the future article stating that its publication would constitute contempt of court. The applicant argued that the law of contempt of court was so vague and uncertain that the restrain imposed on their freedom of expression (Article 10 of the Convention), could not be regarded as "prescribed by law".

Ratio: The Court developed its jurisprudence on the notion of prescribed by law, stating that: "In the Court's opinion, the following are two of the requirements that flow from the expression "prescribed by law". Firstly, the law must be adequately accessible: the citizen must be able to have an indication that is adequate in the circumstances of the legal rules applicable to a given case. Secondly, a norm cannot be regarded as a "law" unless it is formulated with sufficient precision to enable the citizen to regulate his conduct: he must be able - if need be with appropriate advice - to foresee, to a degree that is reasonable in the circumstances, the consequences which a given action may entail" (§49). Applying this test to the present case, it found that the applicants "were able to foresee, to a degree that was reasonable in the circumstances, the consequences of publication of the draft article". Accordingly, the interference on the applicant's freedom of expression was prescribed by law as for the purposes of paragraph 2 of Article 10 of the Convention.

Application: Interestingly, in this case, the Court made it clear that the term "law" referred to both written and unwritten legal provisions: "The Court observes that the word "law" in the expression "prescribed by law" covers not only statute but also unwritten law. Accordingly, the Court does not attach importance here to the fact that contempt of court is a creature of the common law and not of legislation. It would clearly be contrary to the intention of the drafters of the Convention to hold that a restriction imposed by virtue of the common law is not "prescribed by law" on the sole ground that it is not enunciated in legislation: this would deprive a common-law State which is Party to the Convention of the protection of Article 10 (2) (art. 10-2) and strike at the very roots of that State's legal system" (§47).

However, this does not mean that a legal basis has to be absolutely clear. However, what matters is the possibility for an individual to foresee the legal consequences of an act which is regulated by law (see **Hashman and Harrup v. UK, no 25594/94, 25/11/1999, ECHR**).

General principle: When discretion is conferred on public authorities regarding interferences of Convention rights, the law should indicate with reasonable clarity the scope and manner of exercise of the relevant discretion.

Malone v. United Kingdom, no 8691/79, 02/08/1984, ECHR
Facts: The plaintiff claimed that intercepting his telephone conversations, on authority of a warrant by the Secretary of State for Home Affairs, was unlawful, and asked for an injunction against the Metropolitan Police Commissioner for monitoring his telephone. He argued that he had a right of privacy.
Ratio: The court found a violation of Article 8 of the Convention because the interference was not prescribed by law. It considered that: "In the opinion of the Court, the law of England and Wales does not indicate with reasonable clarity the scope and manner of exercise of the relevant discretion conferred on the public authorities. To that extent, the minimum degree of legal protection to which citizens are entitled under the rule of law in a democratic society is lacking".
Application: The *rationale* behind this rule of necessary limitations to discretionary powers of the executive regarding interferences with convention rights is to protect the key principles of the Rule of law.

General principle: The European Court will be reluctant to declare an interference prescribed by law where the legal

provision contains vague terms enabling for clear risks of arbitrariness in the grant of broad discretionary powers.

Gillan and Quinton v. UK, no 4158/05, 12/01/2010, ECHR

Facts: This case concerned Section 44 of the Terrorism Act 2000, which allowed a senior police officer to grant a stop and search authorisation for a designated area where he considered it "expedient" to do so for the prevention of acts of terrorism. One safeguard provided that this grant had to be authorized by the Secretary of State.

Ratio: The Court held that the interference was not prescribed by law and found a violation of Article 8 of the Convention (respect for private life). "The Court notes at the outset that the senior police officer referred to in section 44(4) of the Act is empowered to authorise any constable in uniform to stop and search a pedestrian in any area specified by him within his jurisdiction if he "considers it expedient for the prevention of acts of terrorism". However, "expedient" means no more than "advantageous" or "helpful". There is no requirement at the authorisation stage that the stop and search power be considered "necessary" and therefore no requirement of any assessment of the proportionality of the measure. (...) In the Court's view, there is a clear risk of arbitrariness in the grant of such a broad discretion to the police officer".

Application: Once again, in this case, the reasoning of the Court is relying on the fundamental protection of the rule of law. As the Court stated, in its judgement: "In matters affecting fundamental rights it would be contrary to the rule of law, one of the basic principles of a democratic society enshrined in the Convention, for a legal discretion granted to the executive to be expressed in terms of an unfettered power. Consequently, the law must indicate with sufficient clarity the scope of any such discretion conferred on the competent authorities and the manner of its exercise".

General principle: The Strasbourg Court applies flexibility to certain types of laws that, by their very definition, do not lend themselves to precise legal definitions.

Wingrove v. United Kingdom, no 17419/90, 25/11/1996, ECHR

Facts: In this case, the British Board of Film Classification refused to grant distribution certificate for the applicant's video in order to be published. The latter claimed that the criminal offence of blasphemy, in UK law, was so vague, that it was inordinately difficult to foresee whether a particular publication would constitute an offence.

Ratio: The Court was satisfied that applicant with legal advice could reasonably foresee that scenes in film could fall within the scope of blasphemy, it could not be said that blasphemy law did not afford adequate protection against arbitrary interference. Therefore, the Court held that the impugned restriction was prescribed by law. Interestingly, the Court noted that blasphemy, by very nature, has no precise legal definition - national authorities must be afforded degree of flexibility in assessing whether particular facts fall within definition.

Application: It should be noted that the same solution was adopted by the Court, few years earlier, in the context of obscenity laws (see **Müller v. Switzerland, no 10737/84, 24/05/1988**, ECHR).

Subsidiarity

The principle of subsidiarity in the Convention system means that human rights violations should be reviewed by judges at the most immediate (or local) level that is consistent with their resolution. As Stated by the Court in **Cocchiarella v. Italy, no 64886/01, 29/03/2006**, ECHR : "The machinery of complaint to the Court is thus subsidiary to national systems safeguarding human rights. This subsidiary character is articulated in Articles 13 and 35 § 1 of the Convention".

Accordingly, the Strasbourg Court will refrain from imposing its view if, during national proceedings, domestic judges have fairly reviewed the applicant's case in accordance with the main safeguards enshrined by the European court's case law. One of the main illustrations of this principle which underlines the entire Convention is the admissibility criterion that requires applicants to have exhausted domestic remedies.

The principle of subsidiarity has been recently reinforced by the Member States during the Brighton conference which resulted in the entry into force of Protocol no. 15. Protocol no. 15 amended the preamble of the Convention by adding the following sentence: *"Affirming that the High Contracting Parties, in accordance with the principle of subsidiarity, have the primary responsibility to secure the rights and freedoms defined in this Convention and the Protocols thereto, and that in doing so they enjoy a margin of appreciation, subject to the supervisory jurisdiction of the European Court of Human Rights established by this Convention".*

Margin of appreciation

The margin of appreciation is a jurisprudential concept developed by the Strasbourg Court to improve the flexibility of its review over domestic proceedings. It provides contracting States with a kind of discretion when balancing multiple interests in a specific case. The traditional argument in favour of the recognition of a national margin of appreciation is that local authorities are better placed to assess and balance the interests at stake. Therefore, on this aspect, the margin of appreciation is based on the principle of subsidiarity which requires decisions to be taken at the most immediate level.

General principle: When restricting individuals' rights in order to protect public morals, the Convention leaves to the Contracting States a wide margin of appreciation.

Handyside v. UK, no 5493/72, 07/12/1976, ECHR

Facts: The Little Red Schoolbook is a book for children which had been published in several European and non-European countries. The book urged young people at whom it was directed to take a liberal attitude in sexual matters. Prosecutions were brought against the applicant for possessing obscene publications, under Obscene Publications Act 1959, as amended by the Obscene Publications Act 1964. He claimed that his prosecution breached his freedom of expression under Article 10 pf the Convention.

Ratio: The Court found that there has been no violation of Article 10 of the Convention. It noted that "it is not possible to find in the domestic law of the various Contracting States a uniform European conception of morals. The view taken by their respective laws of the requirements of morals varies from time to time and from place to place, especially in our era which is characterised by a rapid and far-reaching evolution of

opinions on the subject. By reason of their direct and continuous contact with the vital forces of their countries, State authorities are in principle in a better position than the international judge to give an opinion on the exact content of those requirements as well as on the "necessity" of a "restriction" or "penalty" intended to meet them". On the specific question of obscenity laws, it stated that: "The Contracting States have each fashioned their approach in the light of the situation obtaining in their respective territories; they have had regard, inter alia, to the different views prevailing there about the demands of the protection of morals in a democratic society".

Application: In this case, the Strasbourg Court that local authorities are better placed to define public morals, a concept that is country-specific depending on the traditions and culture of each contracting state.

General principle: Not only the nature of the legitimate aim invoked to justify the restriction but also the nature of the activities involved will affect the scope of the margin of appreciation. When a restriction impinges on the enjoyment of the individual's right to private life, the margin of appreciation afforded to the Contracting States is generally narrow.

Dudgeon v. The United Kingdom, no 7525/76, 22/10/1981, ECHR

Facts: This case concerned the criminalisation of homosexual activity. The applicant was a gay activist in Northern Ireland. He was subsequently arrested an interrogated. He claimed that his right to private life under Article 8 of the Convention has been violated.

Ratio: The Court held that the applicant suffered an unjustified interference with his right to private life. Accordingly, it found that there has been a violation of Article 8 of the Convention. The Strasbourg Court considered that "not only the nature of the aim of the restriction but also the nature of the activities involved will affect the scope of the margin of appreciation. The present case concerns a most intimate aspect of private life. Accordingly, there must exist particularly serious reasons before interferences on the part of the public authorities can be legitimate for the purposes of

paragraph 2 of Article 8 (art. 8-2)".

Application: It should be noted that the notion of margin of appreciation is flexible, and the Court will broaden its scope depending on the circumstances of each case.To some extent, the breadth of the margin of appreciation is assessed by the Court, on case by case basis, taking into account the context, the national specificities (such as, for example, the political structure of a contracting State, see **Demuth v. Switzerland, no 38743/97, 2002,** ECHR) and the interests at stake. The Court considered that different historical development of countries and their cultural diversities can explain that domestic authorities should apply the Convention with a certain margin of appreciation. This case by case assessment has been heavily criticized by academics who pointed out a tool used by the Court to discretionarily justify or reject its intervention in State affairs.

However, the Court has developed some jurisprudential criteria to determine the breadth of the margin of appreciation in specific areas, such as freedom of expression, where it had constantly reiterated that margin of appreciation should be particularly narrow when the applicant intended to debate a question of general interest (**Morice v. France [GC], n 29369/10, 23 /04/2015,** ECHR).

General principle: The absence of European consensus speaks in favour of allowing a wider margin of appreciation.

Animal Defenders International v. The United Kingdom, no 48876/08, 22/04/2013, ECHR

Facts: In this case, it should be noted that the Communications Act 2003 prohibited political advertising in television or radio services. The applicant, a non-governmental organisation, was campaigning against the use of animals in commerce, science and leisure and sought to achieve changes in the law. In 2005 it sought to screen a television advertisement as part of a campaign concerning the treatment of primates. However, the Broadcast Advertising Clearance Centre ("the BACC") refused to clear the advert. The applicant claimed that this had violated its rights under Article 10 of the Convention.

Ratio: The Court held that there has been no violation of Article 10 given that domestic authorities enjoyed a wide margin of appreciation in balancing the interest at stake. It

stated that: "The Court would underline that there is no European consensus between Contracting States on how to regulate paid political advertising in broadcasting. It is recalled that a lack of a relevant consensus amongst Contracting States could speak in favour of allowing a somewhat wider margin of appreciation than that normally afforded to restrictions on expression on matters of public interest".

Application: The Court, when examining the existence of European consensus, looks at state practice on a given topic by engaging in comparative law analyses.

Proportionality

As for the criterion of prescription by law, the notion of proportionality only applies to conditional rights, in other words, Articles 8 to 11: the right to respect for private and family life, Freedom of thought, conscience and religion, Freedom of expression, Freedom of assembly and association. The Court's assessment of proportionality intervenes at the end of the review of the justification of an interference to conditional rights, when the Court determines whether the interference was necessary in a democratic society. The doctrine of proportionality ensures that domestic courts have conducted a fair balance between pursuing a legitimate aim and protecting Convention rights.

General principle: The principle of proportionality imposes on contracting States, when pursuing a legitimate aim, to consider using the less restrictive measures in order to justify interferences to a conditional right.

Goodwin v. The United Kingdom, no 17488/90, 27/03/1996, ECHR

Facts: This case concerned a disclosure order granted to private company requiring a journalist to disclose the identity of his source. A fine was subsequently imposed on the journalist for having refused to disclose the identity of his source.

Ratio: The Court concluded that there was not, in sum, a reasonable relationship of proportionality between the legitimate aim pursued by the disclosure order and the means deployed to achieve that aim. The restriction which the

disclosure order entailed on the applicant journalist's exercise of his freedom of expression cannot therefore be regarded as having been necessary in a democratic society, within the meaning of paragraph 2 of Article 10 (art. 10-2), for the protection of Tetra's rights under English law, notwithstanding the margin of appreciation available to the national authorities.

Application: In this case, the Court developed the idea of proportionality as a concept imposing on contracting States to refrain from taking measure that are not strictly necessary to achieve the legitimate aim invoked. If there was a suitable alternative less restrictive to the applicant's rights and the responding State did not make a reasonable use of it, the Court will certainly declare the interference disproportionate.

In addition to this, the Court observes that the nature and severity of the penalty imposed are also factors to be taken into account when assessing the proportionality of the interference (**Sürek V. Turkey (No. 1), no 26682/95, 08/07/1999,** ECHR). Accordingly, a fine of a significant amount of money or a very restrictive measure in terms of its impact on the applicant's rights, will generally speak in favour of the disproportionate nature of the interference to the legitimate aim.

Summary

- The concept of human rights relies on the postulate that individuals have rights simply because they are human beings.

- Human rights have developed through history along the principles of natural law, which comes from the period of Enlightenment.

- The Council of Europe was created in 1949 with three main objectives: the protection of Human Rights, Democracy and the Rule of Law. It is an inter-governmental organization composed of 47 Member States.

- In 1950, the Member States of the Council of Europe adopted the Convention for the Protection of Human Rights and Fundamental Freedoms. As of today, the Convention has 16 protocols. The latest entered into force in August 2018.

- According to Article 46 of the Convention and subsequent practice: all final judgments (Chamber and Grand Chamber) are binding on the respondent states. The Committee of Ministers supervises the enforcement of judgments.

- According to Article 15 of the Convention, temporary derogations are allowed in times of public emergency. However, the second paragraph of Article 15 prohibits derogations to rights as protected by Article 2 (except regarding deaths resulting from lawful acts of war), 3, 4(1) and 7.

- The European Court of Human Rights (hereinafter "the Court") is located in Strasbourg, France. It is composed of 47 judges, each one of them representing one of the Member States.

- The term "jurisdiction" in Article 1 of the Convention refers to the traditional concept of territorial jurisdiction. However, in specific circumstances, the Court also has extra-territorial jurisdiction.

- The Convention allows individual complaints (under Article 34 of the Convention) but also inter-States complaints (Article 33 of the Convention) to be lodged to the European Court of Human Rights for a review of potential violation of human rights as provided for by the Convention.

- The Court, before examining the merits of a case, will first look at its admissibility. Admissibility criteria are listed in Article 34 and 35 of the Convention. The term "person", in line with its traditional legal signification, covers both individuals and legal persons such as companies, trade unions or political parties.

- The idea of traditional negative obligations under the Convention is that a State should refrain from actively interfering with an individual's rights. However according to the theory of positive obligations: Member States are held responsible for their inactivity in protecting from or investigating into human rights violations committed by private actors.

- The Strasbourg Court appreciates the justification of an interference to a conditional right using its traditional test (prescribed by law, pursuing a legitimate aim and necessary in a democratic society).

- The principle of subsidiarity in the Convention system means that human rights violations should be reviewed by judges at the most immediate (or local) level

- The doctrine of proportionality ensures that domestic courts have conducted a fair balance between pursuing a legitimate aim and protecting Convention rights.

Chapter 11 – The Human Rights Act 1998

The necessary adoption of the Human Rights Act 1998

After the adoption of the European Convention on Human Rights in 1950, the question that arose was to clarify the status of this international Treaty in domestic systems. A similar legal issue was raised along the development of European Union Law. For the vast majority of Member States, which are monists, this was not really a problem. Such states treat international law as binding on their domestic legal systems. Where the two forms of law clash, the monist system treats the international law rule as superior and overrides the domestic rule. By contrast, the UK has a dualist legal system. Therefore, its international obligations are not directly incorporated in its domestic legal order. Accordingly, the UK system treats domestic and international legal orders as two separate orders. However, where the UK has incorporated international law rules into its domestic legal system through an enabling act of Parliament, UK courts are bound to uphold those rules as having the same binding force as attached to any other UK legislation.

Because of its dualist system, for many decades, the UK led Europe in terms of violations of the European Convention on Human rights. There was a clear lack of competence for the UK judiciary and Parliament to respect its international obligations, namely because the ECHR was not really incorporated into domestic law. It was also symbolically important for the UK to have a single Act of Parliament embracing the principles and values of European Human Rights Law.

Attempts to incorporate the ECHR into the domestic law of the UK can be traced back to 1968, which saw the publication of Lord Lester's Fabian Society pamphlet, Democracy and Individual Rights. As a result, in the 1990's more intense discussions over a Human Rights Act were launched at Parliament.The HRA 1998 received royal assent on 9 November 1998. It is applicable to England, Scotland, Wales and Northern Ireland. Its aim is to incorporate into UK law the rights contained in the European Convention on Human Rights. The Act makes a remedy for breach of a Convention right available in UK courts, without the need to go to Strasbourg Court.

The duty to take the Strasbourg's jurisprudence into account

Under Section 2 of the Human Rights Act 1998 (hereinafter "the HRA"), UK courts must take into consideration the Strasbourg Court's case law when dealing with cases which raise issues related to Convention rights: "(1) A court or tribunal determining a question which has arisen in connection with a Convention right must take into account any— (a) judgment, decision, declaration or advisory opinion of the European Court of Human Rights, (b) opinion of the Commission given in a report adopted under Article 31 of the Convention, (c) decision of the Commission in connection with Article 26 or 27(2) of the Convention, or (d) decision of the Committee of Ministers taken under Article 46 of the Convention". The Act does not clearly state that UK courts must apply the ECtHR's jurisprudence but that it should take it into account. However, it should be remembered that one of the objectives of the Act is to avoid that individuals have no other choice than lodging application to the Strasbourg Court. Accordingly, in practice, UK judges will, in most of the cases, apply the Strasbourg's case law if it benefits the plaintiff.

General principle: Domestic courts should follow any clear and consistent jurisprudence of the ECHR unless there are special circumstances, or the decisions of the ECHR compel a conclusion fundamentally at odds with the distribution of powers under the UK Constitution.

R (Ullah) v Special Adjudicator [2004] UKHL 26

Facts: The issue in the case was whether a person can be deported from the United Kingdom to a third state where there are known human rights abuses. The plaintiff raised the question of the application of the European Court's case law in his case.

Ratio: The United Kingdom Appellate Committee of the House of Lords dismissed the appeal because the interference with Convention Rights was "flagrant". Lord Bingham made the following comments, with which the other members of the panel agreed: "The House is required by section 2(1) of the Human Rights Act 1998 to take into account any relevant

Strasbourg case law. While such case law is not strictly binding, it has been held that courts should, in the absence of some special circumstances, follow any clear and constant jurisprudence of the Strasbourg court: R (Alconbury Developments Ltd) v Secretary of State for the Environment..., paragraph 26. This reflects the fact that the Convention is an international instrument, the correct interpretation of which can be authoritatively expounded only by the Strasbourg court. From this it follows that a national court subject to a duty such as that imposed by section 2 should not without strong reason dilute or weaken the effect of the Strasbourg case law ... It is of course open to member states to provide for rights more generous than those guaranteed by the Convention, but such provision should not be the product of interpretation of the Convention by national courts, since the meaning of the Convention should be uniform throughout the states party to it. The duty of national courts is to keep pace with the Strasbourg jurisprudence as it evolves over time: no more, but certainly no less".

Application: This case represented the first opportunity for UK Courts to interpret Section 2 of the Human Rights Act. The approach of the United Kingdom Appellate Committee of the House of Lords is quite illustrative of the traditional reluctance of British judges to recognize the legal force of binding international law and would certainly not be similar in most of the other contracting states to the Convention.

General principle: UK courts will generally apply the European Court's case law as a minimum standard and will unlikely replace it by a more generous interpretation of the Convention for the plaintiff.

R v Secretary of State for the Home Department, ex parte Tylor and Anderson [2001] EWCA Civ 1698

Facts: In this case, the plaintiff claimed that the power of the Home Secretary to set tariffs for life sentence prisoners was incompatible with Article 6 of the Convention for lack of independence and impartiality. It should be noted that the power of the Home Secretary to set tariffs for life sentence prisoners had been accepted by the Strasbourg Court as compatible with the convention in its judgement **Wynne v United Kingdom, no**

15484/89, 18/07/1994, ECHR.

Ratio: The Court of Appeal noted that the European Court's case law was in favour of declaring the power of the Home Secretary to set tariffs for life sentence prisoners compatible with the Convention, therefore it would be improper for a domestic Court to decide in a manner which was inconsistent with that approach.

Application: This case illustrates the domestic courts' reluctance to interpret the Convention more generously than the European Court of Human Rights. It should be noted that the case **Wynne v United Kingdom, no 15484/89, 18/07/1994,** ECHR was later overruled by the Strasbourg Court in **Stafford v. The United Kingdom no 46295/99, 28/05/2002,** ECHR and new legislation was subsequently introduced at the domestic level to comply with it.

The Strasbourg's doctrine of proportionality embraced by domestic courts

Section 2 of the HRA enables UK courts to apply the doctrine of proportionality. Before the Act, this doctrine was rejected by domestic courts, preferring to use UK law standards (**R v Home Secretary, ex parte Brind [1991]** 1 AC 696). The doctrine of proportionality only applies to conditional rights. It ensures that domestic courts have conducted a fair balance between pursuing a legitimate aim and protecting Convention rights. Domestic courts, when having to appreciate the justification of interferences to conditional rights, can therefore conduct a balancing exercise to determine whether it was necessary and proportionate.

General principle: UK courts will declare interferences to conditional rights disproportionate when they are inflexible and appear to go beyond what was necessary for the purposes of pursuing the legitimate aim.

R (T) v Chief Constable of Greater Manchester [2013] EWCA Civ 25

Facts: This case concerned statutory provision imposing a blanket statutory scheme requiring disclosure of cautions held in the police national computer. The question asked to the Court was related to the compatibility of those provisions with Article 8 of the

Convention (the right to respect for private and family life).

Ratio: The Court of Appeal held that the *rationale* for the additional level of disclosure (where employers are responsible for children or vulnerable adults) was reasonable. However, the scheme did not control disclosure of information by reference to whether the information is relevant for enabling the employer to assess the suitability of the individual for particular work. Accordingly, such a regime was disproportionate and went beyond legitimate aims of protecting employees and vulnerable individuals. Therefore, the impugned laws were incompatible with Article 8 of the Convention.

Application: As illustrated in this case, the passing of the HRA has resulted on a subsequent use of the doctrine of proportionality by British judges.

General principle: In areas usually reserved to Parliament or the executive where the issue is policy-based, courts will be reluctant apply the proportionality test and will rather show deference to the decision-maker.

R (Countryside Alliance) v Attorney General [2007] UKHL 52

Facts: The Hunting Act was challenged by the plaintiffs. This Act banned the hunting of living animals. The plaintiff claimed that it violated their Convention rights under articles 8, 11, 14 and Art 1 of protocol 1.

Ratio: The House of Lords dismissed the claims and deferred the matter to Parliament which was responsible for regulating hunting because of the recent parliamentary and public debates. The issue was highly political and sensitive, therefore the House of Lords decided not to intervene. In addition to this, it found that Article 8 protected the right to private and family life. Its purpose was to protect individuals from unjustified intrusion by state agents into the private sphere within which they expected to be left alone to pursue their personal affairs and live as they chose. Hunting was a very public activity and a ban did not infringe article 8.

Application: Similarly, in **R (British American Tobacco and others) v Secretary of State for Health [2004]** EWHC 2493 (Admin), the High Court stated that there were areas in which the courts had to be particularly careful when trying to impose its own value judgement upon legislative scheme.

Interpretation of statutory provisions in the light of the Convention

Section 3(1) of the Human Rights Act provides that: *"So far as it is possible to do so, primary and subordinate legislation must be read and given effect in a way which is compatible with Convention rights"*. In other words, British judges, when interpreting UK legislation, must do it in a way which is compatible with the Convention. Section 3(1) of the HRA applies to legislation enacted both before and after 1998. However, this provision is rarely applied by UK courts in practice. In 2017, courts had only made use of Section 3 in 10 cases, almost 20 years after the adoption of the Human Rights Act. The terms "so far as it is possible to do so" in Section 3 are of a crucial importance regarding the practical effect of Convention-compatible interpretations. Generally, interpretations of domestic law as to give it an effect compatible with the Convention is made where the impugned legislation is not expressly contradictory to the Convention.

Such an interpretation is possible in practice only when the wording of domestic law is blurry, where there is room for interpretation, but not in situations where domestic law is obviously incompatible with the Convention. In those situations, Convention-compatible interpretations are impossible for the purposes of Section 3 of the HRA. For instance, Lord Nicholls considers that the wording of domestic legislation renders the interpretation impossible where it would imply a fundamental change of a feature of the law.

General principle: The use of Section 3 of the HRA will sometimes be necessary to adopt an interpretation which linguistically may appear strained. The techniques to be used will not only involve the reading down of express language in a statute but also the implication of provisions.

R v A (Complainant's Sexual History) (No 2) [2001] 2 WLR 1546
Facts: In December 2000 the defendant was due to stand trial in

the Crown Court on an indictment charging him with an offence of rape. The defendant's defence was that sexual intercourse took place with the complainant's consent. The Youth Justice and Criminal Evidence Act 1999 (Section 41), restricted the circumstances in which evidence and questioning about a complainant's prior sexual history in trials concerning sexual offences. The defendant argued that this provision was incompatible with Article 6 of the Convention.

Ratio: The House of Lords made use of Section 3 of the HRA by reading and giving effect to domestic legislation in a way which is compatible with the Convention. In the words of Lord Steyn: "The interpretative obligation under section 3 of the 1998 Act is a strong one. It applies even if there is no ambiguity in the language in the sense of the language being capable of two different meanings (...) Parliament specifically rejected the legislative model of requiring a reasonable interpretation. Section 3 places a duty on the court to strive to find a possible interpretation compatible with Convention rights ... In accordance with the will of Parliament as reflected in section 3 it will sometimes be necessary to adopt an interpretation which linguistically may appear strained. The techniques to be used will not only involve the reading down of express language in a statute but also the implication of provisions".

Application: In this case, Lord Hope's main objection, dissenting, was that the use of Section 3 in such a case resulted on departing from the apparent intention of Parliament in enacting the Youth Justice and Criminal Evidence Act 1999 (Section 41). This decision has subsequently been debated and qualified by commentators as an interpretation *contra legem*. It is therefore considered as the "high water mark" situation for the use of Section 3 of the HRA.

General principle: In order to make a provision convention-compliant, a court may be required to depart from the clear and unambiguous meaning that the provision would otherwise have borne.

Ghaidan v Godin-Mendoza [2004] UKHL 30
Facts: In this case, the main question was related to the right of same sex couples to access similar tenancy benefits as for heterosexual couples. The domestic legislation at stake was s.

76(1) of the Rent Act 1977. The plaintiff argued that the words of the said legislation "as his husband and wife" had to be read down as to give it an effect with was compatible with Article 14 of the Convention (prohibition of discrimination).

Ratio: The House of Lords made use of Section 3 of the HRA to read s. 76(1) of the Rent Act 1977 in a way as to give it an effect which was compatible with Article 14 of the Convention. It affirmed that courts can interpret the language of domestic legislation restrictively or expansively given that what mattered the substance of the legislation and its spirit was rather that its mere wording. Nevertheless, the Lords restricted the use of interpretative powers under Section 3 of the HRA by holding that interpretations that will result on a complete change of the substance of the provision or affect one of its fundamental features would go too far.

Application: Once again, this judgement was highly criticized as making an excessive use of Section 3 of the HRA. However, it should be noted that the present judgement was adopted one year after **Karner v. Austria, no 40016/98, 24/07/2003,** ECHR, judgement of the Strasbourg Court, which found a violation of Article 14 in a similar situation. Therefore there was no doubt about the incompatibility of s. 76(1) of the Rent Act 1977, but the question was rather whether the use of Section 3 of the HRA was appropriate.

Non-binding declarations of incompatibility

Under Section 4 of the HRA, situations where the court does not consider it appropriate to adopt a certain interpretation of the law under section 3, it may make a declaration that the impugned law (Section 4(2) of the HRA 1998 regarding primary legislation and Section 4(4) regarding subordinate legislation) is incompatible with the Convention. However, according to Section 4(5) of the said Act, this power is reserved to the High courts and appellate courts.

As stated earlier, UK courts do not have the power to strike down acts of Parliament, even when they are incompatible with the Convention. This is precisely why the power of judges to declare UK legislation incompatible with the Convention is not legally binding Parliament. Therefore, Parliament may subsequently ignore the courts' call on the incompatibility of domestic legislation, thereby taking the risk that a case might be lodged to the Strasbourg Court.

Nevertheless, in practice, such declarations still put significant political pressure on Parliament to amend the law. Accordingly, in most cases, Parliament will follow the courts' "recommendations" by amending the impugned law in order to render UK law compatible with the Convention. In this respect, some authors have argued that a constitutional convention has arisen in this situation, requiring the relevant minister and Parliament to take steps to remove the incompatibility.

Section 5 (1) of the HRA enables the relevant minister, where issues of incompatibility of law with the Convention are raised in domestic proceedings, to be heard by the courts on the objects and purposes of the legislation in question and any other relevant matter. In this way, courts are able to operate a broad and contextual assessment of the compatibility of the provision at stake with the Convention.

General principle: UK courts may declare legislation incompatible with the Convention where using section 3 of the HRA would give it an effect quite different from that which Parliament intended and would go well beyond any interpretative process.

R (Anderson) v Secretary of State for the Home Department, [2002] UKHL 46
Facts: Section 29 of the Crime (Sentences) Act 1997 left the decision on tariffs for mandatory life term prisoners solely in the hands of the Home Secretary. The plaintiff argued that this provision was incompatible with Article 6 of the European Convention given that the Home Secretary was a member of the executive and was not impartial and independent.
Ratio: The House of Lords held that Section 29 of the Crime (Sentences) Act 1997 was incompatible with a Convention right (that is the right under Article 6 of the European Convention on Human Rights to have a sentence imposed by an independent and impartial tribunal) in that the Secretary of State for the Home Department was acting so as to give effect

to section 29 when he himself decided on the minimum period which must be served by a mandatory life sentence prisoner before he is considered for release. It considered that the impugned provision left it to the Home Secretary to decide whether or when to refer a case to the board, and he was free to ignore its recommendation if it was favourable to the prisoner, the decision on how long the convicted murderer should remain in prison for punitive purposes was his alone. It could not be doubted that Parliament intended this result when enacting section 29 and its predecessor sections. The Lords noted that the use of Section 3 of the HRA would have resulted on the withdrawal of a fundamental feature of the legislation: "To read section 29 as precluding participation by the Home Secretary, if it were possible to do so, would not be judicial interpretation but judicial vandalism: it would give the section an effect quite different from that which Parliament intended and would go well beyond any interpretative process sanctioned by section 3 of the 1998 Act".

Application: It should be noted that in this case, there was a so obvious incompatibility between UK law and the Convention that interpreting in a way which was compatible with Convention rights would have resulted on the withdrawal of a fundamental feature of the legislation. Following this judgement, Parliament voluntarily complied with the non-binding declaration made by the House of Lords by enacting the Criminal Justice Act 2003, s. 269.

General principle: When making use of section 3 of the HRA implies a perilous qualification and reasoning on sensitive issues, courts will rather declare the impugned provision incompatible with the Convention under section 4.

Bellinger v Bellinger, [2003] UKHL 21

Facts: The Matrimonial Causes Act 1973, s. 11(c) made no provision for the recognition of gender reassignment. This section provided that a marriage was void unless the parties were "respectively male and female". Mrs Bellinger had undergone gender reassignment before the wedding. The question at stake was whether, at the time of the marriage, Mrs Bellinger was "female" within the meaning of that expression in the statute. Mrs Bellinger argued that the impugned legislation was incompatible with Articles 8 and 12 of the Convention.

Ratio: The House of Lords upheld that the Matrimonial Causes Act 1973, s. 11(c)
was incompatible with Articles 8 and 12 of the Convention. It recalled that if a provision of primary legislation is shown to be incompatible with a Convention right the court, in the exercise of its discretion, may make a declaration of incompatibility under section 4 of the Human Rights Act 1998. The Lords considered that the use of section 3 was inappropriate because it implied the sensitive issue of qualifying the term "gender".

Application: It should be noted that following this judgement, Parliament voluntarily complied with the non-binding declaration made by the House of Lords by enacting the Gender Recognition Act 2004. The Gender Act only requires the person to demonstrate a desire of gender reassignment for 2 years and a professional medical certificate.

General principle: Where the incompatibility of legislation with the Convention is not obvious, courts may issue "statements" of incompatibility, which are politically less binding than declarations of incompatibility under Section 4 of the HRA.

R. (Nicklinson) v. Ministry of Justice, [2014] UKSC 38
Facts: Until 1961 suicide was a crime in England and Wales and encouraging or assisting a suicide was therefore also a crime. By section 1 of the Suicide Act 1961, suicide ceased to be a crime. However, section 2 of that Act ("Section 2") provided that encouraging or assisting a suicide remained a crime, carrying a maximum sentence of 14 years in prison, but that no prosecutions could be brought without the permission of the Director of Public Prosecutions. It was argued that this provision was incompatible with Article 8 of the Convention.

Ratio: The Supreme Court stated that the question whether the current law on assisted suicide is incompatible with Article 8 lies within the United Kingdom's margin of appreciation, and is therefore a question for the United Kingdom to decide. However, it held that the question whether the current law on assisting suicide is compatible with Article 8 involved a consideration of issues which Parliament was inherently better qualified than the courts to assess, and that under present circumstances the courts had to respect Parliament's assessment. Accordingly, the Supreme Court made a "statement" of incompatibility.

Application: The statement of incompatibility is an alternative for the courts when the use of Section 3 or Section 4 of the HRA would not be appropriate.

General principle: According the European Court of Human Rights, a declaration of incompatibility under Section 4 of the HRA is not an effective remedy as for the purposes of Article 35 (1) of the Convention, which requires applicants to exhaust all domestic remedies before lodging a case to the Strasbourg Court.

Burden and v. United Kingdom, no 13378/05, 29/04/2008, ECHR

Facts: The applicants were unmarried sisters, born in 1918 (89 at time of judgment]) and 1925 (82 at time of judgment) respectively. They were not in a couple relationship but asked to qualify for a civil partnership. Their request has been rejected at domestic level and they argued that it constituted a violation of Article 14 of the Convention combined with Protocol No. 1, Article 1. In this case, the courts have made a declaration of incompatibility which was not remedied for.

Ratio: At the admissibility stage, the Court recalled that the Human Rights Act places no legal obligation on the executive or the legislature to amend the law following a declaration of incompatibility and that, primarily for this reason, the Court has held on a number of previous occasions that such a declaration cannot be regarded as an effective remedy within the meaning of Article 35 § 1. Given that there have to date been a relatively small number of such declarations that have become final, it would be premature to hold that the procedure under section 4 of the Human Rights Act provides an effective remedy to individuals complaining about domestic legislation.

Accordingly, it rejected the government's preliminary objection regarding non-exhaustion of domestic remedies under Article 35 (1). However, it considered that it cannot be excluded that at some time in the future the practice of giving effect to the national courts' declarations of incompatibility by amendment of the legislation is so certain as to indicate that Section 4 of the Human Rights Act is to be interpreted as

imposing a binding obligation.

On the merits of the case, the European Court held, by 15 votes to 2, that there has been no violation of Article 14 combined with Protocol No. 1, Article 1, because the difference in treatment between couples living together, who had married or had registered civil partnerships, and non-couples living together, such as the Burden sisters, could be justified.

Application: The fact that the Strasbourg Court did not acknowledge a declaration of incompatibility as an effective remedy illustrates that the enforcement of the binding nature of the Convention in UK law could be improved. However the European Court acknowledged that this might change in the future, as far as the Parliament is generally complying with such declarations.

In terms of remedial action following a declaration of incompatibility, Section 10(2) of the HRA 1998 provides that the relevant minister, if he considers that there are compelling reasons, may take "remedial action" to amend the relevant legislation as necessary to remove the incompatibility. In this respect, Schedule 2 of the HRA 1998 sets out two procedures for remedial action. The standard procedure requires that a draft amending order be laid before Parliament for 60 days before being approved by both Houses of Parliament. The other procedure allows for urgent action, in which case the order may be laid before Parliament for approval after it is made.

Liability of public authorities for acts and omissions under the Human Rights Act

Section 6(1) of the HRA 1998 makes it: "unlawful for a public authority to act in a way which is incompatible with Convention rights". There is a general obligation for public authorities to act in a way which is compatible with the Convention. The terms "to act" also include omissions of public authorities, as indicated by Section 6(6) which refers to failures to act.

The HRA expressly states that the British Parliament (both houses) is not a "public authority" within the meaning of Section 6, given that its incompatible acts are already sanctioned by other provisions. However, the Scottish and Welsh parliaments, enacting subordinate legislation, qualify as public authorities for the purposes of the said provision.

However this rule does not apply, according to Section 6(2) of the HRA, in two situations:

" (a) as the result of one or more provisions of primary legislation, the authority could not have acted differently; or

(b) in the case of one or more provisions of, or made under, primary legislation which cannot be read or given effect in a way which is compatible with the Convention rights, the authority was acting so as to give effect to or enforce those provisions".

Accordingly, Section 6(2) of the HRA will be invoked by the state as a defence where an individual claims that the acts or omissions of its public authorities were incompatible with the Convention.

General principle: If legislation cannot be read compatibly with Convention rights, a public authority is not obliged to subvert the intention of Parliament by treating itself as under a duty to neutralise the effect of the legislation.

R v Secretary of State for Work and Pensions, ex parte Hooper [2005] UKHL 29

Facts: This case concerned an alleged discrimination (infringing Article 14 of the Convention) in the implementation by the Secretary of State of the 1992 Act relating to the payment of WPt and WMA to widows without making similar payments to widowers.

Ratio: The House of Lords held that the acts and omissions of the Secretary of State incompatible with Convention rights, were immunised by section 6(2)(b). In the words of Lord Hope:

"The situation to which paragraph (a) is addressed arises where the effect of the primary legislation is that the authority has no alternative but to do what the legislation tells it to do. The language of the paragraph tells us that this may be the result of one provision taken by itself, or that it may be the result of two or more provisions taken together. Where more than one provision is involved, they may be part of one enactment or they may be found in several different enactments. The key to its application lies in the fact that the effect of this legislation, wherever it is found, is that a duty is imposed on the authority. If the legislation imposes a duty to act, the authority is obliged to act in the manner which the legislation lays down even if the legislation requires it to act in a way which is incompatible with a Convention right. The authority

has no discretion to do otherwise. *As it is a duty which has been imposed on the authority by or as a result of primary legislation, Parliamentary sovereignty prevails over the Convention right. The defence is provided to prevent the legislation from being rendered unenforceable.*

The situation to which paragraph (b) is addressed on the other hand arises where the authority has a discretion, which it has the power to exercise or not to exercise as it chooses, to give effect to or enforce provisions of or made under primary legislation which cannot be read or given effect to in a way which is compatible with the Convention rights. The source of that discretion may be in a single statutory provision which confers a power on the authority which it may or may not choose to exercise".

Application: Section 6(2) (b) is generally used as an exemption of liability where the executive is merely implementing Parliament's will, also known as judicial deference. However, this section will not apply in many cases, for example where an individual is victim of violence from police.

Section 6 of the HRA 1998 effectively recognises three types of bodies:

- Core public authorities (Section 6(1));
- Functional/hybrid public authorities (Section 6(3) (b));
- Private bodies (Section 6(5)).

Core public authorities

This category includes bodies that are, by their very nature, public authorities. Their public nature is obvious and generally this category will not trigger issues of interpretation. These authorities include, for example: central government departments; local authorities or the police.

General principle: Core public authorities are essentially bodies whose nature is governmental in a broad sense.

Aston Cantlow and Wilmcote with Billesley Parochial Church Council v Wallbank, [2003] UKHL 37
Facts: This case concerned the liability of a lay rector, or lay impropriator, for the repair of the chancel of a church.

Ratio: The House of Lords held that the Parochial Church councils, established by the 1956 Measure, were hybrid public authorities, but not "core" authorities. Their functions had no connection to government, it was a religious organisation. Lord Nicholls clarified the definition of core public authorities as being "essentially bodies whose nature is governmental in a broad sense". He further suggested that the following factors were relevant in determining whether a body is a "core" public authority: (i) the possession of special powers; (ii) democratic accountability; (iii) public funding in whole or in part; (iv) an obligation to act only in the public interest; (v) a statutory constitution. It should also be noted that in this case, the House of Lords indicated that public authorities do not enjoy Convention rights as victims under Article 34 of the Convention.

Application: The definition of core public authority provided by this judgement seems to include, according to The White Paper, "Rights Brought Home": "central government (including executive agencies); local government; the police; immigration officers; prisons; courts and tribunals themselves; and, to the extent that they are exercising public functions".

Functional/hybrid public authorities

By definition, hybrid public authorities exercise activities that are both of public and private nature. Accordingly, they are only bound for the actions of a public nature that they carry out. The distinction between hybrid public authorities and core public authorities has been controversial. This is because the HRA, Section 6(3) (b), provides that public authority includes "any person certain of whose functions are functions of a public nature".

General principle: The mere fact that a body is performing an activity which otherwise a public body would be under a duty to perform cannot mean that such performance is necessarily a public function. Others factors such as the charity purposes of the body, its statutory authority, the control of the core public body over the activity carried out and their relationship of proximity, have to be taken into account.

Poplar Housing and Regeneration Community Association Ltd

v Donoghue [2001] EWCA Civ 595

Facts: The question in this case was whether a housing association, which had taken over a local housing authority's housing stock and was providing rental accommodation on behalf of the local authority (a core public authority), was performing a public function.

Ratio: The court of Appeal rejected an automatic assumption solely based on the nature of the activity carried out by the body in question: "The fact that a body is performing an activity which otherwise a public body would be under a duty to perform cannot mean that such performance is necessarily a public function. A public body, in order to perform its public duties, can use the services of a private body". It held the following factors in the assessment of the hybrid public nature of a body: (i) the fact that a body is a charity or is not motivated by profit does not necessarily mean that it performs a public function; (ii) statutory authority for what is being done can help to establish the act as being public; (iii) the extent of control over the function exercised by a core public body; (iv) proximity of relationship between the private body and the delegating authority. In the present case, the Court of Appeal held that the Poplar Housing and Regeneration Community Association was a functional public authority, namely because of its close relationship with the core public authority delegating the function.

Application: There is no unique definition of hybrid public authorities. The test is rather a combination of several factors, mainly depending on the proximity of relationship between the body and the delegating authority.

General principle: Courts are reluctant to recognize the functional public nature of bodies carrying out commercial activities where the delegating public authority does not exercise a significant control over these activities.

YL v Birmingham City Council [2007] UKHL 27

Facts: The question that was raised before the House of Lords was whether a privately owned, profit-earning care home providing care and accommodation for a publicly funded resident was a hybrid public authority, under section 6(3)(b) of the Human Rights Act 1998? The Southern Cross was taking care of popular housing for the elderly and its residents were 80% founded by the State.

Ratio: The House of Lords held that the private care home was not a functional public authority for the purposes of the HRA 1998. Lord Scott put it: "Southern Cross is a company carrying on a socially useful business for profit. It is neither a charity nor a philanthropist. It enters into private law contracts with the residents in its care homes and with the local authorities with whom it does business. It receives no public funding, enjoys no special statutory powers, and is at liberty to accept or reject residents as it chooses (subject, of course, to anti-discrimination legislation which affects everyone who offers a service to the public) and to charge whatever fees in its commercial judgment it thinks suitable. It is operating in a commercial market with commercial competitors. The position might be different if the managers of privately owned care homes enjoyed special statutory powers over residents entitling them to restrain them or to discipline them in some way or to confine them to their rooms or to the care home premises". One of the concerns of the majority was that 20% of the residents were not publically founded.

Application: It should be noted that in this case, the majority of the House of Lords was split (3-2), which mitigates the authority of this judgement. However, this case illustrates that courts are reluctant to recognize the functional public nature of a body where the activity carried out is mainly commercial and the delegating authority does not exercise a significant control over it.

Private bodies

Section 6(3)(a) of the HRA 1998 acknowledges that courts are "core public authorities". In other words courts' judgments and orders must be compatible with Convention rights, even in proceedings between private parties, allowing Convention rights to affect the substance of private law by virtue of the court's duty, owed to litigants, not to act incompatibly with their rights. Although Section 6(5) identifies private bodies as not bound by the obligations under Section 6, their conduct may be regulated under the indirect horizontal effect of the HRA 1998 which derives from the obligation of courts, as public authorities, to act in a way which is compatible with the Convention, even in proceedings between private parties.

Remedies under the Human Rights Act

Under Section 7(1) of the HRA, a person claiming to be victim to an act or omission from a public authority as being incompatible with the Convention (Section 6), may bring their claim under the Act or any other provision of the Convention by introducing a new proceeding or during any existing proceedings (for example criminal proceedings or judicial review). Section 7(5) imposes a time limit of one year after the complained act or omission occurred.

Nevertheless, as well as for the purposes of Article 34 of the Convention, Section 7(1) of the HRA limits this right to those who are "victims" of a violation of Convention rights. As stated in Chapter 10, the term "victim" includes both direct victims and indirect victims such as relatives of deceased persons or dependants of direct victims. Section 8 (1) of the HRA provides that: *"In relation to any act (or proposed act) of a public authority which the court finds is (or would be) unlawful, it may grant such relief or remedy, or make such order, within its powers as it considers just and appropriate"*. This Section further allows any courts usually entitled to award damages to do so, and in the determination of damages they must follow the ECHR guideline laid down by article 41 of the Convention.

Summary

- For long, there was a clear lack of competence for the UK judiciary and Parliament to respect its international obligations, namely because the ECHR was not really incorporated into domestic law. Attempts to incorporate the ECHR into the domestic law of the UK can be traced back to 1968.

- The HRA 1998 received royal assent on 9 November 1998. It is applicable to England, Scotland, Wales and Northern Ireland. Its aim is to incorporate into UK law the rights contained in the European Convention on Human Rights.

- Under Section 2 of the Human Rights Act 1998, UK courts must take into consideration the Strasbourg Court's case law when dealing with cases which raise issues related to Convention rights.

- Domestic courts, when having to appreciate the justification of interferences to conditional rights, may conduct a balancing exercise to determine whether it was necessary and proportionate.

- Under Section 3 of the HRA, British judges, when interpreting UK legislation, must do it in a way which is compatible with the Convention. However, the wording of domestic legislation renders the interpretation impossible where it would imply a fundamental change of a feature of the law.

- Under Section 4 of the HRA, situations where the court does not consider it appropriate to adopt a certain interpretation of the law under section 3, it may make a declaration that the impugned law is incompatible with the Convention. However, the power of judges to declare UK legislation incompatible with the Convention is not legally binding Parliament.

- In terms of remedial action following a declaration of incompatibility, Section 10(2) of the HRA 1998 provides that the relevant minister, if he considers that there are compelling reasons, may take "remedial action" to amend the relevant legislation as necessary to remove the incompatibility.

- There is a general obligation for public authorities to act in a way which is compatible with the Convention. The terms "to act" also include omissions of public authorities, as indicated by Section 6(6) which refers to failures to act.

- Section 6 of the HRA 1998 effectively recognises three types of bodies: core public authorities (Section 6(1)); functional/hybrid public authorities (Section 6(3) (b)) and private bodies (Section 6(5)).

- Core public authorities include bodies that are, by their very nature, public authorities.

- By definition, hybrid public authorities exercise activities that are both of public and private nature. This is because the HRA, Section 6(3) (b), provides that public authority includes "any person certain of whose functions are functions of a public nature".

- Although Section 6(5) identifies private bodies as not bound by the obligations under Section 6, their conduct may be regulated under the indirect horizontal effect of the HRA 1998 which derives from the obligation of courts, as public authorities, to act in a way which is compatible with the Convention, even in proceedings between private parties.

Chapter 12 – Freedom of Person – Articles 2, 3, 5 & 6 ECHR

Introduction to freedom of person

The rights referred to by "freedom of person and security" are generally considered as being the most important ones. The violation of such rights usually triggers the most intense reaction of public opinion. These rights are: the right to life, the prohibition of torture, inhuman and degrading treatment, the right to liberty and security and the right to a fair trial. Historically, the prohibition of slavery and forced labour (Article 4 of the Convention) has also been studied under this category, however, this Chapter will only focus on the rights under articles 2,3,5 and 6 of the Convention.

These rights are sometimes wrongly labelled as "absolute rights". However it should be noted that all of them can be legally restricted, except for the right to not be tortured (Article 3), which seems to be the only absolute human right (this element will be discussed further below).

The European Convention enshrines a variety of rights, including those that are mainly related to the liberal nature of our democracies such as, for example, the rights to freedom of expression or freedom of association. Although the doctrine of the indivisibility of human rights prohibits any kind of hierarchy, the particular importance historically conferred to the protection of rights related to freedom of person can be explained by the seriousness of the impact of their potential violations on individuals. To some extent, those rights protect individuals from violence and abuse.

Article 2 of the Convention: Right to life
The scope of Article 2 of the Convention

Article 2(1) of the Convention provides that:
"1. Everyone's right to life shall be protected by law. No one shall be deprived of his life intentionally save in the execution of a sentence of a court following his conviction of a crime for which

this penalty is provided by law".

General principle: The right to life, under Article 2 of the Convention, includes a right not to be killed but does not extend to a right to die.

Pretty v. United Kingdom, no 2346/02, 29/04/2002, ECHR

Facts: The applicant, a 43-year old woman, suffered from motor neurone disease, an incurable degenerative disease. She was unable to commit suicide without assistance and it was a crime for her husband to assist her to commit suicide. The applicant's lawyer requested the Director of Public Prosecutions to give an undertaking that her husband would not be prosecuted if he assisted her to commit suicide. The Divisional Court refused an application for judicial review. The applicant claimed that she had a right to die under Article 2.

Ratio: The Court found that there had been no violation of Article 2 in the present case. The consistent emphasis in all the cases brought before the Court under this provision has been the obligation of the State to protect life and the Court was not persuaded that the right to life could be interpreted as involving a negative aspect. The Court held that Article 2 was unconcerned with issues to do with the quality of living or what a person chooses to do with his or her life and it cannot, without a distortion of language, be interpreted as conferring a right to die, nor can it create a right to self-determination in the sense of conferring on an individual the entitlement to choose death rather than life.

Application: In this case, the Court made it clear that it cannot be claimed under Article 2 of the Convention, a right to suicide or assisted suicide. However, this right is recognized in some Member States, such as Switzerland. It should be remembered that the Convention is a minimum standard that the Court applies. Member States can always implement a greater protection of individual rights at the domestic level.

In addition to this, the scope of Article 2 does not seem to cover the right to life of the unborn child (see **Vo v. France, no 53924/00, 08/07/2004**, ECHR).

Regarding the abolition of death penalty, the wording of Article 2 of the Convention created an intense debate. However, Protocol No. 6 provides that death penalty should be abolished in peacetime. Protocol No. 13 later abolished it in all circumstances. The UK and most the vast majority of Member States have ratified both protocols. However, in principle, for the states that did not ratify these protocols, such as Russia, those provisions should not apply to them.

General principle: The adoption of protocols 6 and 13 to the Convention and subsequent State practice indicates that Article 2 of the Convention had been amended so as to prohibit the death penalty in all circumstances.

Al-Saadoon and Mufdhi v. the United Kingdom, no 61498/08, 02/03/2010, ECHR

Facts: This case concerned a complaint by two Iraqi nationals that the British authorities in Iraq had transferred them to Iraqi custody in breach of an interim measure indicated by the European Court under Rule 39 of the Rules of Court, so putting them at real risk of an unfair trial followed by execution by hanging. They claimed that their deportation would amount to a violation of Articles 2 and 3 of the Convention.

Ratio: The Court found a violation of 3 of the Convention considering that death penalty – which caused not only physical pain but also intense psychological suffering as a result of the foreknowledge of death – constituted an inhuman and degrading treatment or punishment. It noted that: "Although the death penalty had not been considered to violate international stàndards when the Convention was drafted, there had since been an evolution towards its complete *de facto* and *de jure* abolition within all the member States of the Council of Europe. Two Protocols to the Convention had thus entered into force, abolishing the death penalty in time of war (Protocol No. 6) and in all circumstances (Protocol No. 13), and the United Kingdom had ratified them both. All but two member States had signed Protocol No. 13 and all but three of the States which had signed it had ratified it. These figures and consistent State practice in observing the moratorium on capital punishment were strongly indicative that Article 2 of the Convention had been amended so as to prohibit the death penalty in all circumstances".

Application: In this case, the Court underlined that Article 2 has certainly been amended in practice as to abolish death penalty in all circumstances. This would apply even to the Member States which did not ratify protocols 6 and 13. Anyways, the Court made it clear that death penalty would constitute inhuman and degrading treatment or punishment as for the purposes of Article 3.

The duty not to interfere with a person's right to life

Article 2 imposes a negative duty on contracting states not to interfere with a person's right to life. In other words, individuals have a right not to be killed by State agents. However, Article 2(2) of the Convention describes the legitimate exceptions to this duty of contracting states to refrain from killing individuals: *"2. Deprivation of life shall not be regarded as inflicted in contravention of this Article when it results from the use of force which is no more than absolutely necessary: (a) in defence of any person from unlawful violence; (b) in order to effect a lawful arrest or to prevent the escape of a person lawfully detained; (c) in action lawfully taken for the purpose of quelling a riot or insurrection".*

General principle: The use of force (potentially lethal) must be no more than "absolutely necessary" for the achievement of one of the purposes set out in sub-paragraphs (a), (b) or (c) of Article 2 of the Convention.

Mccann v. United Kingdom, no 18984/91, 27/09/1995, ECHR
Facts: This case concerned the killing by members of the UK security forces of three members of the IRA (Irish Republican Army) suspected of involvement in a bombing mission. The members of the security forces, believing that the suspects were about to detonate the bomb, shot them dead. Indirect victims brought claims under Article 2 of the Convention. They also alleged that the killings were premeditated.
Ratio: The Court found that there has been a violation of Article 2 of the Convention. However, it rejected the allegations of premeditation as unsubstantiated: it was not established that there was an execution plot at highest level of command in the Ministry of Defence or in Government. It noted that "Provision is one of the most fundamental in the

Convention and must be strictly construed - paragraph 2 does not primarily define instances where it is permitted intentionally to kill an individual, but describes situations where it is permitted to "use force" which may result, as an unintended outcome, in the loss of life - the use of force must be no more than "absolutely necessary" for the achievement of one of the purposes set out in sub-paragraphs (a), (b) or (c)".

Application: In this case, the Court seems to impose strict conditions on contracting states when using lethal force. Despite this decision, it should be noted that courts will generally afford a wide margin of discretion to contracting states when they have demonstrated that they acted in good faith and with reasonable diligence (see **Bubbins v. United Kingdom, no 50196/99, 17/03/2005**, ECHR).

The positive obligation to preserve life from public and private threats

According to the doctrine of positive obligations, contracting states also have to take measures to protect individuals where their lives are at risk. This obligation applies where the death is caused by state officials but also where it is caused by a private individual and the State has not taken due care to safeguard an individual's life. In these situations, applicants allege that the State has failed to protect their rights to life.

General principle: The primary duty under Article 2 imposes on contracting states to secure the right to life by putting in place effective criminal-law provisions to deter the commission of offences against the person backed up by law-enforcement machinery for the prevention, suppression and sanctioning of breaches of such provisions. Article 2 of the Convention may also imply, in certain circumstances, a positive obligation on the authorities to take preventive operational measures to protect an individual whose life is at risk from the criminal acts of another individual.

Osman v. United Kingdom, no 23452/94, 28/10/1998, ECHR
Facts: This case concerned a teacher who developed an attachment for one of his pupils at school. The teacher later attacked the

family. This attack caused the dead of the father and wounded the child. The applicant, the widow of the deceased husband, claimed that the authorities had failed to comply with their positive obligation under Article 2 given that the police had been given information which should have made it clear that the individual posed a danger to their lives.

Ratio: The Court held that there has been no violation of Article 2 of the Convention. It the view of the Court: "the applicants have failed to point to any decisive stage in the sequence of the events leading up to the tragic shooting when it could be said that the police knew or ought to have known that the lives of the Osman family were at real and immediate risk from". The Strasbourg Court considered that the police could not be held responsible for having attributed greater weight to the teacher's presumption of innocence. It noted that in the present circumstances, the police considered insufficient to give rise to a reasonable suspicion.

Application: In this case, the Court enshrines two types of positive obligations, imposing on the contracting states to, on the first hand, adopt procedural safeguards in the form of criminal law deterring the commission of offences, and in the other hand, to take preventive operational measures to protect an individual whose life is at risk from the criminal acts of another individual. However, the Court made it clear that this latter obligation should not be construed disproportionately or as to impose an unreasonable burden on contracting states.

The positive obligation to carry out an effective investigation

In addition to the substantive obligations imposing on the State to preserve life before the criminal act is committed, a procedural duty to carry out an effective investigation *a posteriori* also exists.

General principle: Article 2 imposes a duty on contracting state to conduct official and effective investigations, with reasonable promptness, when individuals had been killed as a result of the use of force. The authorities must also take reasonable steps to secure evidence.

Hugh Jordan v. United Kingdom, no 24746/94, 04/05/2001, ECHR

Facts: The Applicant, Mr. Hugh Jordan, alleged that his son was unjustifiably shot and killed by a police officer, and that there was no effective investigation into, or redress for, his death. He submitted that the failure to investigate into his son's killing breached the authorities' duty to carry out an effective investigation under Article 2 of the Convention.

Ratio: The Court held that there has been a failure to comply with the procedural obligation imposed by Article 2 of the Convention and that there has been, in this respect, a violation of that provision. It noted that the proceedings for investigating the use of lethal force by the police officer shown in this case to disclose the following shortcomings: "lack of independence of the police officers investigating the incident from the officers implicated in the incident and lack of public scrutiny and information to the family".

Application: It should be noted that the Strasbourg Court, in this case, upheld that the authorities investigating the killing should be somehow independent from those who allegedly committed the killing. When conducting such investigations, the relevant authorities should have, as a main objective, the identification of those responsible and if the use of force was not justifiable, their punishment.

The Court has later added that the expression "effective investigation" requires contracting states to allow the victims' relatives to effectively participate in the investigation (see **Paul and Audrey Edwards, no 46477/99, 14/03/2002,** ECHR).

Article 3 of the Convention: Prohibition of torture, inhuman and degrading treatment and punishment

Article 3 of the Convention provides with a strict prohibition of what is generally referred to as "ill-treatments": "No one shall be subjected to torture or to inhuman or degrading treatment or punishment".

Definitions of torture, inhuman treatment or punishment and degrading treatment and punishment

In order to conclude to a violation of Article 3 of the Convention, the alleged treatment must reach a threshold of "an intense level of severity". The level of severity is gradually increasing from degrading treatment to inhuman treatment and lastly the gravest treatment: torture.

General principle: The European Court defines torture as a "deliberate inhuman treatment causing very serious and cruel suffering", inhuman treatment as "causing actual bodily injury, at least intense physical and mental suffering" and degrading treatment as treatment resulting on feelings of victims such as "fear, anguish and inferiority capable of humiliating and debasing them and possibly breaking their physical or moral resistance".

Ireland v. the United Kingdom, no 5310/71, 18/01/1978, ECHR
Facts: Individuals from Northern Ireland were subjected by the UK forces to the "Five techniques" interrogation measures which consist, *inter alia*, on wall standing (forcing detainees to remain in a stress position for hours at a time); hooding (keeping a bag over detainees heads at all times, except during interrogation) and subjection to continuous loud noise. These interrogations were part of a series of "extrajudicial measures of detention and internment of suspected terrorists". The Republic of Ireland brought this application to the attention of the Strasbourg Court against the UK in one of the first inter-state applications it had to examine.
Ratio: The Court held that the "Five techniques" of interrogation, as applied in the case by the UK forces in this case, violated Article 3 of the Convention as they constituted inhuman and degrading treatment but were not severe enough to constitute torture.
Application: The Court, in the present case, enshrined that a finding of torture is reserved to the most serious ill-treatments constituting aggravated and deliberate forms of inhuman treatment. It should be noted that the Court received a request for revision in this case and dismissed it on 20 March 2018. The applicants alleged that new facts arose recently, as to demonstrate that some of the ill-treatments in this case amounted to torture. However the

Court considered that those facts: "by their nature, had no decisive influence on the judgment".

General principle: Judicial corporal punishment, as a particularly degrading form of institutionalised violence, is incompatible with Article 3 of the Convention.

Tyrer v. United Kingdom, no 5856/72, 25/04/1978, ECHR
Facts: A 15-year-old-boy has been found guilty of assault and convicted by the local juvenile court to a punishment which consisted on birching him on his bare buttocks. This was in accordance with the law of Isle of Man.
Ratio: The Court found that the judicial corporal punishment inflicted on the applicant amounted to degrading punishment within the meaning of Article 3 of the Convention. The Court noted that the applicant was subjected to a punishment in which the element of humiliation attained the level inherent in the notion of "degrading punishment" and the indignity of having the punishment administered over the bare posterior aggravated its degrading nature.
Application: In this case, the Court made it clear that not all forms of corporal punishment will give rise to a violation of Article 3. As the Court stated: "the assessment is, in the nature of things, relative: it depends on all the circumstances of the case and, in particular, on the nature and context of the punishment itself and the manner and method of its execution".

General principle: Article 3 of the Convention imposes a positive obligation on contracting states to ensure that adequate legal protection that deters and sanctions the use of ill treatments in private spheres.

A v. United Kingdom, no 25599/94 , 23/09/1998, ECHR
Facts: Investigation at domestic level demonstrated that a young boy had been beaten by his stepfather with considerable force on several occasions. The applicant claimed that the British authorities had a positive obligation to protect the boy from such treatments.
Ratio: The Court upheld that beating a young boy with a garden cane, applied with considerable force on more than one occasion, reaches level of severity prohibited by Article 3.

Accordingly, there has been a violation of Article 3 of the Convention.

The Court also noted that: "the obligation on the High Contracting Parties under Article 1 of the Convention to secure to everyone within their jurisdiction the rights and freedoms defined in the Convention, taken together with Article 3, requires States to take measures designed to ensure that individuals within their jurisdiction are not subjected to torture or inhuman or degrading treatment or punishment, including such ill-treatment administered by private individuals (..) Children and other vulnerable individuals, in particular, are entitled to State protection, in the form of effective deterrence, against such serious breaches of personal integrity".

Application: In this case, the Court emphasises that the failure to comply with positive obligations relies on the lack of sufficient legal protection in domestic law to deter and sanction the application of violent chastisement. Following this case, the UK complied with this judgement by adopting Section 54 of the Children Act 2004.

The absolute prohibition of the use of torture

The prohibition of torture and its negative counterpart, the right to not be subjected to torture, is certainly the only absolute human rights universally recognized at the international level. In public international law, according to some authors, it is one of the only provisions of the *jus cogens*, a form of universal law that applies to any states regardless of their consent to these rules.

Torture is prohibited by the Convention even in times of war of public emergencies, which means that once a breach has been found, there can be no justification for that breach.

General principle: Torture and inhuman or degrading treatment cannot be inflicted even in circumstances where the life of an individual is at risk.

Gäfgen v. Germany [GC], no 22978/05, 01/06/2010, ECHR

Facts: The applicant suffocated an eleven-year-old boy to death and hid the body somewhere. He was taken to the police station for interrogation where he was threatened by police officers with physical pain and, if necessary, to subject him to such pain in order to make him reveal the boy's location. Police officers thought that the boy could still be saved. This situation has been referred to as "the ticking bomb issue". The applicant claimed that this treatment violated his rights under Article 3 of the Convention.

Ratio: The Court noted that the applicant was handcuffed and thus in a state of vulnerability, so the threat to use violence he had received must have caused him considerable fear, anguish and mental suffering. Despite the police officers' motives, the Court reiterated that torture and inhuman or degrading treatment could not be inflicted even in circumstances where the life of an individual was at risk. In conclusion, the Court upheld that the method of interrogation to which the applicant had been subjected was found to be sufficiently serious to amount to inhuman treatment prohibited by Article 3.

Application: This case illustrates the strict test applied by the Court to find a violation in a case of ill-treatment on the merits: as far as it is demonstrated that the treatment amounts to torture, inhuman or degrading treatment, the breach of Article 3 of the Convention cannot be justified.

Indirect violations of Article 3 of the Convention

Throughout its jurisprudence, the Strasbourg has developed the doctrine of indirect violations of Article 3 of the Convention. The violation is indirect because it is not directly committed by the responding state. The violation might rather be committed in the third State where the deported individual would be subjected to a real risk that of treatment or punishment in breach of Article 3. Therefore the violation by the Member States, by deporting the individual where he would risk ill treatments, is indirect.

General principle: The extradition of an individual to a third State where it exists a real risk that he will be subjected to torture or inhuman degrading treatment is prohibited by Article 3 of the Convention.

Soering v. United Kingdom, no 14038/88, 07/07/1989, ECHR

Facts: In this case, a German national was to be extradited by the United Kingdom to the USA where he was to stand in trial for the murder of his step parents. Although the UK had received diplomatic guarantees that he would not be convicted to death penalty, the applicant claim that he could still be subjected to the "death row phenomenon", which allegedly constituted a breach of his rights under Articles 2 and 3 of the Convention.

Ratio: The Court held that, having regard to the very long period of time spent on death row in such extreme conditions, with the ever present and mounting anguish of awaiting execution of the death penalty, and to the personal circumstances of the applicant, especially his age and mental state at the time of the offence, the applicant's extradition to the United States would expose him to a real risk of treatment going beyond the threshold set by Article 3 (art. 3).

Application: This landmark case constituted a basis for further jurisprudential developments of the Strasbourg Court who later found that indirect violations of Articles 2 and 6 are also covered by the Convention.

Article 5 of the Convention: Right to liberty and security of the person

Article 5 (1) provides that: "Everyone has the right to liberty and security of person. No one shall be deprived of his liberty save in (…) accordance with a procedure prescribed by law".

It should be noted that Article 5 of the Convention does not deal with the freedom of movement (which is already enshrined by Article 2 of Protocol no. 4), but rather with the right of an individual's liberty. It protects individuals from arbitrary arrest and detention. However, this right is limited by an important number of possible restrictions. Therefore, as for Article 6 of the Convention, it mainly protects individuals from procedural violations.

Lawful arrests and detentions under Article 5(1)

According to Article 5(1)(a) of the Convention: "No one shall be deprived of his liberty save in the following cases and in accordance with a procedure prescribed by law: (a) the lawful detention of a person after conviction by a competent court". This is a traditional restriction of liberty which is accepted in all contracting states. Imprisonment following a lawful conviction can even sometimes be considered a duty for the State in order to protect public order and security of other individuals where the detainee might represent a threat to society.

General principle: There must be a sufficient connection between a finding of guilt by a competent court and any subsequent detention.

Stafford v. United Kingdom [GC], no 46295/99, 28/05/2002, ECHR

Facts: The applicant, convicted to life imprisonment for murder in 1967, was released on licence in 1979. In 1994 he was sentenced to six years' imprisonment for conspiracy to forge travellers' cheques and passports. The Home Secretary refused to release him on licence on the ground that he might commit other proprietary offences.

Ratio: The Court held that there has been a violation of Article 5 (1) of the Convention. In the present case, it noted that the applicant had to be regarded as having exhausted the punishment element for his offence of murder and his continued detention after expiry of the sentence for forgery could not be regarded as justified by his punishment for murder.

Application: It should be noted that the Court considers that Article 5 of the Convention prohibits continued detention after the expiry of a fixed sentence, even in circumstances of previous conviction to life imprisonment.

Article 5(1)(b) of the Convention provides that: "No one shall be deprived of his liberty save in the following cases and in accordance with a procedure prescribed by law: (b) the lawful arrest or detention of a person for noncompliance with the lawful order of a court or in order to secure the fulfilment of any obligation prescribed by law". Once again, this is a traditional restriction to right to liberty and security, which deals with the enforcement and execution of judicial decisions.

According to article 5(1)(c) of the Convention: *"No one shall be deprived of his liberty save in the following cases and in accordance with a procedure prescribed by law: "c) the lawful arrest or detention of a person effected for the purpose of bringing him before the competent legal authority on reasonable suspicion of having committed an offence or when it is reasonably considered necessary to prevent his committing an offence or fleeing after having done so".*

This category is generally referred to lawful detention following arrest or "pre-trial detention". Because this type of detention can be subjected to arbitrary abuses, the Strasbourg Court has developed strict requirements in order to justify it

General principle: Authorities must provide, at least, facts and information capable of demonstrating that the arrested person was reasonably suspected of having committed the offence for the purposes of Article 5(1)(c) of the Convention.

Fox, Campbell and Hartley v. United Kingdom, no 12244/86, 30/08/1990, ECHR

Facts: The applicants were arrested on suspicion of participation to terrorist acts under Section 1 of the Northern Ireland (Emergency Provision) Act 1978. They claimed that the arrest was not reasonably necessary, as infringing their rights under article 5(1)(c) of the Convention. The only reason for their arrest given by the British authorities was that the applicants had been convicted 7 years earlier.

Ratio: The Strasbourg Court held that there has been a breach of Article 5(1)(c) of the Convention. It noted that having a ""reasonable suspicion" presupposes the existence of facts or information which would satisfy an objective observer that the person concerned may have committed the offence. What may be regarded as "reasonable" will however depend upon all the circumstances. In this respect, terrorist crime falls into a special category. Because of the attendant risk of loss of life and human suffering, the police are obliged to act with utmost urgency in following up all information, including information from secret sources".

Application: In this case, the Court stated that the mere fact that the applicants had been convicted few years earlier was not sufficient to demonstrate that the authorities had reasonable suspicion that they committed the offence.

The right to be informed for reasons of arrest and charge under Article 5(2)

Article 5(2) of the Convention provides that: "Everyone who is arrested shall be informed promptly, in a language which he understands, of the reasons for his arrest and of any charge against him". This right is closely related to the procedural obligations under Article 6 of the Convention: right to a fair trial. It is a safeguard of the rule of law which imposes on contracting states to provide the suspect with transparency of the investigations and proceedings.

General principle: An interval of few hours between the arrest and the notification of the reasons for the arrest does satisfy the criterion of promptness under Article 5(2) of the Convention.

Murray (Margaret) v. United Kingdom, no 14310/88, 28/10/1994, ECHR

Facts: The applicant was arrested and informed of the reasons for his arrest, under suspicion of participation to terrorist acts, after two hours of detention. He claimed that he was not promptly informed of the reasons of his arrest.

Ratio: The Court held that there has been no violation of Article 5(2) in the present case, considering that an interval of a few hours between arrest and interrogation did not fall outside constraints of time imposed by notion of promptness. It accepted that reasons for arrest, where they are not sufficiently indicated when the applicant is taken into custody, could be brought to the arrested person's attention during subsequent interrogation.

Application: In this case, the Court applies flexibility to the criterion of prompt information of the reasons of the arrest. The expression "few hours" seems to cover a maximum of approximately 7 or 8 hours before informing the detainee of the reasons for the arrest.

The right of arrested or detained individuals to be brought promptly before a judge under Article 5(3)

According to Article 5(3): *"Everyone arrested or detained in accordance with the provisions of paragraph 1 (c) of this Article shall be brought promptly before a judge or other officer authorised by law to exercise judicial power and shall be entitled to trial within a reasonable time or to release pending trial. Release may be conditioned by guarantees to appear for trial".*

This safeguard is one of the most important against arbitrary arrest from the executive. The judge or relevant "officer" should be independent from the executive when deciding on the detention of the detainee and more precisely as to whether the latter should be kept in detention until his trial or released.

General principle: A detention of four days or more without being brought to a judge for trial or release is inconsistent with the notion of promptness for the purposes of Article 5(3) of the Convention.

Brogan v. United Kingdom, no 11209/84, 29/11/1988, ECHR
Facts: The applicants were arrested under Section 12 of the Prevention of Terrorism1984 Act for suspicion of participation to terrorist acts. They were detained for 4 days. None of the applicants was brought before a judge or other officer authorised by law to exercise judicial power, nor were any of them charged after their release. They claimed that this constituted a violation of their right to be brought promptly before a judge under Article 5(3) of the Convention.
Ratio: The Court found that there has been a violation of Article 5(3) of the Convention. Even the shortest of the four periods of detention, namely the four days and six hours spent in police custody, falls outside the strict constraints as to time permitted by the first part of Article 5 (3). According to the Court, the scope for flexibility in interpreting and applying the notion of "promptness" is very limited.
It noted that the mere fact that a detained person is not charged or brought before a Court does not in itself amount to a violation of the first part of Article 5 (3). No violation of Article 5 (3) can arise if the arrested person is released "promptly" before any judicial control of his detention would have been feasible.
Application: It should be noted that the context of public emergency threatening the life of the nation (as illustrated by the notification of the Secretary General of the use of Article 15 of the Convention), might change the solution adopted in the present case (see **Brannigan and McBride v United Kingdom, no 14553/89, 26/05/1993**, ECHR).

The right to challenge lawfulness of detention under Article 5(4)

The right to challenge lawfulness of detention is enshrined by Article 5(4):"Everyone who is deprived of his liberty by arrest or detention shall be entitled to take proceedings by which the lawfulness of his detention shall be decided speedily by a court and his release ordered if the detention is not lawful".

It should be noted that this Article is not concerned with the conditions of detention, which are rather covered by Article 3 and, on some occasions, Article 8 of the Convention (see **Winterwerp v. Germany, no 6301/73, 24/10/1979,** ECHR).

Accordingly, Article 5 is only concerned with the lawfulness of the decision to place an individual in detention, including the evidence on which the decision was made. This specific provision confers on the individual a right to access a Court in order to order a release if the detention is not lawful.

Article 6 of the Convention: Right to a fair trial

The most important part of Article 6(1) provides the following: *"In the determination of his civil rights and obligations or of any criminal charge against him, everyone is entitled to a fair and public hearing within a reasonable time by an independent and impartial tribunal established by law".*

Article 6 on the right to a fair trial is on top of the list of the most violated articles, with approximately 25% of the violations found by the Court related to this provision in 2018. Most of these cases are concerned with the breach of the requirement of "reasonable time" of the fair trial. Importantly, it should be noted that Article 6 applies equally to civil and criminal proceedings.

The right of access to a Court

The right of access to a Court other than pending pre-existing proceedings is implicit in Article 6 of the Convention and has been developed throughout the Court's jurisprudence.

General principle: Article 6(1) does not only guarantee the right to a fair trial in legal proceedings already pending, but also secures a right to introduce new proceedings for individuals in order to commence an action to have their rights

and obligations determined.

Golder v. United Kingdom, no 4451/70, 21/02/1975, ECHR
Facts: The applicant, a prisoner, was refused by the prison authorities permission to meet a solicitor with a view to introduce libel proceedings against a prison officer. He claimed that the refusal violated his rights under Article 6(1) of the Convention.
Ratio: The Court found that there has been a violation of the applicant's right of access to Court, under Article 6(1) of the Convention. It noted that the said provision "does not state a right of access to the courts or tribunals in express terms. It enunciates rights which are distinct but stem from the same basic idea and which, taken together, make up a single right not specifically defined in the narrower sense of the term. It is the duty of the Court to ascertain, by means of interpretation, whether access to the courts constitutes one factor or aspect of this right (...) The principle whereby a civil claim must be capable of being submitted to a judge ranks as one of the universally "recognised" fundamental principles of law; the same is true of the principle of international law which forbids the denial of justice. Article 6(1) must be read in the light of these principles (...) It follows that the right of access constitutes an element which is inherent in the right stated by Article 6(1)".
Application: As noted by the Court in its reasoning when construing Article 6 (1) as encompassing a right of access to a Court, the main *rationale* behind this solution relies on the Rule of law. In this respect, the Court stated in this case that: "in civil matters one can scarcely conceive of the rule of law without there being a possibility of having access to the courts".

The right to a public hearing before an independent and impartial tribunal

The Rule of law protects citizens from arbitrary use of power, tyranny and authoritarianism. In this connection, the independence of the judiciary is of paramount importance in order to ensure that legal disputes are resolved fairly by independent and impartial judges. Such guarantees result in citizens having confidence in the administration of justice, which legitimizes the entire system.

The requirement to hold a "public hearing" is subject to several exceptions. This is apparent from the text of Article 6(1) itself, which contains the proviso that "the press and public may be excluded from all or part of the trial (...) where the interests of juveniles or the private life of the parties so require, or to the extent strictly necessary in the opinion of the court in special circumstances where publicity would prejudice the interests of justice".

While a public hearing constitutes a fundamental principle enshrined by Article 6(1), the obligation to hold such a hearing is not absolute (see **De Tommaso v. Italy [GC], no 43395/09, 23/02/2017**, ECHR § 163). It should be noted that the Court considers that it is only in proceedings before a court of first and only instance that the right to a public hearing under Article 6(1) entails an entitlement to an oral hearing (see **Fredin v. Sweden, no 18928/91, 23/02/1994**, ECHR).

General principle: The right to a public hearing of an independent and impartial tribunal includes freedom from the appearance of executive and political bias.

McGonnell v. United Kingdom, no 28488/95, 08/02/2000, ECHR
Facts: The applicant was refused planning permission for residential use by the Deputy Bailiff of Guernsey. The Deputy Bailiff of Guernsey was a member of several state committees and also presided different courts. He was even involved in the passing of legislation that had been applied to the applicant's case. The latter alleged that his right to a public hearing before an independent and impartial tribunal under Article 6(1) had been violated.
Ratio: The European Court found a violation of Article 6(1) in the applicant's case. It noted that "the Bailiff's functions were not limited to judicial matters and the Court does not accept that when he acts in a non-judicial capacity he merely occupies positions rather than exercising functions - even a purely ceremonial role must be classified as a "function" (...) Any direct involvement in the passage of legislation or of executive rules is likely to be sufficient to cast doubt on the judicial impartiality of a person later called on to determine a dispute

over whether reasons exist to permit a variation from the wording of the legislation or rules".

Application: In this case, it should be noted that any direct involvement in the passage of legislation or of executive rules is likely to be sufficient to cast doubt on the judicial impartiality of a person. Member States should observe a strict separation of functions between the executive and the judiciary in order to comply with the requirements of an independent and impartial judiciary under Article 6(1) of the Convention.

The right to a public hearing within a reasonable time

Under Article 6(1), the right to a fair trial should be secured to any individuals within a reasonable time. There are multiple reasons justifying the need of this safeguard. The most important ones have been mentioned by Lord Bingham in **HM Advocate v Watson, Burrows and JK** [2002] UKPC D1: "The Strasbourg case law makes plain the object of the reasonable time requirement: to ensure that accused persons do not lie under a charge for too long and that the charge is determined; to protect a defendant against excessive procedural delays and prevent him remaining too long in a state of uncertainty about his fate; to avoid delays which might jeopardise the effectiveness and credibility of the administration of justice".

General principle: The requirement of reasonable timing applies to the length of judicial proceedings, including appeal. What amounts to a "reasonable time" depends on the particular circumstances of each case, having regard in particular to its complexity as well as the conduct of the parties and the relevant authorities.

Robins v. United Kingdom, no 22410/93, 23/09/1997, ECHR
Facts: The applicants' proceedings lasted for more than 4 years, including first instance judgements and subsequent appeals on the costs of the proceedings. They claimed that the length of the proceedings had breached their right to a fair trial within a reasonable time under Article 6(1) of the Convention.
Ratio: The Court held that has been a violation of Article 6(1) in that the applicants' "civil rights and obligations" were not determined within "a reasonable time".

In particular, it noted that it took over four years to resolve what may be regarded as a relatively straightforward dispute over costs.

Application: In this case, the Court emphasises that the length of the proceedings should be assessed on an overall basis, looking at the reasonableness of the delay in processing the applicant's case.

The right to effective participation to the trial

Article 6(1) confers the right on every individual to present legal arguments to support their case before the courts. This right applies equally to both parties in civil proceedings, which, in principle, should be placed on an equal footing before the tribunal (see **Row and Davis v. United Kingdom [GC], no 28901/95, 16/02/2000,** ECHR).

General principle: In certain cases, especially where the outcome of the proceedings is particularly serious, the right of individuals to put their case forward in a proper and effective manner might include the indispensable assistance of a lawyer during hearings.

P, C and S v. United Kingdom, no 56547/00, 16/07/2002, ECHR
Facts: The applicants were the mother and father of a child which has been subject to a care order by a local judge. The child was felt to be in danger from his mother. The parents could not be effectively represented in the proceedings related to the care order and the subsequent adoption proceedings. Their child was placed for adoption without a possibility for them to be heard with legal representation. They claimed that this breached their right to effective participation to the trial.
Ratio: The Court found a breach of Article 6(1) of the Convention for lack of legal representation in proceedings concerning child care. The procedures adopted not only gave the appearance of unfairness but prevented the applicants from putting forward their case in a proper and effective manner. The assistance of a lawyer during the hearings was thus indispensable.
Application: The Court, when assessing if the right to effectively participate to the trial, will take into account contextual elements, such as the complexity of the case or the seriousness of its

outcome.

The right to effectively participate to the trial is often complemented by the right to legal assistance in criminal proceedings which is enshrined by Article 6(3)(c). Article 6(3)(c) provides with the following: "Everyone charged with a criminal offence has the following minimum rights: to defend himself in person or through legal assistance of his own choosing or, if he has not sufficient means to pay for legal assistance, to be given it free when the interests of justice so require". In criminal proceedings, where the defendant has no sufficient financial resources to pay for a lawyer and if the interests of justice demand it, the defendant has a right to be represented with free legal aid.

General principle: The particular vulnerability of the defendant and the complexity of the case may justify that he should be provided free legal aid.

Granger v. United Kingdom, no 11932/86, 28/03/1990, ECHR
Facts: The applicant was of modest intelligence with a poor command of English and poor comprehension of written material. He was charged with a criminal offence and his demand for free legal aid had been refused, even on appeal.
Ratio: The Court concluded that there had been a violation of paragraph 3 (c), taken together with paragraph 1, of Article 6. The Court considered that the question whether the interests of justice required a grant of legal aid must be determined in the light of the case as a whole. In that respect not only the situation obtaining at the time the decision on the application for legal aid was handed down but also that obtaining at the time the appeal was heard are material.
Application: The right to free legal assistance should be assessed on a case-by-case basis, taking into account contextual elements. The scope of this right guarantees legal assistance during trial but also during detention and interrogation where the interests of justice so require (see **Brennan v. United Kingdom, no 39846/98, 16/10/2001,** ECHR).

The right to be presumed innocent and to remain silent

The right to be presumed innocent is enshrined by Article 6(2) of the Convention: "Everyone charged with a criminal offence shall be presumed innocent until proved guilty according to law". The right to remain silent, also known as the rule against "self-incrimination", stems from the combination of Article 6(1) and Article 6(2).

The presumption of innocence implies that it is not for the defendant to prove his innocence but rather for the State has the burden to prove the guilt. Accordingly, the right to remain silent flows from the presumption of innocence and ensures protection of the defendant from unreasonable pressure to confess.

General principle: Where a defendant is legally compelled to give statements to inspectors relating to offences that he allegedly committed prior to the interrogation, the crucial factor in order to determine whether or not it constitutes a violation of the right to remain silent under Article 6(1) depends on the use made of those statements by the prosecution at trial.

Saunders v. the United Kingdom, no 19187/91, 17/12/1996, ECHR
Facts: The applicant, director and chief executive of a company, was suspected of being involved in an unlawful share-support operation. He was obliged under sections 434 and 436 of the Companies Act 1985 to answer the questions put to him by the inspectors in the course of nine lengthy interviews of which seven were admissible as evidence at his trial. The applicant claimed that his right to remain silent had been breached during the trial.
Ratio: The Court held that there has been a violation of Article 6(1) of the Convention because the applicant had been legally compelled to give statements to inspectors which were used by the prosecution at trial.
It recalled that, although not specifically mentioned in Article 6 of the Convention, the right to silence and the right not to incriminate oneself are generally recognised international standards which lie at the heart of the notion of a fair procedure under Article 6 and applies to all types of criminal proceedings. It is primarily concerned with respecting the will of an accused person to remain silent.
Application: In, this judgement, the Court stated that the right to

remain silent had to be strictly protected regardless of the complexity of the case.

General principle: The right not to incriminate oneself is limited, it prohibits forced self-incrimination where the defendant is compelled to confess in prosecutions related to acts or omissions related to an offence which he is suspected of having previously committed.

Allen v. United Kingdom (dec.), no 76574/01, 10/09/2002, ECHR

Facts: The applicant faced the risk of imposition of a penalty of a maximum of GBP 300 if he persisted in refusing to make a declaration of assets. He eventually accepted to make a declaration on the Inland Revenue. He was prosecuted for having issued a false declaration of assets, which constituted an offense under domestic law. He submitted before the Strasbourg Court that he could not be charged for this offense because he had no other choice but to incriminate himself, which violated his rights under Article 6(1) of the Convention.

Ratio: The Court declared the application inadmissible, holding that no facts of this case disclosed any infringement of the right to silence or privilege against self-incrimination or that there has been any unfairness contrary to Article 6 (1) of the Convention. The Court noted that: "The applicant was charged with and convicted of the offence of making a false declaration of his assets to the Inland Revenue. In other words, he lied, or perjured himself through giving inaccurate information about his assets. This was not an example of forced self-incrimination about an offence which he had previously committed; it was the offence itself".

Application: It should be noted that the circumstances of this case are different from those in **Saunders v. the United Kingdom, no 19187/91, 17/12/1996**, ECHR where the applicant was charged with two years imprisonment. In addition to this, the applicant had demonstrated to be in bad faith for issuing a false declaration which constituted in itself an offence and was in no way a forced self-incrimination.

Summary

- The rights referred to by "freedom of person and security" usually trigger the most intense reaction of public opinion. These rights are: the right to life, the prohibition of torture, inhuman and degrading treatment, the right to liberty and security and the right to a fair trial.

- Although the doctrine of the indivisibility of human rights prohibits any kind of hierarchy, the particular importance historically conferred to the protection of rights related to freedom of person can be explained by the seriousness of the impact of their potential violations on individuals.

- The right to life, under Article 2 of the Convention, includes a right not to be killed but does not extend to a right to die. The adoption of protocols 6 and 13 to the Convention and subsequent State practice indicates that Article 2 of the Convention had been amended so as to prohibit the death penalty in all circumstances.

- Article 2 imposes a negative duty on contracting states not to interfere with a person's right to life. In other words, individuals have a right not to be killed by State agents.

- According to the doctrine of positive obligations, contracting states also have to take measures to protect individuals where their lives are at risk. This obligation applies where the death is caused by state officials but also where it is caused by a private individual and the State has not taken due care to safeguard an individual's life.

- In addition to the substantive obligations imposing on the State to preserve life before the criminal act is committed, a procedural duty to carry out an effective investigation *a posteriori* also exists.

- In order to conclude to a violation of Article 3 of the Convention, the alleged treatment must reach a threshold of "an intense level of severity". The level of severity is gradually increasing from degrading treatment to inhuman treatment and lastly the gravest treatment: torture.

- Torture is prohibited by the Convention even in times of war of public emergencies, which means that once a breach has been found, there can be no justification for that breach.

- The extradition of an individual to a third State where it exists a real risk that he will be subjected to torture or inhuman degrading treatment is prohibited by Article 3 of the Convention.

- Lawful arrests and detentions under Article 5(1) is a traditional restriction of liberty which is accepted in all contracting states.

- Since "pre-trial detention" can be subjected to arbitrary abuses, the Strasbourg Court has developed strict requirements in order to justify it.

- The right to be informed for reasons of arrest and charge under Article 5(2) is a safeguard of the rule of law which imposes on contracting states to provide the suspect with transparency of the investigations and proceedings.

- A detention of four days or more without being brought to a judge for trial or release is inconsistent with the notion of promptness for the purposes of Article 5(3) of the Convention.

- The right to challenge lawfulness of detention under Article 5(4) is only concerned with the lawfulness of the decision to place an individual in detention, including the evidence on which the decision was made.

- Article 6 on the right to a fair trial is on top of the list of the most violated articles, with approximately 25% of the violations found by the Court related to this provision in 2018. Importantly, it should be noted that Article 6 applies equally to civil and criminal proceedings.

- The independence of the judiciary is of paramount importance in order to ensure that legal disputes are resolved fairly by independent and impartial judges.

- Under Article 6(1), the right to a fair trial should be secured to any individuals within a reasonable time. This is mainly to ensure that accused persons do not lie under a charge for too long and to avoid delays which might jeopardise the effectiveness and credibility of the administration of justice.

- Article 6(1) confers the right on every individual to present legal arguments to support their case before the courts. It applies equally to both parties in civil proceedings, which, in principle, should be placed on an equal footing before the tribunal.

- In criminal proceedings, where the defendant has no sufficient financial resources to pay for a lawyer and if the interests of justice demand it, the defendant has a right to be represented with free legal aid.

- The presumption of innocence implies that it is not for the defendant to prove his innocence but rather for the State has the burden to prove the guilt. Accordingly, the right to remain silent flows from the presumption of innocence and ensures protection of the defendant from unreasonable pressure to confess.

Chapter 13 – The right to private and family life – Article 8 ECHR

Introduction to Article 8 of the Convention

Article 8 of the Convention protects the sacred private sphere surrounding a person's individuality. It allows personal development of individuals free from undue restrictions. Examples of public interferences in an individual's private life include unjustifiable surveillance. However, the right to protect for private and family life also has a horizontal effect. It prohibits private interferences such as intrusions by the Media or breaches of confidentiality.

The right to private and family life is the right to "individuality" by excellence. Everyone is entitled to decide to make choices affecting their personal life and to make them public or to keep them for their private sphere. The Court, throughout its jurisprudence, has interpreted the concept of private life extensively as to encompass various issues related to individuals' privacy. This idea is illustrated by Laws LJ's statements in the case **R (Wood) v Commissioner of Police of the Metropolis [2009]** EWCA Civ 414: *"the content of the phrase "private and family life" is very broad indeed. Looking only at the words of the article, one might have supposed that the essence of the right was the protection of close personal relationships. While that remains a core instance, and perhaps the paradigm case of the right, the jurisprudence has accepted many other facets; so many that any attempt to encapsulate the right's scope in a single idea can only be undertaken at a level of considerable abstraction".*

Article 8 (1) provides that: "Everyone has the right to respect for private and family life, his home and his correspondence". Private life, family life, home and correspondence are the main rights protected by this provision. Therefore, these concepts will be presented in turn. These rights enshrined by Article 8 are not closed, nor are they clearly defined which results on overlaps sometimes.

It should also be noted that Article 8 is a conditional right, which means that it can be subjected to justifiable restrictions or interferences. As articles 9,10 and 11, in order to justify a restriction the responding State must demonstrate that it was prescribed by law, pursuing a legitimate aim and was necessary in a democratic society. These restrictions are regulated by the second paragraph of Article 8.

The right to respect for private life

The right to respect for private life has been interpreted by the Strasbourg Court as encompassing several issues such as physical and mental integrity, sexual orientation or State surveillance for example.

General principle: The scope of private life is limited. It does not apply to hunting activities where such activities are prohibited by law, even where performed on private lands.

R (Countryside Alliance) v Attorney General, [2006] EWCA Civ 817

Facts: The plaintiffs were convicted to a fine, under the Hunting Act 2004, for having organized hunting activities with dogs, which was clearly prohibited by the Act. They submitted that these activities were performed on private lands and that their right to private life under Article 8 of the Convention had been violated.

Ratio: The Court of Appeal dismissed the plaintiffs' submissions. It held that such an interpretation of private life was over-reaching. The ban on hunting with dogs did not result on a lack of respect for the applicants' private or family life in the present case.

Application: While examining a case and the potential violation of one of the articles of the Convention, it should be remembered that the scope of the provision is the first step to look at in order to determine whether or not this Article of the Convention applies to the facts of the case.

Importantly in connection with the scope of Article 8 of the Convention, the Court has accepted that a form of private life can be enjoyed in the employment sphere (see **Halford v. UK, no 20605/92, 25/06/1997,** ECHR).

General principle: The right to respect for private life includes a right to physical and moral integrity.

Costello-Roberts v. UK, no 13134/87, 25/03/1993, ECHR
Facts: It this case, a young boy was subjected to corporal punishment in a private school in accordance with its internal disciplinary rules. The applicants submitted that this treatment breached their rights under articles 3 and 8 of the Convention.
Ratio: The Court held, in the circumstances of the case, that there had been no violation of articles 3 and 8 of the Convention given that the corporal punishments of this private school were not intense or administered with significant force. However, it recalled more importantly that Article 8 included a right to physical and moral integrity and stated that: "The Court does not exclude the possibility that there might be circumstances in which Article 8 could be regarded as affording in relation to disciplinary measures a protection which goes beyond that given by Article 3".
Application: In the context of the protection of physical and moral integrity, Article 8 can be invoked where the minimum threshold for the application of Article 3 regarding degrading treatments is not reached. In this context, Article 8 constitutes an interesting alternative.

General principle: Searches on the person that reach a minimum threshold of intrusiveness in an individual's private sphere constitute interferences with rights under Article 8 of the Convention.

R (Gillan) v Commissioner of Police of the Metropolis and Another, [2006] UKHL 12
Facts: The question raised before the House of Lords related to the compatibility with the Convention of searches on the person in application the Terrorism Act 2000. Those were ordinary superficial searches of the person and an opening of bags, similar to which passengers generally submit at airports. However the plaintiffs claimed that such searches were not compatible with Article 8 of the Convention.
Ratio: The House of Lords held that there had been no violation of Article 8 in the circumstances of the case.

However, Lord Bingham noted that a search of the person could result on an interference in an individual's right to private life where the intrusion reaches a certain level of seriousness.

Application: In this case, the Strasbourg Court extended the minimum threshold test, initially conceived for the application of Article 3 of the Convention, to Article 8 of the Convention. Examples of searches that would certainly reach the minimum level of seriousness include a very detailed search of the body and belongings of a person, including a search in the mobile phone, infringing with the privacy of personal data.

General principle: The criminal prohibition on homosexual conduct between consenting adults in private constitutes a continuing interference with individuals' rights to respect for their private life (which includes his sexual life) within the meaning of Article (1).

Dudgeon v. UK, no 7525/76, 22/10/1981, ECHR

Facts: This case concerned the criminalisation of homosexual activity. The applicant was a gay activist in Northern Ireland. He was subsequently arrested an interrogated. He claimed that his right to private life under Article 8 of the Convention had been violated.

Ratio: The Court held that the applicant suffered an unjustified interference with his right to private life. Accordingly, it found that there had been a violation of Article 8 of the Convention. The Court noted that "In the personal circumstances of the applicant, the very existence of this legislation continuously and directly affects his private life (...): either he respects the law and refrains from engaging – even in private with consenting male partners - in prohibited sexual acts to which he is disposed by reason of his homosexual tendencies, or he commits such acts and thereby becomes liable to criminal prosecution".

Application: It is one of the first cases where the Court made clear that sexual life should be considered as a part of the private sphere which is protected by Article 8 of the Convention.

In this respect, the Court later held that consensual sexual activity between five adults in the applicant's home was a also a matter of private sexual behaviour protected by article 8 of the Convention (see **ADT v. UK, no 35765/97, 31/07/2000**, ECHR). In this case, the Court overruled the argument of public disapproval of such behaviours which was submitted by the UK to justify the interference with the applicant's rights.

General principle: Surveillance by the State in the form of recordings by listening devices constitutes an undisputed interference with the right to private life.

Khan v. UK, no 35394/97, 12/05/2000, ECHR
Facts: A conversation in the course of which the applicant admitted his involvement in the importation of drugs was recorded by the police. The police had installed a listening device in the house of B., which the applicant was visiting. The latter claimed that this surveillance breached his rights to respect for private life.
Ratio: The Court found that there was an interference in the applicant's rights. It noted that: "it is not disputed that the surveillance carried out by the police in the present case amounted to an interference with the applicant's rights under Article 8 (1) of the Convention". Given that the interference was not "in accordance with the law", the Court concluded that there had been a violation of Article 8 of the Convention.
Application: It should be noted that, following this judgement of the Strasbourg Court, the Regulation of Investigatory Powers Act 2000, regulating similar surveillance, was passed by the UK Parliament. In the context of surveillance by the State, it should be noted that the ECHR recently found that the United Kingdom's bulk data-collection programs violated Article 8 of the Convention for failure to incorporate adequate privacy safeguards and oversight (see **Big Brother Watch and other v. UK, no 58170/13, 13/09/2018**, ECHR, but note that this case has been referred to the Grand Chamber on February 2019).

The right to respect for family life

The right to "family life" under Article 8 of the Convention has been interpreted extensively by the Court. It is not restricted to the constraints of the traditional notion of family. The idea is to protect everyone's family sphere and develop free and normal relationship within this sphere. The right to family life is often concerned in disputes involving spouses, partners and children. Along with

Article 12 of the Convention, the right to respect for family life guarantees the right to marry, but not the right to divorce (see **Johnston v. Ireland, no 9697/82, 18/12/1986,** ECHR). However, as stated above, the right to private life is not restricted to martial relationships.

General principle: The notion of "family life" in Article 8 of the Convention is not confined solely to marriage-based relationships and may encompass other *de facto* "family ties" where parties are living together outside marriage.

Kroon v. The Netherlands, no 18535/91, 27/10/1994, ECHR
Facts: This case concerned the legal impossibility in Dutch law for a married woman to deny the paternity of her husband for her child and thereby enable recognition by the biological father. She claimed that her right to family life had been violated.
Ratio: The Court found that there had been a violation of Article 8 of the Convention. It noted that "in the instant case it has been established that the relationship between the applicants qualifies as "family life". There is thus a positive obligation on the part of the competent authorities to allow complete legal family ties to be formed between Mr Zerrouk and his son Samir [the biological father and the child]".
Application: The right to respect for family life is related to the protection of family sphere which includes other family ties that those based on marriage.

General principle: "Private life" incorporates the right to respect for both the decisions to become and not to become a parent.

Evans v. UK, no 6339/05, 10/04/2007, ECHR
Facts: The applicant and her partner J. started fertility treatment. They were informed that, in accordance with the provisions of the Human Fertilisation and Embryology Act 1990 ("the 1990 Act"), it would be possible for either of them to withdraw their consent at any time before the embryos were implanted in the applicant's uterus. Their relationship ended and J. subsequently informed the applicant about the withdrawal of his consent. The applicant complained that domestic law permitted her former partner to withdraw his consent to the storage and use of the embryos, thus

violating her right to become a parent under Article 8. Conversely, J. submitted that without his consent, this operation would violate his own rights to respect for family life, as he would be forced into paternity against his will.

Ratio: The Court found that there had been no violation of Article 8 of the Convention considering that national authorities had struck a fair balance between the competing interests at stake. It noted that there was no European consensus in the field; therefore the margin of appreciation afforded to the respondent State had to be a wide one. Accordingly, the Court stated that it "did not consider that the applicant's right to respect for the decision to become a parent in the genetic sense should be accorded greater weight than J.'s right to respect for his decision not to have a genetically-related child with her".

Application: In cases where national authorities are confronted to conflicts of rights or interests of such a nature, the Court generally affords a wide margin of appreciation to contracting states. The Court noted: *"In the difficult circumstances of the case, whatever solution the national authorities might adopt would result in the interests of one of the parties being wholly frustrated"*. However, importantly, the Court clarified that Article 8 applies to decisions related to parenthood, including a right to become a parent and a right not to become a parent.

General principle: A prisoner may also complain that his right to respect for family life has been interfered with, if for example prison rules do not allow him and his wife to be provided with artificial insemination enabling them to have a child together.

Dickson v. UK [GC], no 44362/04, 04/12/2007, ECHR

Facts: The applicants were a married couple who met through a prison correspondence network while serving prison sentences. They requested artificial insemination facilities to enable them to have a child together, arguing that it remained the applicants' only realistic hope of having a child together, given the wife's age and the husband's release date. They complained that the authorities' refusal breached their rights under Article 8 of the Convention.

Ratio: The Court found that, in the absence of a balancing exercise of proportionality of the interests at stake, the

authorities' decision had to be seen as falling outside any acceptable margin of appreciation so that a fair balance had not been struck between the competing public and private interests involved. Accordingly, there had been a violation of the applicants' rights under Article 8 of the Convention. The Court further noted that "Convention rights were retained on imprisonment, so that any restriction had to be justified, either on the grounds that it was a necessary and inevitable consequence of imprisonment or that there was an adequate link between the restriction and the prisoner's circumstances. A restriction could not be based solely on what would offend public opinion".

Application: In this case, after recalling that Convention rights were retained on imprisonment, the Court emphasized that the right to become a genetic parent under Article 8 also had to be secured for prisoners.

The right to respect for the home

Article 8 of the Convention also guarantees the right to respect for the home, protecting that right from public and private intrusions or disturbances. The right to respect for the home does not confer a right to have a home but rather ensures that home life is respected. This right is closely related to the rights under Article 1 Protocol 1 (right to property).

General principle: Unannounced visits by the police to registered sex offenders for monitoring purposes do not violate Article 8 of the Convention, as long as they are not overly frequent and do not lead to disclosure of private information to neighbours.

R (M) v Hampshire Constabulary [2014] EWCA Civ 1651
Facts: The plaintiff, a registered sex offender, was subjected to unannounced visits by the police at his home under Section 325 of the Criminal Justice Act 2003.If the police had a warrant, they were allowed to enter by force in case the offender would not let them in. He claimed that this possibility violated his right to respect for the home under Article 8 of the Convention.
Ratio: The Court of Appeal held that the police visits for monitoring purposes had not violated the plaintiff's rights

given that they were prescribed by law and pursued a legitimate aim of protecting vulnerable persons. In addition to this, nothing from the instant case illustrated that these visits had been conducted disproportionately.

Application: It should be remembered that Article 8 is a conditional right. Therefore, although an intrusion in an individual's home might constitute an interference, it may still be justified by a legitimate aim if this intrusion was prescribed by law and applied proportionately.

General principle: There is no explicit right in the Convention to a clean and quiet environment, but where an individual is directly and seriously affected by noise or other pollution, an issue may arise under Article 8.

Hatton v. UK, no 36022/97, 08/07/2003, ECHR

Facts: The applicants, who all lived on the flight path of Heathrow airport, complained that from 1993 the level of noise from aircraft taking off and landing during the night increased substantially, as a result of which they and their families experienced considerable sleep disturbance. They submitted that these disturbances violated their rights to respect for their homes.

Ratio: The Court did not find that, in substance, the authorities overstepped their margin of appreciation by failing to strike a fair balance between the right of the individuals affected by those regulations to respect for their private life and home and the conflicting interests of others and of the community as a whole. Accordingly, there had been no violation of Article 8 of the Convention. In this respect, the Court noted that: "Article 8 may apply in environmental cases whether the pollution is directly caused by the State or whether State responsibility arises from the failure to regulate private industry properly. In both contexts regard must be had to the fair balance that has to be struck between the competing interests of the individual and of the community as a whole; and in both contexts the State enjoys a certain margin of appreciation in determining the steps to be taken to ensure compliance with the Convention".

Application: Although it did not find that there was a violation in the present case, the Court stressed in this judgement that claims may be brought to the attention of the Court on serious and direct impact of noise or pollution regarding an individual's rights under Article 8 of the Convention.

The right to respect for correspondence

The fourth category under Article 8 of the Convention protects individuals' right to communicate with others. This right applies to private communications with family or friends but also to professional communications in a business context.

General principle: The notions of "private life" and "correspondence", within the meaning of Article 8, encompass telephone conversations which are intercepted by the police for the purposes of the prevention and detection of crime.

Malone v. United Kingdom, no 8691/79, 02/08/1984, ECHR
Facts: The plaintiff claimed that intercepting his telephone conversations, on authority of a warrant by the Secretary of State for Home Affairs, was unlawful, and asked for an injunction against the Metropolitan Police Commissioner for monitoring his telephone. He argued that he had a right to privacy.
Ratio: The Court held that there had been a violation of Article 8 of the Convention. The Court noted: *"the existence in England and Wales of laws and practices which permit and establish a system for effecting secret surveillance of communications amounted in itself to an "interference with the exercise" of the applicant's rights under Article 8, apart from any measures actually taken against him".*
Application: Although originally devised to communication by letters, the notion of correspondence has been progressively extended to any form of modern communication.

General principle: A prisoner's right to communicate with counsel out of earshot of the prison authorities is particularly important given that the lawyer-client relationship is, in principle, privileged.

Campbell v. UK, no 13590/88, 25/03/1992, ECHR
Facts: This case concerned the control by prison authorities in Scotland of a prisoner's correspondence to and from his solicitor and with the European Commission of Human Rights. He

complained that these interceptions breached his right to respect for the correspondence.

Ratio: The Court held that there had been a violation of Article 8 of the Convention in this case. It noted that: "It is clearly in the general interest that any person who wishes to consult a lawyer should be free to do so under conditions which favour full and uninhibited discussion (...) In the Court's view, similar considerations apply to a prisoner's correspondence with a lawyer concerning contemplated or pending proceedings where the need for confidentiality is equally pressing, particularly where such correspondence relates, as in the present case, to claims and complaints against the prison authorities".

Application: The right of prisoners to respect for the correspondence with their lawyer enjoys a high degree of protection given the importance of the interests at stake.

Justifiable restrictions under Article 8(2)

Under Article 8(2): "There shall be no interference by a public authority with the exercise of this right except such as is in accordance with the law and is necessary in a democratic society in the interests of national security, public safety or the economic well-being of the country, for the prevention of disorder or crime, for the protection of health or morals, or for the protection of the rights and freedoms of others". It is important to recall that conditional rights, such as articles 8,9,10 and 11 allow for lawful restrictions. The Strasbourg Court appreciates the justification of an interference to a conditional right using its traditional test (prescribed by law, pursuing a legitimate aim and necessary in a democratic society).

A restriction prescribed by law

In accordance with key principles of the Rule of law, the requirement of prescription by law should present a minimum standard of certainty and clarity. The clarity of laws guarantees that individuals are able to regulate their conduct in accordance with the law.

General principle: When discretion is conferred on public

authorities regarding interferences to Article 8 of the Convention, the law should indicate with reasonable clarity the scope and manner of exercise of the relevant discretion.

Malone v. United Kingdom, no 8691/79, 02/08/1984, ECHR

Facts: The plaintiff claimed that intercepting his telephone conversations, on authority of a warrant by the Secretary of State for Home Affairs, was unlawful, and asked for an injunction against the Metropolitan Police Commissioner for monitoring his telephone. He argued that he had a right to privacy.

Ratio: The court found a violation of Article 8 of the Convention because the interference was not prescribed by law. It considered that: "In the opinion of the Court, the law of England and Wales does not indicate with reasonable clarity the scope and manner of exercise of the relevant discretion conferred on the public authorities. To that extent, the minimum degree of legal protection to which citizens are entitled under the rule of law in a democratic society is lacking".

Application: The *rationale* behind this rule of necessary limitations to discretionary powers of the executive regarding interferences with Convention rights is to protect the key principles of the Rule of law.

General principle: If the exercise of powers conferred to the police interferes with an individual's rights under Article 8 of the Convention, this interference is not "in accordance with the law" where the powers are neither sufficiently circumscribed nor subject to adequate legal safeguards against abuse.

Gillan and Quinton v. UK, no 4158/05, 12/01/2010, ECHR

Facts: This case concerned Section 44 of the Terrorism Act 2000, which allowed a senior police officer to grant a stop and search authorisation for a designated area where he considered it "expedient" to do so for the prevention of acts of terrorism. One safeguard provided that this grant had to be authorized by the Secretary of State.

Ratio: The Court held that the interference was not prescribed by law and found a violation of Article 8 of the Convention (respect for private life). The Court noted that "the large

number of searches involved and the reports by the independent reviewer indicating that the powers were being used unnecessarily, the Court found that there was a clear risk of arbitrariness in granting such broad discretion to the police officer. The risk of the discriminatory use of the powers against ethnic minorities was a very real consideration and the statistics showed that black and Asian persons were disproportionately affected".

Application: The Court underlined in this judgement that restrictions to rights under Article 8 of the Convention should be subjected to strict scrutiny. The protection of these rights is ensured, *inter alia*, by the legal safeguards of prescription by law against arbitrariness.

General principle: An interference with Article 8 rights which has no legal basis in domestic law amounts to a breach without the need of assessing its legitimate aim and necessity.

Copland v. UK, no 62617/00, 03/04/2007, ECHR

Facts: The applicant, a public teacher, worked for a college of further education. Her telephone, e-mail and internet usage were subjected to monitoring at the deputy principal's instigation to make sure that she did not use public facilities for personal purposes. The college did not have a policy on monitoring at the material time and English law did not provide with such a possibility. The applicant submitted that these interceptions breached her rights under Article 8 of the Convention.

Ratio: The Court found unanimously that there had been a violation of the applicant's rights under Article 8 of the Convention. Telephone calls from business premises were *prima facie* **covered by the notions of "private life" and "correspondence". Accordingly, the Court concluded that: "while leaving open the question whether the monitoring of an employee's use of a telephone, e-mail or internet at the place of work might be considered "necessary in a democratic society" in certain situations in pursuit of a legitimate aim, the Court concluded that, in the absence of any domestic law regulating monitoring at the material time, the interference was not "in accordance with the law"".**

Application: It is important to note that the three steps of the test devised by the Convention to appreciate the lawfulness of a restriction to conditional rights are cumulative. Therefore, when a restriction is not prescribed by law for example, there is no need to look at its legitimate aim or necessity. Similarly, where the restriction did not pursue any of the legitimate aims listed by Article 8(2), there is automatically a breach without having to assess its necessity in a democratic society.

A restriction pursuing a legitimate aim which is necessary in a democratic society

A justifiable restriction to a right under article 8(1) should pursue one or several legitimate aim(s) provided for by Article 8 (2). These legitimate aims are listed by Article 8(2): "national security, public safety or the economic well-being of the country, the prevention of disorder or crime, the protection of health or morals, or the protection of the rights and freedoms of others". It should be noted that in general responding states invoke several legitimate aims given that there are overlapping situations where they seek to interfere with rights for more than one reason.

Nevertheless, the doctrine of proportionality ensures that domestic courts have conducted a fair balance between pursuing a legitimate aim and protecting Convention rights. Accordingly, as stated by Article 8 of the Convention, even though a restriction is prescribed by law and pursues a legitimate aim, it remains to be demonstrated that it was necessary in a democratic society. The following cases provide examples of Article 8(2) in operation and illustrate the variety of legitimate aims which has to be assessed together with the criterion of necessity in a democratic society in order to appreciate the lawfulness of the restriction.

General principle: Despite accepting that surveillance by the State is intended to protect national security and the prevention of crime, the Strasbourg Court may still declare it unnecessary or disproportionate and conclude to a violation of Article 8 of the Convention.

Segerstedt-Wiberg v. Sweden, no 62332/00, 06/06/2006, ECHR
Facts: The applicants' personal data relating to their political opinions, affiliations and activities were stored by police following bomb threats. They brought the case to the attention of the

Strasbourg Court claiming that it breached their rights under Article 8 of the Convention. The responding State maintained that the interference pursued one or more legitimate aims: the prevention of crime, in so far as the first applicants' own safety was concerned by the bomb threats, and the interests of national security with regard to all the applicants.

Ratio: The Court held that there had been a violation of Article 8 of the Convention in the case of four out of five applicants. Although it accepted, in its judgement, that: "the storage of the information in question pursued legitimate aims, namely the prevention of disorder or crime, in the case of the first applicant, and the protection of national security, in that of the remainder of the applicants", the Court declared that these interferences were not necessary in a democratic society because they were disproportionate to the applicants' right to respect for private life.

Application: Generally, the Court affords a wide margin of appreciation to contracting states where national security issues are at stake. However, it does not mean that any interference to Article 8 in such contexts will be automatically accepted by the Court.

General principle: While the searching of visitors in prison with respect to drugs may be considered a legitimate preventive measure protecting the health of prisoners, strip-searches will constitute disproportionate interferences if they are carried out without respecting procedures protecting the dignity of those being searched.

Wainwright v. UK, no 12350/04, 26/09/2006, ECHR

Facts: The applicants were a mother and her son whose father was incarcerated. It should be noted that the son had cerebral palsy and severe arrested social and intellectual development. Since the father was suspected of being involved in the supply and use of drugs within the prison, the prison governor ordered that all of his visitors be strip-searched. The applicants went to the prison to visit the father. They were subsequently subjected to intimate body searches including examinations of their sexual organs. They claimed that these searches breached their rights under Article 8 of the Convention.

Ratio: The Court held that there had been a violation of the applicants' rights under Article 8 of the Convention. It

accepted that: "the endemic drugs problem in the prison and the prison authorities' suspicion that the inmate had been taking drugs, the searching of visitors could be considered a legitimate preventive measure protecting the health of prisoners". However, the Court concluded that it was not satisfied that the searches had been proportionate to that aim, given the manner in which they had been carried out.

Application: Once again in this case, the Court stresses that the acceptance of a legitimate aim does not automatically establish the lawfulness of a restriction. One has still to assess the necessity of this restriction and, particularly in this case, its proportionality to the legitimate aim invoked by the responding State.

Summary

- Article 8 of the Convention protects the sacred private sphere surrounding a person's individuality. It allows personal development of individuals free from undue restrictions.

- Article 8 (1) provides that: Private life, family life, home and correspondence are the main rights protected by this provision.

- Article 8 is a conditional right, which means that it can be subjected to justifiable restrictions or interferences. These restrictions are regulated by the second paragraph of Article 8.

- The right to respect for private life has been interpreted by the Strasbourg Court as encompassing several issues such as physical and mental integrity, sexual orientation or State surveillance for example.

- The right to "family life" under Article 8 of the Convention has been interpreted extensively by the Court. The idea is to protect everyone's family sphere and develop free and normal relationship within this sphere.

The right to respect for family life is related to the protection of family sphere which includes other family ties that those based on marriage.

- "Private life" incorporates the right to respect for both the decisions to become and not to become a parent. A prisoner may also complain that his right to respect for family life has been interfered with.

- Article 8 of the Convention also guarantees the right to respect for the home, protecting that right from public and private intrusions or disturbances.

- The right to respect for correspondence protects individuals' right to communicate with others. This right applies to private communications with family or friends but also to professional communications in a business context. The right of prisoners to respect for the correspondence with their lawyer enjoys a high degree of protection given the importance of the interests at stake.

- It is important to recall that conditional rights, such as articles 8,9,10 and 11 allow for lawful restrictions. The Strasbourg Court appreciates the justification of an interference to a conditional right using its traditional test (prescribed by law, pursuing a legitimate aim and necessary in a democratic society).

- The three steps of the test devised by the Convention to appreciate the lawfulness of a restriction to a condition right are cumulative. Therefore, for example, when a restriction is not prescribed by law, there is no need to look at its legitimate aim or necessity.
- The doctrine of proportionality ensures that domestic courts have conducted a fair balance between pursuing a legitimate aim and protecting Convention rights.

Accordingly, as stated by Article 8 of the Convention, even though a restriction is prescribed by law and pursues a legitimate aim, it remains to be demonstrated that it was necessary in a democratic society.

Chapter 14 – Freedom of Expression – Article 10 ECHR

Introduction to Freedom of Expression

Freedom of expression is considered to be an indicator of the democratic nature of a State. The Strasbourg Court often refers to this right as being one of the fundamental pillars of democratic societies: "Freedom of expression constitutes one of the essential foundations of a democratic society and one of the basic conditions for its progress and for each individual's self-fulfilment" (see **Palomo Sánchez and others v. Spain, no 28955/06, 12/09/2011,** ECHR).

The ECHR attributes special attention to the protection of freedom of expression as it relies on one of the objectives of the Council of Europe: the protection of democracy. As Fenwick puts it, in order for a democracy to flourish, individuals and particularly the press should be free to disseminate ideas, opinions or information about governmental or public affairs. Free debates where diverse ideas are exchanged are inherent to the political functioning of a democracy.

The *rationale* behind this link often made between freedom of speech and democracy is that democratic participation of individuals is not possible without being able to freely express ideas and opinions.

Historically, this right was enshrined by the most important national bills or charters of rights. For instance, the First amendment of the United States Constitution illustrates the importance traditionally attached to this right: "Congress shall make no law (…) abridging the freedom of speech, or of the press" (the 1791 Bill of Rights). The fact that this right is enshrined in first position of the amendments reflects its fundamental importance in the American society. Freedom of expression is also enshrined by Article 19 of the Indian Constitution and Article 11 of the French Declaration of the Rights of Man and of the Citizen.

As article 8, freedom of expression is a conditional right that can be lawfully restricted by national authorities if the interference with Article 10(1) is justifiable under Article 10(2). In order to appreciate the lawfulness of such a restriction, one should apply the traditional three-step-test (prescribed by law, pursuing a legitimate and necessary in a democratic society)

The scope of freedom of expression

Article 10(1) of the European Convention on Human Rights provides that: "Everyone has the right to freedom of expression. This right shall include freedom to hold opinions and to receive and impart information and ideas without interference by public authority and regardless of frontiers".

One of the most important concepts in the jurisprudence of the Court is the respect for pluralism. In the words of the Court, freedom of expression "is applicable not only to "information" or "ideas" that are favourably received or regarded as inoffensive or as a matter of indifference, but also to those that offend, shock or disturb. Such are the demands of pluralism, tolerance and broadmindedness without which there is no democratic society" (see **Morice v. france [GC], no 29369/10, 23/04/2015**, ECHR).
Article 10 of the Convention is applicable to a variety of forms of expression, including a form of behaviour (see **Semir Güzel v. Turkey, no 29483/09, 13/09/2016**, ECHR), a particular clothing (see **Stevens v. UK (dec.), no 11674/85, 03/03/1986**, ECHR), an artistic performance (see **Ulusoy and others v. Turkey, no 34797/03, 03/05/2007**, ECHR), the publication of a book (see **Öztürk v. Turkey [GC], no 22479/93, 28/09/1999**, ECHR) or a poster (see **Chorherr v. Austria, no 13308/87, 25/08/1993**, ECHR). In addition to this, it applies to different types of speech: such as, *inter alia*, commercial speech (see **Sekmadienis Ltd. v. Lithuania, no 69317/14, 30/01/2018**, ECHR) and political speech (see **Sürek v. Turkey (No. 1), no 26682/95, 08/07/1999**, ECHR).

General principle: The right to freedom of expression applies to prisoners. The refusal by public authorities to provide access to a manuscript written by a prisoner to revise it and publish it constitutes an interference with his rights under Article 10(1) of the Convention.

Nilsen v. UK (dec.), no 36882/05, 09/03/2010, ECHR

Facts: This case concerned measures taken by prison service to prevent a serial killer to publish an autobiographical work. The applicant spent four years writing an autobiography in prison which contained detailed accounts of the killings and the abuse, dismemberment and disposal of the bodies. His solicitor sent the manuscript to the prison authorities who refused to pass it to the applicant. The latter argued that this refusal infringed his right to freedom of expression.

Ratio: The Court acknowledged that the refusal to return the manuscript to enable the applicant to revise it in prison with a view to publication amounted to an interference. However, it considered that it was prescribed by law and pursued the legitimate aim of protecting health or morals and the reputation or rights of others. As to whether the interference was necessary in a democratic society, the Court noted that the fact that the perpetrator of such crimes sought to publish for personal satisfaction his own account of the killing and mutilation of his victims was an affront to human dignity, one of the fundamental values underlying the Convention. The interference thus corresponded to a pressing social need and was proportionate to the legitimate aims pursued; the Court accordingly declared the application inadmissible as manifestly ill-founded.

Application: The Court made it clear in this case that Article 10 of the Convention is applicable in prison. It should be noted that although the Court held the refusal constituted an interference, it concluded that it was necessary in a democratic society.

General principle: Freedom of expression implies a right to receive or impart information. Freedom to receive information, referred to in paragraph 2 of Article 10 of the Convention prohibits a government from restricting a person from receiving information that others wish or may be willing to impart to him.

Open Door and Dublin Well Woman v. Ireland, no 14234/88, 29/10/1992, ECHR

Facts: An injunction was granted by the Supreme Court in March 1988 restraining the applicants (counselling agencies) inter alia from providing pregnant women with information concerning abortion facilities abroad. It should be noted that these counselling agencies advised about abortion abroad given that abortion was strictly restricted under Irish law. The applicants claimed that this injunction breached their rights to receive information.

Ratio: The Court accepted that the impugned injunction interfered with corporate applicants' freedom to impart information. Given that Irish law protected the right to life of the unborn, which was based on profound moral values concerning the nature of life, the restriction thus pursued the legitimate aim of protection of morals. However, the Court concluded that the restraint imposed on the applicants from receiving or imparting information was disproportionate given the absolute nature of the injunction which imposed a "perpetual" restraint without taking into account the age and health of women or the reasons for seeking counselling on termination of pregnancy. Accordingly, it held that there had been a violation of Article 10 of the Convention.

Application: This is a landmark judgement of the Strasbourg Court regarding freedom to receive information. However, it should be noted that, in this case, the Court did not tackle the question of the right to abortion but only the right to be informed about abortion, particularly when abortion is not effectively accessible in a Member State.

The discussion of questions of general interest

Determining whether a speech can contribute to a debate of general interest is a fundamental step and one of the most important factors for assessing the proportionality of interferences with freedom of expression. Therefore, a high level of protection is generally afforded by the Court to speeches contributing to debates of general interest.

The *rationale* behind it is related to the effectivity of the right of the public to receive information: if no one is able to talk about questions of public interests, the right of the public to receive information is not effective. Accordingly, a speech that tackles a problem that the public would have an interest in being informed about has to be highly protected from undue restrictions.

General principle: Public interest ordinarily relates to matters which affect the public to such an extent that it may legitimately take an interest in them, which attract its attention or which concern it to a significant degree, especially in that they affect the well-being of citizens or the life of the community. This is also the case with regard to matters which are capable of giving rise to considerable controversy, which concern an important social issue, or which involve a problem that the public would have an interest in being informed about.

Satakunnan Markkinapörssi Oy and Satamedia Oy v. Finland [GC], no 931/13, 27/06/2017, ECHR
Facts: The applicants published a newspaper providing information on the taxable income and assets of Finnish taxpayers. The national Data Protection Board restrained the applicants' research and ordered a restriction from processing taxation data. The applicants claimed that this restriction violated their rights under Article 10 of the Convention and argued, *inter alia*, that their speech contributed to a debate of general interest.
Ratio: The Court found that there had been no violation in the applicant's freedom of expression. However it provided a detailed definition of questions contributing to debates of general interest. It noted that the Finnish legislative policy of rendering taxation data publicly accessible was the need to ensure that the public could monitor the activities of government authorities. However, taking the publication as a whole and in context the Court was not persuaded that publication of taxation data in the manner and to the extent done by the applicant companies (the raw data was published as catalogues *en masse*, almost verbatim) had contributed to such a debate or indeed that its principal purpose was to do so.
Application: In this case, the Court devised a definition of questions contributing to a debate of public interest. Interestingly, it held in the present case that it was not convinced that the applicant's "speech" was effectively contributing to such a debate. Such findings illustrate how important the element of general interest is when appreciating the proportionality of interferences to freedom of expression.

Accordingly, the Strasbourg Court has progressively recognized the following topics as contributing to questions of general interest: the functioning of the judiciary (see **Morice v. france [GC], no 29369/10, 23/04/2015**, ECHR), the protection of public health and the environment (see **Mamère v. France, no 12697/03, 07/11/2006**, ECHR) the establishment of historical facts (see **Dink v. Turkey, no 2668/07, 14/09/2010**,ECHR) and the role of television in a democratic society (see **Ricci v. Italy, no 30210/06, 08/10/2013**, ECHR).

General principle: There is little scope under Article 10 (2) of the Convention for restrictions on political speech or on debate of questions of public interest.

Animal Defenders International v. The United Kingdom, no 48876/08, 22/04/2013, ECHR

Facts: The Communications Act 2003 prohibited political advertising in television or radio services. The applicant, a non-governmental organisation, was campaigning against the use of animals in commerce, science and leisure and sought to achieve changes in the law. In 2005 it sought to screen a television advertisement as part of a campaign concerning the treatment of primates. However, the Broadcast Advertising Clearance Centre ("the BACC") refused to clear the advert. The applicant claimed that this refusal had violated its rights under Article 10 of the Convention.

Ratio: The Court held that there had been no violation of Article 10 of the Convention. However it recalled that "As to the breadth of the margin of appreciation to be afforded, it is recalled that it depends on a number of factors. It is defined by the type of the expression at issue and, in this respect, it is recalled that there is little scope under Article 10 § 2 for restrictions on debates on questions of public interest". Accordingly, it concluded that the protection of animals contributed to a question of public interest.

Application: The fact that a speech contributes to a public debate may also serve when determining the margin of appreciation afforded to responding states, a step which is closely related to the assessment of the proportionality of the interference.

Competing interests and restrictions pursuing legitimate aims under Article 10(2)

Article 10(2) of the Convention allows for lawful restrictions to the rights enshrined by Article 10(1): "The exercise of these freedoms, since it carries with it duties and responsibilities, may be subject to such formalities, conditions, restrictions or penalties as are prescribed by law and are necessary in a democratic society, in the interests of national security, territorial integrity or public safety, for the prevention of disorder or crime, for the protection of health or morals, for the protection of the reputation or rights of others, for preventing the disclosure of information received in confidence, or for maintaining the authority and impartiality of the judiciary".

Freedom of expression and national security

Numerous examples of legal provisions of UK law allow restrictions to freedom of expression in order to protect national security. For example, the Official Secrets Act 1989 makes it a criminal offence for members of the security and intelligence services to disclose information without lawful authority. In such context, it is considered that national security should prevail over freedom of expression.

National security is a legitimate aim laid down by Article 10(2) which allows for lawful restrictions on Freedom of expression. Traditionally, the jurisprudence affords a certain margin of appreciation to national authorities given the utmost importance of the interests at stake. However, one should be very careful while assessing the lawfulness of such restrictions that can lead to abuses and arbitrariness, particularly when criminal convictions are conducted as a result of the speech.

General principle: Although Article 10 of the Convention does not in terms prohibit the imposition of prior restraints on publication, the dangers inherent in such restrictions are such that they call for the most careful scrutiny. This is especially so as far as the press is concerned, for news is a perishable commodity and to delay its publication, even for a short period, may well deprive it of all its value and interest.

Observer and Guardian v. The United Kingdom, no 13585/88, 26/11/1991, ECHR
Facts: Interlocutory injunctions, for two separated periods, were

granted restraining newspapers from publishing details of unauthorised memoirs, the "Spycatcher" alleging unlawful conduct by Security Service and information obtained from their author a former employee of the Service. While the applicants claimed that this restriction had violated their rights under Article 10 of the Convention, the UK government submitted that it pursued, *inter alia*, the legitimate aim of national security.

Ratio: The Court upheld that there had been a violation of the applicants' rights under Article 10 of the Convention regarding the second period. The Court noted that as a matter of fact, on 14 July 1987, Spycatcher was published in the United States of America. As regards national security interests, the purpose of restrictions had become confined to promotion of efficiency and reputation of Security Service and their continuation prevented newspapers from purveying information, already available, on matter of legitimate public concern. Accordingly, the interference was therefore no longer "necessary in a democratic society".

Application: The Court, throughout its jurisprudence, stresses that although prior restraints on publication are not prohibited as such, they impose a strict scrutiny. In this regard, the mere promotion of efficiency and reputation of security services and their continuation cannot justify restrictions allegedly pursuing the legitimate aim of national security.

General principle: Where the views expressed do not comprise incitements to violence - in other words unless they advocate recourse to violent actions or bloody revenge, justify the commission of terrorist offences in pursuit of their supporter's goals or can be interpreted as likely to encourage violence by expressing deep-seated and irrational hatred towards identified persons - Contracting States must not restrict the right of the general public to be informed of them, even on the basis of national security.

Dilipak v. Turkey, no 29680/05, 15/09/2015, ECHR
Facts: The applicant, a journalist, published an article criticising the intervention of certain commanding officers of the armed forces in government policy. He was subsequently charged with the offence of denigrating the armed forces. While the applicant claimed that this restriction had violated his rights under Article 10

of the Convention, the responding State submitted that it pursued the legitimate aim of national security and defence of law and order.

Ratio: The Court held that there had been a violation of the applicant's rights under Article 10 of the Convention in the present case. It noted that in expressing his reaction to the remarks made by the generals, which he saw as inappropriate intervention by the military in politics, the applicant had been conveying his ideas and opinions on an issue which was unquestionably a matter of general interest in a democratic society. As to the article written by the applicant, it had in no way been "gratuitously offensive" or insulting and had not incited others to violence or hatred. Accordingly, the restriction complained of had not been justified by a pressing social need, had in any event not been proportionate to the legitimate aims pursued and therefore had not been necessary in a democratic society.

Application: In this case the Court laid down an important criterion which has to be taken into consideration when assessing the risk caused by a speech to national security. The potential impact of the speech, based on the content and nature of such speech, helps to determine whether or not it might incite or provoke violence.

Freedom of expression and the prevention of disorder and crime

A speech can be lawfully restricted to prevent disorder or crime. In the balance of competing interests, the protection of order and security seems to justify that these legitimate aims should prevail over freedom of expression. While relevant examples of cases involving the prevention of disorder mainly imply restrictions on speeches criticising military service or advocating for demilitarization, other examples of cases related to the prevention of crime include measures intended to prohibit the commission of criminal offences.

General principle: Although the nature of a speech is hostile to military service, as far as it does exhort the use of violence or incite armed resistance, rebellion, or immediate desertion, a restriction on the said speech cannot be justified on the ground

of prevention of disorder.

Ergin v. Turkey (no. 6), no 47533/99, 04/05/2006, ECHR
Facts: This case concerned the criminal conviction of a journalist by a military Court for publishing an article criticising the ceremony to mark departures for military service. He was found guilty of incitement to evade military service and sentenced to two months' imprisonment, commuted to a fine. While the applicant claimed that this restriction had violated his rights under Article 10 of the Convention, the responding State submitted that it pursued the legitimate aim of prevention of disorder.
Ratio: The Court held that there had been a violation of the applicant's rights under Article 10 of the Convention in the present case. The Court noted that the offending article had been published in a newspaper on sale to the general public and did not seek, either in its form or in its content, to precipitate immediate desertion. Accordingly, the applicant's criminal conviction did not correspond to a pressing social need and was accordingly not "necessary in a democratic society".
Application: The Strasbourg Court accepts restrictions pursuing the legitimate aim of the prevention of disorder on speeches that are hostile to the military if it can be demonstrated that such speeches exhort the use of violence or incite armed resistance, rebellion, or immediate desertion.

General principle: A journalist cannot claim an exclusive immunity from criminal liability for the sole reason that, unlike other individuals exercising the right to freedom of expression, the offence in question was committed during the performance of his or her journalistic functions.

Pentikäinen v. Finland [GC], no 11882/10, 20/10/2015, ECHR
Facts: The applicant covered a demonstration in his capacity as a journalist and photographer. When the demonstration turned violent, he decided not to obey police orders intended at dispersing the crowd. He was later arrested and convicted for not obeying police orders during a demonstration. The applicant claimed that he was performing his journalistic functions. The contracting state submitted that the restriction was intended to prevent disorder and crime.

Ratio: The Court held that there had been no violation of the applicant's rights under Article 10 of the Convention. It noted that paragraph 2 of Article 10 does not guarantee a wholly unrestricted freedom of expression even with respect to media coverage of matters of serious public concern. In particular, and notwithstanding the vital role played by the media in a democratic society, journalists cannot, in principle, be released from their duty to obey the ordinary criminal law on the basis that, as journalists, Article 10 affords them a cast-iron defence. The Court emphasised that the conduct sanctioned by the criminal conviction was not the applicant's journalistic activity as such, but his refusal to comply with a police order at the very end of a demonstration which had been judged by the police to have become a riot.

Application: This landmark case of the Grand Chamber laid down the principle that journalists are not exempted from respecting criminal law and subsequently gave rise to other cases. The Court applied this principle in a case where a journalist bought a gun to illustrate an article and demonstrate how easy it was to get one (see **Salihu and others v. Sweden (dec.) no 33628/15, 10/05/2016**, ECHR) and in a case concerning the conviction of journalists for possessing and using radio equipment to intercept confidential police communications (see **Brambilla and others v. Italy (dec.), no 22567/09 , 23/06/2016**, ECHR).

Freedom of expression and the protection of health and morals

The protection of health and morals is frequently invoked in combination by responding states. These legitimate aims justify the existence, all across Europe, of obscenity laws. For instance, in the UK, the Obscenity Act 1959 (as amended I 1964) makes it a criminal offence punished by up to three years' imprisonment, for a person to publish an obscene article. The first section of the said Act defines an obscene article as a material which tends to corrupt or deprave its reader.

It should be noted that restrictions on speeches pursuing the protection of health or morals where the targeted audience is vulnerable to depravation, for example young kids, tend to justify the necessity of such interference (see **Société de conception de presse et d'édition et Ponson v. France, no 26935/05,**

05/03/2009, ECHR).

General principle: There is no uniform conception of morality in domestic laws of contracting states. Therefore, national authorities, which are in principle in a better position to assess the necessity for any restriction on freedom of expression, are afforded a wide margin of appreciation.

Handyside v. The United Kingdom, no 5493/72, 07/12/1976, ECHR

Facts: The Little Red Schoolbook, an "educative book for teenagers", had been published in in several European countries such as Denmark, Belgium, Finland and France. This book was aimed at children and adolescents aged from twelve to eighteen and contained a 26-page section concerning "Sex". In the UK 1,069 copies of the book were provisionally seized together with leaflets, posters, showcards, and correspondence relating to its publication and sale. The author of the book, the applicant, claimed that this restriction had violated his rights under Article 10 of the Convention. The responding State submitted that the restriction was intended to protect morals.

Ratio: The Court held that there had been no breach of Article 10 of the Convention in the present case. It noted that the book "included above all in the section on sex and in the passage headed "Be yourself" in the chapter on pupils, sentences or paragraphs that young people at a critical stage of their development could have interpreted as an encouragement to indulge in precocious activities harmful for them or even to commit certain criminal offences. In these circumstances, despite the variety and the constant evolution in the United Kingdom of views on ethics and education, the competent English judges were entitled, in the exercise of their discretion, to think at the relevant time that the Schoolbook would have pernicious effects on the morals of many of the children and adolescents who would read it".

Application: As mentioned earlier, the lack of European consensus often results on a greater margin of appreciation afforded to national authorities. In the context of obscene publications, the lack of European consensus is due to the diversity of cultures and traditions in the 47 Member States of the Council of Europe.

General principle: The refusal to allow a poster campaign promoting human cloning and "geniocracy" and the possibility that the campaign's writings and ideas had led to sexual abuse of minors by some of its members, pursued the legitimate aim of the protection of health and morals.

Mouvement Raëlien suisse v. Switzerland [GC] - 16354/06, 13/07/2012, ECHR

Facts: The applicant was a non-profit association whose declared aim was to make initial contact and establish good relations with extraterrestrials. It promoted human cloning. The association sought permission from the police to put up posters which featured, among other things, pictures of extraterrestrials' faces and a flying saucer and displayed the movement's website address and telephone number. The authorisation was denied and the applicant subsequently invoked Article 10 of the Convention in domestic proceedings. The responding State submitted that the restriction was intended to protect public health and morals.

Ratio: The Court, holding that the interference with Article 10 of the Convention was proportionate, found that there had been no violation of the applicant's freedom of expression. It noted that whilst some of the reasons for the ban on the posters taken separately might not be capable of justifying it, the domestic authorities had been entitled to consider that in view of the situation as a whole and to conclude that the ban had been indispensable. Accordingly the national authorities had not overstepped the broad margin of appreciation afforded to them in this case; the grounds for their decisions had been "relevant and sufficient" and had corresponded to a "pressing social need".

Application: In this case, the Court recalled the subsidiary nature of the Convention mechanism, noting that it did not see any serious reason to substitute its own assessment for that of the court of last instance, which had examined the question carefully and in line with the principles laid down in the Court's case-law.

Freedom of expression and the protection of rights of others

The protection of reputation, which is illustrated in domestic orders by defamation laws, is very frequently invoked by contracting parties to justify a restriction pursuing the protection of rights of others. Some member states prohibit defamation at the domestic level through civil laws; others make it a criminal offense.

General principle: Where the restriction on an individual's freedom of speech protects the reputation of a politician the limits of acceptable criticism are wider as such than as regards a private individual. Unlike the latter, the former inevitably and knowingly lays himself open to close scrutiny of his every word and deed by both journalists and the public at large, and he must consequently display a greater degree of tolerance.

Lingens v. Austria, no 9815/82, 08/07/1986, ECHR
Facts: The applicant was fined for publishing in local magazine comments about the behaviour of the Austrian Chancellor, such as "basest opportunism", "immoral" and "undignified". Under the Austrian criminal code the only defence was proof of the truth of these statements. He claimed that this fine had breached his rights under Article 10 of the Convention and the responding state invoked the protection of rights of others.
Ratio: The Court found that there had been a breach in the applicant's rights under Article 10 of the Convention. The Court affirmed that "a careful distinction needs to be made between facts and value-judgments. The existence of facts can be demonstrated, whereas the truth of value-judgments is not susceptible of proof. The Court notes in this connection that the facts on which Mr. Lingens founded his value-judgment were undisputed, as was also his good faith. Under paragraph 3 of Article 111 of the Criminal Code, read in conjunction with paragraph 2, journalists in a case such as this cannot escape conviction for the matters specified in paragraph 1 unless they can prove the truth of their statements. As regards value-judgments this requirement is impossible of fulfilment and it infringes freedom of opinion itself, which is a fundamental part of the right secured by Article 10 of the Convention".
Application: In this case, the Strasbourg Court stressed that, although member states could, in certain circumstances, restrict freedom of expression in order to protect the reputation of others, there were still limits of acceptable criticism. These limits are wider for politicians who are, because of their official functions,

publically exposed to comments and criticisms.

The ECHR has accepted that the protection of rights of others, under Article 10(2) of the Convention, may also encompass offence to others on religious grounds. National laws protecting religious sensibilities have generally been upheld as compatible.

General principle: Those who choose to exercise the freedom to manifest their religion, irrespective of whether they do so as members of a religious majority or a minority, cannot reasonably expect to be exempt from all criticism.

Otto Preminger v. Austria, no 13470/87, 20/09/1994, ECHR

Facts: This case was related to the seizure and forfeiture of a film considered blasphemous. The domestic Court described the film as follows: "God the Father is presented both in image and in text as a senile, impotent idiot, Christ as a cretin and Mary Mother of God as a wanton lady with a corresponding manner of expression". The applicant, the author of the film, argued that the seizure violated his rights under Article 10 of the Convention.

The contracting state submitted that the said interference pursued the legitimate aim of protection of the rights of others, namely the right of citizens not to be insulted in their religious beliefs by public expression of others' views.

Ratio: The Court found that there had been no violation in the applicant's freedom of expression under Article 10 of the Convention. It noted that those who choose to exercise the freedom to manifest their religion must tolerate and accept the denial by others of their religious beliefs and even the propagation by others of doctrines hostile to their faith. However, recalling that national authorities had considered that the film constituted an abusive attack on Roman Catholic religion and that they did not overstep their margin of appreciation.

Application: Even though, in this case, the Court finds that the restriction was lawful to protect the right of Roman Catholic believers, it emphasised that they must accept a reasonable degree of public criticism. Accordingly, restrictions to freedom of expression are not lawful where imposed on comments that do not reach this degree of criticism.

Freedom of expression and the protection of the authority and impartiality of the judiciary

Protecting the authority an impartiality of the judiciary is a significant legitimate aim provided that the duties and discretion of judges do not enable them to reply to personal attacks by using the media for example in the same way that politicians and other public figures can do.

This objective is also closely related to the core principles of the Rule of law which include the independence and impartiality of the judiciary. In this respect, under the Convention, the state may have a duty to interfere with freedom of expression if, for example, the right to a fair trial or the presumption of innocence would be prejudiced by publication of information about the proceedings. Accordingly, several examples in domestic legislation prescribe such interferences. For instance, the Perjury Act 1911 makes it an offence for a person sworn in as a witness to make a statement during judicial proceedings which he or she knows to be false. Other examples include section 2 of the Contempt of Court Act 1981 providing that a person can be held liable for publications which create a substantial risk that pending legal proceeding will be seriously prejudiced.

General principle: The term "judiciary" comprises the machinery of justice or the judicial branch of government as well as the judges in their official capacity. The phrase "authority of the judiciary" includes, in particular, the notion that the courts are, and are accepted by the public at large as being, the proper forum for the ascertainment of legal rights and obligations and the settlement of disputes relative thereto; further, that the public at large have respect for and confidence in the courts' capacity to fulfil that function.

The Sunday Times v. The United Kingdom n°6538/74, 26/04/1979, ECHR
Facts: The applicant, a British newspaper, published an article on titled the Thalidomide, a drug taken by pregnant women allegedly causing birth defects to new-borns, and criticizing English law for failing to tackle this issue. In this article, a footnote announced another article to be published later on the same topic. In

November 17, 1972, the Divisional Court of the Queen's Bench granted an injunction in order to restrain the publication of the future article stating that its publication would constitute contempt of Court. The applicant argued that this injunction breached his rights under Article 10 of the Convention. The contracting state submitted that the said interference pursued the legitimate aim of protection of the authority and impartiality of the judiciary.

Ratio: The Court held that there had been a violation in the applicant's rights under Article 10 of the Convention, considering that the said restriction was not necessary in a democratic society. However, the Court interestingly noted that the majority of the categories of conduct covered by the law of contempt related either to the position of the judges or to the functioning of the courts and of the machinery of justice: "maintaining the authority and impartiality of the judiciary" was therefore one purpose of that law.

Application: This judgement provides with significant developments on how to interpret the legitimate aim of maintaining the authority and impartiality of the judiciary under Article 10(2). Domestic laws on the position of judges or the functioning of the judiciary seem to be pursuing such an objective. It should also be noted that following this judgement, the UK subsequently amended its law through the Contempt of Court Act 1981.

The nature and severity of the restriction or penalty imposed

As for the contribution to a debate of public interest, the nature and severity of penalty imposed is another crucial factor to be taken into account when assessing the proportionality of an interference. In the words of the Strasbourg Court: "The Court observes in this connection that the nature and severity of the penalty imposed are factors to be taken into account when assessing the proportionality of the interference" (see **Sürek v. Turkey (no 1) [GC], no 26682/95, 26682/95**, ECHR).

This core principle of the ECHR's jurisprudence on freedom of expression applies to both penalty imposed on the basis of criminal law (imprisonment, fines) and other restrictions taken on the basis of civil law (injunctions, refusals). The idea of proportionality is perfectly reflected in this principle the potential harm that can be caused to society by freedom of expression. Accordingly, a speech should not be, in principle, subject to severe restrictions or penalties.

General principle: In principle, the Court considers that peaceful and non-violent forms of expression should not be made subject to the threat of imposition of a custodial sentence.

Murat Vural v. Turkey, no 9540/07, 21/10/2014, ECHR
Facts: The applicant was sentenced to thirteen years' imprisonment in 2007 after being found guilty of an offence under the Law on Offences committed against Atatürk for having poured paint on one if his statues. In addition to this, he was unable to vote or to get elected during this period. However, it should be noted that the applicant was conditionally released in 2013. He claimed to have exercised his rights under Article 10 of the Convention and that the penalty imposed was extremely severe.
Ratio: The Court held unanimously that there had been a violation of the applicant's rights under Article 10 of the Convention considering that the penalty imposed as a result of the exercise of freedom of expression was disproportionate to the legitimate aims pursued. The Court underlined that it was struck by the extreme severity of the penalty foreseen in domestic law and imposed on the applicant that was over thirteen years of imprisonment. While in the present case, the applicant's acts involved a physical attack on property, the Court did not consider that the acts were of a gravity justifying a custodial sentence as provided for by domestic law.
Application: This is a perfect example of a disproportionate restriction on freedom of expression: national authorities cannot convict an individual to 13 years' solely for having poured paint on a sculpture. However, the Court has later stated that the imposition of an imprisonment penalty was not, as such, a disproportionate restriction (see **Perrin v. UK (dec.), no 5446/03, 18/10/2005**, ECHR).

General principle: Where alternative restrictions are available to pursue a legitimate aim, national authorities should make use of the less drastic ones for the purposes of proportionality of the interference.

Kaos GL v. Turkey, no 4982/07, 22/11/2016, ECHR

Facts: This case concerned the seizure and confiscation for more than five years of all copies of edition of a magazine containing article on "pornography". All the copies of the magazine published by the applicant, an association promoting the rights of the LGBT community, were seized by the domestic authorities from 2006 to 2012. The applicant argued that this seizure and confiscation breached his rights under Article 10 of the Convention.

Ratio: The Court held that the interference with the exercise of the applicant's right to freedom of expression was disproportionate and concluded to a violation of Article 10 of the Convention. It considered that there was no justification for blocking the access of the whole general public to the impugned issue of the magazine. In that connection, the domestic authorities had not attempted to implement any preventive measure less drastic than the seizure of all copies of the issue, such as prohibiting its sale to persons under the age of eighteen or requiring special packaging with a warning for minors, or even withdrawing the publication from the newspaper kiosks, stopping short of seizing subscriber copies. The Court thereby stated that the confiscation of the copies of the magazine and the delay of five years and seven months in distributing the publication could not be considered as proportionate to the aim pursued.

Application: In order to appreciate the proportionality of a restriction to Article 10 of the Convention, one has to look at the circumstances of the case to determine if there were less drastic alternatives for national authorities to pursue the legitimate aim invoked.

Summary

- Freedom of expression is considered to be an indicator of the democratic nature of a State. It constitutes one of the essential foundations of a democratic society and one of the basic conditions for its progress. The *rationale* behind this link often made between freedom of speech and democracy is that democratic participation of individuals is not possible without being able to freely express ideas and opinions.

- One of the most important concepts in the jurisprudence of the Court is the respect for pluralism. Freedom of expression is applicable not only to information or ideas that are favourably received or regarded as inoffensive, but also to those that offend, shock or disturb.

- Determining whether a speech can contribute to a debate of general interest is a fundamental step and one of the most important factors for assessing the proportionality of interferences with freedom of expression. Therefore, a high level of protection is generally afforded by the Court to speeches contributing to debates of general interest.

- National security is a legitimate aim laid down by Article 10(2) which allows for lawful restrictions on freedom of expression. Traditionally, the jurisprudence affords a certain margin of appreciation to national authorities given the utmost importance of the interests at stake.

- A speech can be lawfully restricted to prevent disorder or crime. While relevant examples of cases involving the prevention of disorder mainly imply restrictions on speeches criticising military service or advocating for demilitarization, other examples of cases related to the prevention of crime include measures intended to prohibit the commission of criminal offences.

- The protection of health and morals is frequently invoked in combination by responding states. There is no uniform conception of morality in domestic laws of contracting states. Therefore, national authorities, which are in principle in a better position to assess the necessity for any restriction on freedom of expression, are afforded a wide margin of appreciation.

- The protection of reputation, which is illustrated in domestic orders by defamation laws, is very frequently invoked by contracting parties to justify a restriction pursuing the protection of rights of others. The ECHR has accepted that the protection of rights of others, under Article 10(2) of the Convention, may also encompass offence to others on religious grounds. National laws protecting religious sensibilities have generally been upheld as compatible

- Protecting the authority an impartiality of the judiciary is closely related to the core principles of the Rule of law which include the independence and impartiality of the judiciary.

- As for the contribution to a debate of public interest, the nature and severity of penalty imposed is another crucial factor to be taken into account when assessing the proportionality of an interference. The idea of proportionality is perfectly reflected in this principle the potential harm that can be caused to society by freedom of expression. Accordingly, a speech should not be, in principle, subject to severe restrictions or penalties.

Chapter 15 – Judicial review: Preliminaries and procedure

Introduction to Administrative Law and Judicial Review

The mandate and missions of the State administration requires that government, local authorities or courts are able to use special public prerogatives for example to purchase property compulsorily or to impose imprisonment. These powers are, of course, granted to public authorities almost exclusively by means of statutes which – at least in theory – delineate the extent and scope of those powers.

Judicial review is often seen as the major way in which the legality of administrative action is controlled. It is the cornerstone of administrative law. This is the mechanism by which the courts are able to scrutinise the decision-making processes and the legality of actions or decisions taken by public authorities and officials. Under judicial review proceedings, judges are thus capable of examining the legality of public decisions.

Similar procedures exist in a large number of other European states. This is an approach which stresses the role played by the law in the control of administrative activities, and is underpinned by the doctrine of *ultra vires* which imposes on public bodies the obligation to lawfully act within the limits of the powers given to it.

Historically, the massive expansion of the administrative state over the last hundred years, with the state taking on responsibility for education, health provision, energy, social services and housing; logically imposed on public bodies to operate within the bounds of legality. Consequently, administrative law is defined as the legal framework through which public bodies may deliver better, in other words more transparent and fair, public services.

Judicial review has evolved along with important jurisprudential developments in the 1960's. Initially restricted to certain domains, it now touches almost every aspect of public decision-making such as, for example: planning, financial services, immigration and asylum, public transport, social security, university discipline, controls on broadcasting, and environmental regulation.

The definition and objectives of Judicial Review

In the words of H. Barnett: "Judicial review represents the means by which the courts control the exercise of governmental power. Government departments, local authorities, tribunals, state agencies and agencies exercising which are governmental in nature must exercise their powers in a lawful manner". Accordingly, as stated earlier, the rationale behind judicial review stems from the core principles of the Rule of law.

The Rule of law imposes on rulers to respect and act in compliance with law. As a result, for example, those exercising power can only act on the basis of a legal provision, subjected to the will and limited to the terms provided for by Parliament, as a justification of their action. Judicial review ensures that this principle is respected. Lord Phillips famously stated: *"The common law power of the judges to review the legality of administrative action is a cornerstone of the rule of law in this country and one that the judges guard jealously"*.

Throughout the development of case law on judicial review, key elements of this procedure have arisen. Firstly, judicial review can be brought against one or several bodies, regardless of their rank in the hierarchy of the administration (from a Secretary of State to a Parole Board). We will see below that judicial review proceedings may also be introduced against bodies that are not, in a strict sense, public authorities.

Judicial review is not confined to "executive actions" of governmental bodies; it can also include reviewing the decision-making process of judicial bodies of inferior courts. It should be noted that judicial review, technically speaking, is brought in the name of the Crown.

General principle: The objective of judicial review is not to appellate a public law decision on the merits but rather to examine the legality of the decision-making process.

Chief Constable of the North Wales Police v Evans [1982], 1 WLR 1155

Facts: The claimant argued that he was unjustly dismissed as a probationary constable. The Chief Constable interviewed him and asked him to resign rather than formally firing him on the grounds that Evans married a woman much older than himself, that he was keeping four dogs in a police council house, which had a one dog limit, and that he and his wife lived a "hippy" lifestyle. He tried to challenge the legality of the decision under judicial review.

Ratio: The Court found the probationer police constable to have been unlawfully induced the claimant to resign, but the court could not order his reinstatement. The House granted instead a declaration: "affirming that, by reason of his unlawfully induced resignation, he had thereby become entitled to the same rights and remedies, not including reinstatement, as he would have had if the chief constable had not unlawfully dispensed with his services under regulation 16(1)". Lord Brightman concluded: *"Judicial review is concerned, not with the decision, but with the decision-making process. Unless that restriction on the power of the court is observed, the court will in my view, under the guise of preventing the abuse of power, be itself guilty of usurping power be itself guilty of usurping power".*

Application: In this case, the Court made it clear that the purpose of judicial review was not to question a decision itself. Courts should not serve as appellate jurisdictions but rather as operators of a review of the legality of decision-making processes. As Lord Green MR stated in **Associated Provincial Picture Houses Ltd v Wednesbury Corporation [1948]** 1 KB 223: *"it is not an appellate authority to override a decision of the local authority, but as a judicial authority which is concerned, and concerned only, to see whether the local have contravened the law by acting in excess of the powers which Parliament has confided in them".*

Modern debates over Judicial Review

Historically, the British constitutional system has been compared by Dicey to the French constitutional system which distinguishes administrative and civil jurisdictions. In the UK, it was decided that state officials were held to account before ordinary courts, without such separation.

However, this view has been reversed later on along with the modern development and nature of judicial review. The High Court historically has exercised the power of judicially controlling the actions of public authorities. In 2000, the Crown Office List, a branch of the High Court in charge of the processing of judicial review applications, was renamed the "Administrative Court". In addition to this, section 22 of the Crime and Courts Act 2013 allows immigration, asylum and application for nationality to be transferred from the Administrative Court to the Upper Tribunal. Therefore, though changes have been made to confer to specialist judges the examination of judicial review cases, there is still no clear-cut separation between two different orders of jurisdictions as it is the case in France.

Judicial review is subject to many criticisms as it has been devised by the judges, for the judges and against the executive. Indeed, judicial review is a product of common law. It is the courts themselves, and not Parliament, who created, defined and significantly expanded judicial review. Judges are not elected and because of social inequalities, not representative of the society. Accordingly, judges do not enjoy the same legitimacy than MPs or elected members of the executive.

To some extent, striking down decisions of the administration can be seen as a form of judicial activism, especially regarding the recent developments that extended the powers of judges under judicial review. However, it should be remembered that the executive is neither elected *per se*, and the powers of judges to review the legality of its action is strictly limited, as it will be developed below.

Amenability of a Decision to Judicial Review

As a general rule, only public law decisions are amenable to judicial review. The typical situation in which judicial review is the appropriate legal course of action is when a government body is carrying out a public function. However, both non-governmental bodies and inferior courts are also subject to judicial review.

It is generally accepted that public law decisions of government ministers and departments are subject to judicial review.

Bodies subject to judicial review

General principle: The Home Secretary's actions, as actions of any other government minister, are subject to challenges in judicial review.

R (Venables and Thompson) v Home Secretary [1997] UKHL 25

Facts: The claimants argued that the Home Secretary had unlawfully decided not to release them from prison, after they were convicted of murder as children. The Home Secretary took into account public petitions demanding the murderers to be imprisoned for life. They sought to challenge this decision under judicial review.

Ratio: The House of Lords held by 3 votes to 2, that the Home Secretary acted unlawfully by taking into account irrelevant considerations (a public petition) and failing to take into account relevant considerations (progress in detention). Lord Steyn considered the following: "The Home Secretary misunderstood his duty. This misdirection by itself renders his decision unlawful".

Application: Governmental bodies are traditionally subject to judicial review. In this case, the House of Lords made it clear that judicial review can be brought against any public body, regardless of their rank in the hierarchy of the administration.

In addition to public bodies of central government, decisions of local authorities and devolved institutions are also subject to judicial review. The scope of judicial review encompasses inferior courts' decisions including The Crown Court, The Magistrates' Court, The Coroners' Court, the Election Courts and Tribunals.

Judicial review also represents a possible course of legal action against decisions of non-governmental bodies exercising public law powers. Historically, the courts looked at the source of a body's power when deciding whether it would be subject to judicial review. If the body was created by or exercised power pursuant to statute, its decisions would normally be considered amenable to judicial review. However, in addition to the source of powers, courts nowadays look at the nature of such powers, determining whether or not they are *de facto* governmental in nature.

General principle: If a private body is exercising a public law function, or if the exercise of its functions has public law consequences, these elements may be sufficient to bring the body within the reach of judicial review.

R v Panel of Take-overs and Mergers, ex parte Datafin [1987] QB 815
Facts: The claimant sought judicial review of a Panel which was a non-governmental body and had not been established by an Act of Parliament or under royal prerogative. It was a body established to regulate the City Code in London.
Ratio: The Court of Appeal underlined that judicial review was an adaptable procedure and could be extended to a body which performed public law duties. The Panel was a powerful body taking important decisions on the regulation of the financial activity of the City of London. Accordingly it was a *de facto* public body that was subject to judicial review. Lloyd LJ stated: "If the source of power is a statute, or subordinate legislation under a statute, then clearly the body in question will be subject to judicial review (...) if the body is exercising a public law function, or if the exercise of its functions have public law consequences, then that may be sufficient to bring the body within the reach of judicial review."
Application: For the first time, judicial review was accepted to challenge actions of a body that was not, *per se*, part of public administration. This extensive approach has been reinforced by the Civil Procedure Rules Part 54.1(2)(a)(ii) which defines judicial review in terms of a claim to review the lawfulness of a decision or action "in relation to the exercise of a public function".

Application of the Datafin principle

General principle: Not all non-governmental regulatory authorities exercise public functions. Only those exercising governmental functions.

R v Disciplinary Committee of the Jockey Club, ex parte Aga Khan, [1993] 2 All ER 853
Facts: In this case, the decision of the Jockey Club was being

challenged under judicial review. This private body regulated horse racing in Britain (licences and authorisations were provided for race meetings).

Ratio: The Court of Appeal held that, although the decision of the Jockey Club affected the public, it was not a public body (in terms of history, constitution and membership) and did not exercise governmental functions. It noted that the powers of the Jockey Club to regulate horse racing were derived from an agreement between private parties.

Application: It should be noted that not all regulatory authorities exercise public functions. This case should be contrasted with **R v Panel of Take-overs and Mergers, ex parte Datafin [1987]** QB 815 where the defendant was a powerful body regulating financial activity, which was considered by the Court of Appeal to be a public law duty.

General principle: Powers which are sufficiently public in nature are powers that the administration of the State would have to exercise in the absence of performance by a private body.

R v Chief Rabbi of the United Hebrew Congregation of GB and Commonwealth, ex parte Wachmann, [1993] 2 All ER 249
Facts: On the ground of suspected adultery, the Chief Rabbi of the Jewish religion exiled the claimant from the religion. The latter sought to challenge this decision under judicial review.

Ratio: The High Court refused to subject the functions of the Chief Rabbi to jurisdiction of judicial review. It noted that for a body to be amendable to judicial review, it must have some connection to government. The functions of the Chief Rabbi were in essence religious and spiritual and were such that the government would not seek to discharge them in his absence.

Application: One has to look at the traditional conception of public law duties when appreciating the public nature of powers exercised by non-governmental bodies. The body will not be subject to judicial review if the function performed is not likely to be otherwise performed by the State. However, it should be noted that even if private regulatory authorities are not subject to judicial review, courts, in the course of private law proceedings, may also apply certain administrative principles (for instance the duty to act fairly, see **Nagle v Feilden [1966]**, 2 QB 633).

Procedural exclusivity

The O'Reilly principle

The exclusivity principle provides that public law rights should be enforced through judicial review (Pt. 54 of the Civil Procedure Rules). The aim of this principle is to protect the administration from unrestricted potential challenge of its action. It also prevents "busybodies" to introduce abusive legal actions.

General principle: Where a claimant argues that a public law issue is at stake, he must use the special judicial review procedure to enforce this public law right. Bringing a public law issue by any other ordinary action would amount to an abuse of process of the court.

O'Reilly v Mackman [1983] 2 AC 237
Facts: Four prisoners were convicted to disciplinary penalties by the Visitors Board. In order to challenge this decision for alleged bias, they decided to use private law proceedings.
Ratio: The Court held that the prisoners had used the wrong procedure. It noted that judicial review was the exclusive procedure for challenging public law decisions and that private law matters were to be dealt with by ordinary action. Accordingly, it would be contrary to public policy to evade the procedural protection afforded to public bodies under judicial review. Lord Diplock however conceded that: "I have described this as a general rule (...) there may be exceptions, particularly where the invalidity of the decision arises as a collateral issue in a claim from infringement of a right of the claimant arising under private law, or where none of the parties objects to the adoption of the procedure by writ or originating summons".
Application: In this case, the Court laid down a general principle which was intended to be restricted with legitimate exceptions, as Lord Diplock announced it. The court determined that judicial review was the exclusive procedure for challenging public law decisions and that private law matters were to be dealt with by ordinary action. To bring a public law challenge any other way would amount to an abuse of process of the court.

General principle: Where private rights depended upon prior public law decisions, the judicial review process should ordinarily be used.

Cocks v Thanet District Council [1981] UKHL 10
Facts: The claimant, a homeless person, argued that he had a right to be provided with accommodation under the Housing (Homeless Persons) Act 1977. He sought to enforce the obligation on the respondent to house him permanently by an action in the county court. The defendant claimed that this was an abuse of process as he should have used judicial review.
Ratio: The House of Lords held that it would be an abuse of court process to allow the claimant to seek relief in respect of his claim otherwise than by an application for judicial review. Where the action impugned the authority's performance of its statutory duties as a pre-condition to enforcing private law rights, the correct way was to do so within judicial review proceedings. The authority's decision could not be challenged by an ordinary action.
Application: In this case, the House of Lords applied the principle laid down in **O'Reilly v Mackman [1983]** 2 AC 237, making it clear that in cases involving private and public rights, where private rights depended upon prior public law decisions, the exclusivity principle should be applied.

Exceptions to the O'Reilly rule: Mixed Public/Private Law

The principle of procedural exception is subject to several exceptions which allows for a flexible application.

General principle: It is not an abuse of process for a claimant to use ordinary proceedings to enforce a private law right where it incidentally involved challenging a public law decision.

Roy v Kensington and Chelsea and Westminster Family Practitioner Committee (FPC) [1992] 1 AC 624
Facts: The claimant, a doctor practicing for the NHS, suffered a reduction of practice allowance of 20% by the Family Practitioner Committee because he was not dedicating enough time to his NHS

missions. The claimant brought a private action against the Family Practitioner Committee for breach of contract. The respondent sought to have the action struck out as an abuse of process given that he should have introduced judicial review.

Ratio: The House of Lord considered that it was not an abuse of process to use ordinary proceedings to enforce a private law right where it incidentally involved challenging a public law decision. In the present case, the claimant's main purpose was to enforce a private law right and the challenge of a public law decision was merely incidental. In the words of Lord Lowry, delivering the unanimous opinion: "an issue, which was concerned exclusively with public right, should be determined in judicial review proceedings. However, where a litigant was asserting a private law right, which incidentally involved the examination of a public law issue (the FPC's decision), he was not debarred from seeking to establish that right by ordinary action. Dr Roy had a bundle of private law rights, including the right to be paid for work done, which entitled him to sue for their alleged breach. It was not an abuse of the process of the court to proceed as Dr Roy had done".

Application: In this case, the House of Lords limited the scope of application of the principle of procedural exclusivity. One should look at the main purpose of the claimant where both private law and public law rights are involved.

General principle: Respondents have a right to invoke a public law issue and challenge a public law decision in their defence in private law proceedings.

Wandsworth London BC v Winder [1985] AC 461

Facts: A local council brought private legal proceedings against a council tenant for arrears of rent and possession of his flat. The respondent argued that the recent increase of rents, through a resolution of the local council, were abusive and *ultra vires*.

Ratio: The House of Lords held that, even though the respondent did not initiate the proceedings, he had a right to challenge the local authority's decision in his defence. In the present case, it considered that the local Council had acted unreasonably.

Application: The House of Lords accepted a defence based on the unlawfulness of a public decision to discharge defendant from an obligation under private law. It should be noted that this right to raise a public law issue in an individual's defence also exists in criminal proceedings (see **Boddington v British Transport Police [1999] 2 AC 143**).

Another exception to the procedural exclusivity principle is the consent of the parties. As announced by Lord Diplock in **O'Reilly v Mackman [1983]** 2 AC 237, where the parties to a case jointly agree that a remedy can be sought under ordinary private procedures, the principle of procedural exclusivity cannot be applied against their will.

Standing in judicial review

The question here is to determine who can seek judicial review? A claimant should have sufficient interest in judicial review. This is the traditional *locus standi* which is one of the first requirements for introducing any legal proceedings. Section 31(3) of the Senior Courts Act 1981 stipulates that: "The court shall not grant leave unless it considers that the applicant has sufficient interest in the matter to which the application relates".

General principle: In complex cases on judicial review, standing may be assessed at the substantive hearing together with the merits.

IRC v National Federation of Self-Employed and Small Businesses [1982] AC 617
Facts: A national organization representing small businesses sought judicial review on the Inland Revenue's treatment of a category of workers that were given amnesty of past tax. The organization argued that this treatment was unlawful as it constituted discrimination between taxpayers. The Court of Appeal considered that they had standing.
Ratio: The House of Lords held that the organization had no standing to seek judicial review, thereby overturning the Court of Appeal's findings. It noted that a mere body of taxpayers did not have sufficient interest in asking the Court to investigate the tax affairs' of other taxpayers. As Lord Scarman stated: "It is wrong in law, as I understand the cases, for the court to attempt an assessment of the sufficiency of an

applicant's interest without regard to the matter of his complaint. If he fails to show, when he applies for leave, a prima facie case, or reasonable grounds for believing that there has been a failure of public duty, the court would be in error if it granted leave".

Application: In this case, the House of Lords made a distinction between the assessment of the standing of simple cases that can be definitively decided at leave stage and more complex cases which require an assessment when full factual and legal information about the case is available.

Individuals

Two categories of individuals may seek judicial review. The first category is individuals who are directly affected by a public law decision. Standing raises no issue where a decision was taken following an individual request of the claimant. For instance, where a public body refuses a construction permit for the claimant, they will have no difficulty to prove that they have been directly affected by this decision. However, individual "busybodies" (for example a friend who is upset on the claimant's behalf) cannot pretend to have been directly affected by the decision. The second category is an exception to this rule.

General principle: Individuals with a genuine public or constitutional interest in actions of a public body may have standing to challenge it in judicial review.

R v Secretary of State for Foreign and Commonwealth Affairs, ex parte Rees-Mogg [1995] 1 W.L.R. 386

Facts: A peer in the House of Lords, also former editor of an important Newspaper having written multiple articles on European affairs, sought to challenge in judicial review the decision of the Foreign Secretary to ratify the Maastricht Treaty. The question of standing arose.

Ratio: The House of Lords rejected the claimant's arguments on the merits. However, it accepted that the claimant had standing to challenge the decision as an individual with a genuine constitutional interest. As Lord LJ noted: "we accept without question that Lord Rees-Mogg brings the proceedings because of his sincere concern for constitutional issues".

Application: This second category of individuals who may seek judicial review is an exception to the busybodies' rule. Where claimants cannot demonstrate that they had been directly affected by a public law decision, they can submit that they had a constitutional interest in challenging such a decision.

In the context of genuine public interest see **R (Feakins) v Secretary of State for the Environment, Food and Rural Affairs [2003]** EWCA Civ 1546, where Dyson LJ considered that "if a claimant has no sufficient private interest to support a claim to standing, then he should not be accorded standing merely because he raises an issue in which there is, objectively speaking, a public interest".

It should be noted that Section 6(1) of the Human Rights Act 1998 creates a new head of incompatibility with human rights in judicial review proceedings, where standing is established if the claimant proves to be a "victim" for the purposes of Section 7 of the HRA.

Groups and organizations

Groups and organisations include *inter alia* associations, federations, foundations, NGOs, and pressure or interest groups. As for individuals, groups or organisations having standing in judicial review are divided into two categories. They are recognised bodies who are not only acting in their own interest but rather for the general public interest.

The first category of groups having standing in judicial review is composed of groups acting on behalf of the public interest. On this issue there had been jurisprudential debates over the appreciation of the action of such groups on behalf of the public interest when introducing judicial review proceedings.

General principle: Individuals who have no standing to challenge a public law decision cannot pretend to acquire it just because they formed themselves into a group or a company.

R v Secretary of State for the Environment, ex parte Rose Theatre Trust Co Ltd [1990] 1 QB 504

Facts: An interest group sought judicial review of a decision refusing to schedule a theatre as an ancient monument. The group consisted of people with expertise in archaeology, theatre, literature, and other fields, and also included local councillors and an MP.

Ratio: The Court held that the claimant had no standing in judicial review as members of the public in general had insufficient interest in challenging the refusal of scheduling the building in judicial review. Schiemann J held that individuals who did not have standing would not gain it just because they formed themselves into a group or a company in order, as he saw it, to engineer this status.

Application: In this case, the Court adopted a quite restrictive approach to standing which has been heavily criticised following this judgement. Its authority should be assessed globally together with later case-law.

General principle: An organization may have standing where in the absence of its involvement in the proceedings, the people it represents might not have an effective way of bringing the disputed issues to court.

R v Secretary of State for the Environment, ex parte Greenpeace Ltd (No 2) [1994] 4 All ER 329
Facts: Greenpeace, a well-known NGO advocating for environmental protection sought judicial review to challenge decisions to vary authorisations concerning radioactive waste in Cumbria. The question of standing arose.

Ratio: The claimant was granted standing by the Court. It noted that the pressure group was a well-established organisation protecting the environment and noted that it had 2500 members in the region affected by the public law decision. The court's view was that, without Greenpeace's involvement, the people it represented might not have had an effective way of bringing the disputed issues to court. Individual members of the organization did not have the same expertise as the organization. Claims brought individually would have resulted on far less well-informed challenges of the decision.

Application: In this case, the Court adopted a rather liberal approach on standing. In the further development of case-law on this issue, this approach has been quite predominant (see, for example, **R v Secretary of State for Foreign and Commonwealth Affairs, ex parte World Development Movement Ltd [1995]** 1 WLR 386).

The second category of groups that has standing in judicial review is groups acting on behalf of the interests of its members. These groups include trade unions, professional bodies or associations representing residents of a neighbour-hood.

Public bodies

Noteworthy, not only private persons can bring proceedings in judicial review against public law decisions but also public bodies. There are multiple examples in the courts case-law including a local government against a decision from a central authority or a Police department against a decision of the Magistrates' Court (see **R (Chief Constable of Great Manchester Police) v Salford Magistrates Court and Hookway [2011]** EWHC 1578).

Time limit

Part 54.5(1) of the CPR provides that: "a claim must be filed (a) promptly and (b) in any event no later than 3 months after the grounds to make the claim first arose". The time limit for bringing a judicial review complaint is short and strictly applied. Part 54.5(2) of the CPR stipulates that time cannot be extended by agreement between the parties.

The time limit is not particularly short compared to other European countries. For example, in France, the time limit to bring a *recours pour excès de pouvoir* before administrative courts is two months. This requirement of promptness ensures good administration. The administration cannot function properly if its actions are eternally challengeable before the courts.As a consequence, judicial review can sometimes be rejected because it was not filed promptly. However, under Section 26(1) of the Senior Courts Act 1981, a Court may only do so if it *"considers that the granting of the relief sought would be likely to cause substantial hardship to, or substantially prejudice the rights of, any person or would be detrimental to good administration"*.

Since 2013 and following the 4th Amendment of the Civil Procedure, special rules regarding time limit for judicial review apply to planning decisions (6 weeks) and public procurement (30 days).

Ouster Clauses

An ouster clause is a provision included in a piece of legislation to exclude judicial review of acts and decisions of the executive. As result, the clause strips the courts of their supervisory judicial function over disputed action of a public body. Courts are generally reluctant to enforce such clauses considering that it represents a threat to the Rule of law.

General principle: Total ouster clauses are to be construed as narrowly as possible.

Anisminic v Foreign Compensation Commission [1969] 2 AC 137

Facts: The Foreign Compensation Act 1950 provided that determinations of the Foreign Compensation Commission (FCC) "shall not be called into question in any court of law". The claimant sought judicial review of a determination of the FCC, on the ground of illegality.

Ratio: The House of Lords held that the ouster clause did not prevent the claimant from challenging the decision under judicial review. It noted that Ouster clauses (like those in the Foreign Compensation Act 1950) had to be construed as narrowly as possible such that the claim was not barred.

Application: The decision illustrates the courts' reluctance to give effect to any legislative provision that attempts to exclude their jurisdiction in judicial review. Even when such exclusion is relatively clearly worded, courts will generally hold that it does not preclude them from scrutinising the legality of the decision.

Partial ouster clauses on time limit are generally accepted. They provide that for a specific action of a public body, the time limit for challenging it under judicial review is shorter than the normal time limit of 3 months. In this respect, the Section 54.5(3) Civil Procedure Rule provides that the normal time limit does "not apply when any other enactment specifies a shorter time limit for making the claim for judicial review".

Exhaustion of Alternative Remedies

The exhaustion of alternative remedies is another requirement for a judicial review application to be amenable.

General principle: In principle, judicial review is not granted if an alternative remedy is available to the claimant.

R v Inland Revenue Commissioners, ex parte Preston [1985] AC 835

Facts: The applicant was involved in a tax dispute with the Inland Revenue Commission. His claims were rejected in first instance. In most cases, the remedy of a taxpayer lies in the appeal procedures provided by the tax statutes. However, he decided to bring a claim under judicial review. The Court had to determine if this was possible.

Ratio: The House of Lords granted judicial review considering that the appeal procedure did not operate in the circumstances of his case. However, it emphasised that the taxpayer is expected to use the appeal procedure, where it is available, rather than resort to judicial review.

Application: When appreciating the admissibility of a judicial review application, one has to look at the alternative legal remedies available to the claimant. All of them should be exhausted or unavailable for a case to be amenable under judicial review.

Procedure in Judicial Review

The claimant (formerly the applicant) for judicial review, before bringing his case to the Court, should try to achieve a settlement with the public body. The Pre-action protocol requires the claimant to first write to the future defendant identifying the issues at stake. The claim for should be transmitted to the Court containing the public law decision being challenged and the remedy sought.

The second phase of the procedure is permission to apply for judicial review. This is a filtering system which requires claimants to ask the Court for permission to apply. In practice, permission is granted to arguable cases. Indeed, it is a first *prima facie* assessment of the merits of a case. If the permission is rejected, the claimant can request reconsideration at an "oral renewal". If this is again rejected, the claimant can appeal to the Court of Appeal.

Most of the cases are rejected at the permission stage. In 2015, the Ministry of justice said that: "The proportion of all cases lodged found in favour of the claimant at a final hearing has reduced (...) to 1% in 2013 and has remained the same in 2014". However, it should be noted that it also reported that the vast majority of cases that settled (before the permission at the pre-action stage) did so in favour of claimants.

The final stage, the substantive hearing, enables the Court to assess whether or not the defendant has infringed one or more of the grounds of judicial review. The assessment of the grounds of review will be studied in the next chapters. It should be noted, however, that it rests on the claimant to prove that the defendant has acted unlawfully.

Summary

- Judicial review is often seen as the major way in which the legality of administrative action is controlled. It is the cornerstone of administrative law. Judicial review is the mechanism by which the courts are able to scrutinise the decision-making processes and the legality of actions or decisions taken by public authorities and officials.

- The Rule of law imposes on rulers to respect and act in compliance with law. Accordingly, the *rationale* behind judicial review stems from the core principles of the Rule of law.

- The purpose of judicial review was not to question a decision itself. Courts should not serve as appellate jurisdictions but rather as operators of a review of the legality of decision-making processes.

- As a general rule, only public law decisions are amenable to judicial review. Judicial review can be brought against any public body, regardless of their rank in the hierarchy of the administration.

- Judicial review also represents a possible course of legal action against decisions of non-governmental bodies exercising public law powers. Powers which are sufficiently public in nature are powers that the administration of the State would have to exercise in the absence of performance by a private body.

- A claimant should have sufficient interest in judicial review. This is the traditional *locus standi* which is one of the first requirements for introducing any legal proceedings. Individuals, groups and public bodies may have sufficient interest to seek judicial review.

- The exclusivity principle provides that public law rights should be enforced through judicial review. This principle is subject exception is subject to several exceptions which allows for a flexible application.

- In principle, judicial review is not granted if an alternative remedy is available to the claimant.

- The time limit to bring a judicial review is 3 months after the grounds to make the claim first arose. Since 2013 and following the 4th Amendment of the Civil Procedure, special rules regarding time limit for judicial review apply to planning decisions (6 weeks) and public procurement (30 days).

- The Pre-action protocol requires the claimant to first write to the future defendant identifying the issues at stake in order to try to achieve a settlement. The second phase of the procedure is permission to apply for judicial review.

Chapter 16 – Grounds of Judicial Review: Illegality

Introduction to Grounds of Judicial Review

Traditionally, the notion of grounds of judicial review refers to the legal arguments, generally accepted by common law, to challenge a public law decision. In practice, they will be invoked by the claimant seeking judicial review. A stated earlier, it rests on the claimant to demonstrate that the defendant acted unlawfully. For example, the claimant will argue that the decision is unlawful on the ground of illegality or procedural impropriety. It should be noted that a judicial review claim can be based on several grounds. Judicial review can be sought on different grounds. We will focus on Illegality in this chapter but other grounds of judicial review such as Unreasonableness/Irrationality (Chapter 17), Procedural Impropriety (Chapter 18) and Legitimate Expectation (Chapter 19) will also be studied.

Lord Diplock, in the CGHQ case (**Council of Civil Service Unions v Minister for the Civil Service [1985]** AC 374) identified three grounds: "The first ground I would call illegality, the second irrationality and the third procedural impropriety". However, this list has never been devised to be exhaustive. Accordingly, the ground of legitimate expectations arose along with the important evolution of judicial review in the last decades. Traditionally, grounds of judicial review are divided between two categories: substantive judicial review (illegality, irrationality and legitimate expectations) and procedural judicial review (procedural impropriety).

The ground of illegality

The Rule of law imposes on rulers to respect and act in compliance with law. As a result, for example, those exercising power can only act on the basis of a legal provision, subjected to the will and limited to the terms provided for by Parliament, as a justification for their action. The ground of illegality is the perfect example to the most this idea. It ensures that the exercise of power is confined within the limits afforded by law.

Lord Diplock, in the CGHQ case stated that: "By "illegality" as a ground for judicial review, I mean that the decision-maker must understand correctly the law that regulates his decision-making powers and must give effect to it". Accordingly, the ground of illegality is mainly concerned with the misinterpretation or wrongful application of public law powers.

However, this ground is by no means merely limited to the assessment of whether or not a public power existed as to entitle the decision maker to act. Indeed, when appreciating the illegality of a decision, one should for example look at: whether the decision-maker acted beyond their powers, in abuse of discretion, for an improper purpose, whether the power was wrongfully delegated or whether the public law decision constituted a breach of the ECHR.

Simple illegality - the Doctrine of *Ultra Vires*

The doctrine of *ultra vires* refers to public law decisions actions exceeding powers conferred by law. Conversely, a decision maker acting *intra vires* acts within the limits of his powers. The notion of *ultra vires* is associated to the doctrine of Parliamentary sovereignty. The executive should act within the limits of the powers conferred by Parliament. Accordingly when assessing whether a decision maker has acted *ultra vires* one has to look at Parliament's will. For example, a police officer acts *ultra vires* when he arrests someone for a minor offence without having the power to do so.

General principle: When interpreting Parliament's will to confer powers to the executive, it should be presumed that Parliament did not intend to authorise the infringement of fundamental or constitutional rights except if it is expressly authorised by statute.

R v Secretary of State for the Home Department, ex parte Leech (No 2), [1994] QB 198
Facts: Prison rules permitted interception of prisoners'

correspondence including letters with their lawyers. The Prison Rules 1964, r 33(3) allowed the prison governor to stop the letters of inordinate length or those that were "objectionable". The claimant sought judicial review arguing that the fact that correspondence with lawyers during pending cases was also stopped constituted an action *ultra vires*.

Ratio: The Court of Appeal declared that the application of Prison Rule 33 to correspondence between prisoners and lawyers concerning pending trials was *ultra vires*. It noted that it could not have been Parliament's intention to infringe with prisoners' access to Court via their lawyers. This interfered with a constitutional right to the free flow of communications between a solicitor and a client about contemplated legal proceedings. The interference could only be authorised by express words in the statute or by necessary implication.

Application: In this case, the Court stressed that a statute providing a public body with public law powers cannot be interpreted as to authorise infringements of constitutional rights (unless Parliament expressly intended it).

General principle: A statutory power to provide residents of a local council with facilities to wash their clothes does not allow for the establishment of a commercial laundry service.

Attorney General v Fulham Corporation [1921] Ch 44

Facts: In this case, a local authority had the power to provide wash-houses for residents to wash their clothes in under the Wash-houses Acts 1846-78. The local authority created a laundry with employees, paid by the customers, who washed their clothes. The claimant argued that this was *ultra vires*.

Ratio: The Court held that the local council acted *ultra vires*. It recalled that the defendant, a statutory body, was to be restrained from acting outside its powers. The Court considered that the Wash-houses Acts 1846-78 only permitted the local council to provide washhouses for residents where they could use the facility to wash their own clothes, not to create a laundry business where employees were paid by the customers.

Application: This old case provides an illustrative example of simple illegality which basically means that the defendant acted beyond the boundaries of his powers as determined by statute.

General principle: Although in principle a public body may not do what is not expressly authorised by statute, courts accept such conducts where they are fairly incidental to these powers.

Attorney-General v Crayford Urban District Council [1962] 2 All ER 147

Facts: A district council had arrangements with an insurance company for council tenants. This payment for insurance was collected together with the council rent. It was argued that the council had no legal power to arrange insurance with a private insurance company for council tenants and collect the money for the company.

Ratio: The Court of Appeal held that the Council acted *intra vires* under general acts of management within the scope of Section 111 of the Housing Act 1957. It noted that the Council, by facilitating insurance of the effects of the council tenants, was somehow ensuring that the rents could be paid in case of fire or storm. Making sure that council tenants were paying their rent was part of its mission therefore it acted within the limits of its powers.

Application: In this case, the Court limited the strict approach adopted in previous cases. It stressed that in order to function properly; public bodies should enjoy a certain margin of appreciation.

Wrongful delegation of power

As a general constitutional rule, where a public body is empowered to take a decision, it should not delegate this power to another body. The rationale behind this rule relies on the fact that the delegation would, in essence, go against Parliament's will, which decided to confer this power to a particular body. As a consequence of wrongful delegation, the empowered public body does not fulfil its obligation and the wrong person in law is exercising public law powers.

The delegation of power is not an issue when the enabling Act of Parliament expressly provides that the power can be delegated.

For example, Section 101 of the Local Government Act 1972 authorises local authorities to delegate some of their functions to committees, council officers or other local authorities.

General principle: Judicial or quasi-judicial public powers affecting a person's rights cannot be delegated to other public bodies if not expressly authorised by law.

Barnard v National Dock Labour Board [1953] 2 QB 18

Facts: The Dock Workers Order 1947 established the National Dock Labour Board and expressly authorised the delegation of disciplinary powers such as the suspension of dock workers to local dock boards. The claimant had been suspended by the secretary of a local board and argued that this decision was *ultra vires*. The secretary of the local board agrees that this power had been delegated to him by the local board.

Ratio: The Court of Appeal held that the power of suspension was a quasi-judicial power that could not be delegated by a local board to its secretary. It noted that decision which affected person's rights could not be delegated if not expressly authorised by law. Therefore the decision to suspend the claimant taken by the local board was unlawful and was declared a nullity.

Application: In this case, the Court of Appeal applied the traditional principle that powers should not be delegated unless it is expressly authorised by law.

The Carltona principle

General principle: Regarding delegation of power in central government, ministers are presumed, in the absence of evidence to the contrary, allowed to delegate powers to civil servants within their departments, even if the law does not expressly authorise it.

Carltona v Commissioners of Works [1943] 2 All ER 560

Facts: The claimants owned a factory which was to be requisitioned. They sought a judicial review of the lawfulness of the order making the requisition, arguing that the power of requisition derived from the 1939 Regulations had been implemented not by the Minister as required, but by an official within the Ministry of Works and Planning. They relied on the general principle providing that delegation is only possible where expressly allowed by law.

Ratio: The Court dismissed the claimants' arguments considering that that civil servants acted not on behalf of but in the name of their ministers. Accordingly, the requisition of the civil servant was not a delegated act; it was the act of the Minister himself. In the words of Lord Green MR: "The functions which are given to ministers are functions so multifarious that no minister could ever personally attend to them. (…) The duties imposed upon ministers and the powers given to ministers are normally exercised under the authority of ministers by responsible officials of the department. Public business could not be carried on if that were not the case. Constitutionally, the decision of such an official is, of course, the decision of the minister. The minister is responsible".

Application: It should be however noted that the well known Carltona principle only applies to central government. As noted above, the delegation of local governance is regulated by the Local Government Act 1972.

The limits to the Carltona principle

First of all Carltona principle will logically not apply where statute, expressly or by necessary implication, makes it clear that the power must be exercised by the minister in person. In addition, this principle is limited by other exceptions.

General principle: In order for the Carltona principle to apply, there should be a sufficient degree of accountability and proximity in the relationship between the Minister and the relevant official making the decision.

R (Bourgass) v Secretary of State for Justice [2015] UKSC 54
Facts: The claimants, prisoners, sought judicial review against a decision by the prison authorities to submit individual inmates to long periods of solitary confinement. Prison Rule 45(2) requires that a prisoner shall not be removed under this rule for a period of more than 72 hours without the authority of the Secretary of State.
Ratio: The Supreme Court held that the action was not rightfully delegated to the prison services which were not

sufficiently accountable to the Secretary of State. There was an insufficiently close link between the prison authorities and the Secretary of State. Therefore the prison services could not order the solitary confinement of inmates for long periods without the authorisation of the public body initially empowered by law to take such a decision.

Application: In this case, the Supreme Court laid down an exception to the Carltona principle. This principle is only applicable where there is a close link of accountability between the Minister and his or her civil servants working in his department. This criterion is not satisfied where the alleged delegation took place between the Secretary of State and prison services.

Abuse of discretion

Public law discretion conferred by law to decision-makers should not be abused. Fettering discretion, taking irrelevant factors into account or ignoring relevant factors affect the legality of a public law decision. Although by definition discretion implies a margin of appreciation which is necessary for deciding, it does not mean that it is completely free from any judicial control. In this respect, on the basis of judicial review, courts will be reluctant to recognize absolute discretions.

Fettering of discretion

Public bodies conferred with public law discretions should exercise them rather than restricting themselves. In other words, in certain circumstances, exercising discretion may become a duty.

General principle: The statutory discretion to set a date for the implementation of an enacted Act of Parliament imposes a continuing obligation to consider bringing it into force and cannot be fettered.

R v Secretary of State for Home Department ex p Fire Brigades Union [1995] 2 All ER 244

Facts: This case concerned the use of prerogative powers by the Home Secretary to introduce a criminal injuries compensation scheme. More precisely, the Home Secretary refused to consider whether to bring the statutory criminal injuries compensation scheme (enacted in 1988) into force.

Ratio: The House of Lords ruled that using prerogative power, while refusing to implement a statutory scheme which had been enacted in an Act of Parliament was unconstitutional because it infringed Parliament's will. It noted that the statutory discretion to set a date for the implementation of an enacted Act of Parliament imposed a continuing obligation to consider bringing it into force and could not be fettered.

Application: In this case, the House of Lords stressed that a discretion conferred to a public body may imply a duty to exercise it, especially when it relates to implementing Parliament's will.

General principle: The discretion of pursuing or not an important investigation m   y be be justified by wider public considerations such as national security or diplomatic interests.

R (Corner House Research) v Director of the Serious Fraud Office [2008] UKHL 60

Facts: The Director of the Serious Fraud Office decided to halt investigations into allegations of bribery in relation to arms contracts with Saudi Arabia for reasons related to national security and diplomatic interests. The Administrative Court had declared the decision unlawful for having fettered a public law discretion.

Ratio: The House of Lords reversed the decision of first instance considering that the Director legitimately decided that the public interest in pursuing an important investigation into alleged bribery was outweighed by wider public considerations of national security and diplomatic interests. Lord Bingham concluded that: "The Director was confronted by an ugly and obviously unwelcome threat. He had to decide what, if anything, he should do. He did not surrender his discretionary power of decision to any third party, although he did consult the most expert source available to him in the person of the Ambassador and he did, as he was entitled if not bound to do, consult the Attorney General who, however, properly left the decision to him".

Application: The House of Lords, by reversing the Administrative Court's decision, held that the discretion of not pursuing an important investigation could be justified by wider public considerations.

General principle: The rigid or blanket exercise of a discretion that binds a decision-maker, resulting on the outcome of a particular case being decided in advance or without proper consideration, may constitute an abuse of discretion.

R v Secretary for the Environment, ex parte Brent LBC, [1983] 3 All ER 321
Facts: This case concerned a refusal by the Secretary of State to hear further representations from local authorities with regard to their rate support grants.
Ratio: The Court held that the exercise Secretary of State's discretion was abused as it constituted a blanket rule resulting on the outcome of a particular case being decided in advance or without proper consideration. It concluded that: "it would of course have been unrealistic not to accept that it is certainly probably that, if the representations had been listened to by the Secretary of State, he would have nevertheless have adhered to his policy (…) we are not prepared to hold that it would have been a useless formality for the Secretary of State to have listened to the representations".
Application: It should be remembered from this case that public bodies generally have a duty to listen to relevant actors before taking a decision. Lord Reid puts it **in British Oxygen v Board of Trade [1971]** AC 610: *"What the authority must not do is to refuse to listen at all"*.

Irrelevant and relevant factors

A public law decision may be unlawful because its author took into account irrelevant factors. This irregularity may constitute an abuse of discretion.

General principle: When exercising a public law discretion, there are considerations to which regard must be had and other considerations to which regard must not be had.

R v Somerset County Council, ex parte Fewings [1995] 3 All ER 20
Facts: The claimants sought judicial review of a decision from a

local council to ban deer hunting. The local council viewed the activity as morally repulsive.

Ratio: At the first instance level, the Divisional Court held the decision to be unlawful as, in the words of Lords LJ "the councillor's moral view on hunting" were irrelevant factors. The Court of Appeal confirmed this decision on different grounds. However, Simon Brown LJ, dissenting, stated that: "It is important to bear in mind (...) that there are in fact three categories of consideration. First, those clearly (whether expressly or impliedly) identified by the statute as considerations to which regard must be had. Second, those clearly identified by the statute as considerations to which regard must not be had. Third, those to which the decision-maker may have regard if in his judgment and discretion he thinks it right to do so. There is, in short, a margin of appreciation within which the decision-maker may decide just what considerations should play a part in his reasoning process".

Application: Regarding the authority of this case, one should bear in mind that the findings of Lords LJ on the irrelevancy of certain factors were not upheld by the Court of Appeal. Nevertheless this case teaches us that a sort of control from the courts is exercised over factors that are relevant and irrelevant for a decision maker when adopting a public law decision.

General principle: In some cases, the failure to take into account a relevant factor may result on the unlawfulness of a public law decision.

R v Immigration Appeal Tribunal, ex parte Singh [1986] 1 WLR 910

Facts: The claimant challenged the decision of an immigration adjudicator to deport him to his home country. The claimant was a musician who performed functions as a priest in a Sikh community. He claimed that he was active in the local community and that his deportation would negatively impact upon the community.

Ratio: The House of Lords held that the decision was unlawful as the immigration adjudicator failed to take into account the relevant factor of third parties' interest in the deportation of the claimant. It considered that the deportation of the claimant

would negatively impact upon the local Sikh community. Accordingly the immigration adjudicator's decision was unlawful for abuse of discretion.

Application: In its judgement, the House of Lords enshrined the opposite cornerstone to **R v Somerset County Council, ex parte Fewings [1995]** 3 All ER 20. Accordingly, a public law decision may be unlawful because the decision had taken irrelevant factors but also because of failure to take into account relevant factors.

Improper purpose

A decision maker acts illegally if he uses a power conferred to him by Parliament for a particular purpose pursuing a different objective. In the words of Fordham, an improper motive is "where the decision-maker was motivated by some aim or purpose regarded by the law as illegitimate".

General principle: Powers conferred on public bodies should be exercised to promote the object and policy of the Act as expressed by Parliament's intention.

Padfield v Minister of Agriculture [1968] 1 All ER 694

Facts: Under the Agricultural Marketing Act 1958 the minister had a power to refer complaints to a committee of investigation. The claimants made such a request and the minister decided to refuse because he believed he could be embarrassed by an unfavourable report. The claimants sought judicial review against this decision and argued that this decision was driven by an improper purpose.

Ratio: The House of Lords held that the impugned decision was unlawful because the minister's discretion was exercised for a wrongful or improper purpose. It noted that the said discretion was not unlimited and was conferred on him to promote the object and policy of Parliament's intention which was expressed through the Agricultural Marketing Act 1958. According to Lord Reid: 3The Minister's discretion must be conferred from a construction of the Act read as whole, and for the reasons I have given it would infer that the discretion (...) has been used by the Minister in a manner which is not in accordance with intentions of the statute which conferred it".

Application: In this case, the House of Lords emphasised that public bodies, when exercising their powers, should respect the purpose for which their powers were conferred on them by Parliament.

General principle: The purpose of the power conferred by Parliament to the Home Office to revoke TV licenses is not to make revenue but rather to ensure that licences are not fraudulently used or obtained.

Congreve v Home Office, [1976] QB 629

Facts: In this case, the cost of colour television increased and the applicant, in order to avoid paying more, renewed his licence in advance. The Home Office informed him that unless he paid the difference, his licence would be revoked allegedly exercising its powers under the Wireless Telegraphy Act 1949. The claimant sought judicial review arguing that the purpose of the power to revoke licenses, as intended by Parliament, was not commercial and the impugned decision was thereby unlawful.

Ratio: The Court of Appeal held that the demand for payment was an unlawful exercise of power. It stated that the implied purpose of the power to revoke television licences was not to raise revenue, but rather to ensure that such licences were not wrongfully used or obtained.

Application: In this case, the Court of Appeal emphasised that where a statute does not clearly indicate its purpose, courts should look at the statute as a whole to extract from it an implicit purpose.

Errors of law: Misinterpreting the Law

The courts review errors of law which derive from the misinterpretation or misunderstanding by a public body of its statutory powers to act. Examples of such errors include the wrongful interpretation of a word of the statute and its legal meaning. Errors of law are not restricted to the mere determination of whether or not a public power existed (also known as questions of jurisdiction).

General principle: A public body that wrongfully applies rules of a scheme that it should implement and misunderstands their meaning commits an error of law.

Anisminic v Foreign Compensation Commission [1969] 2 AC 137

Facts: The Foreign Compensation Act 1950 authorised the Foreign Compensation Commission (FCC) to decide on compensation claims of companies that were nationalised after the Suez conflict of 1956. The claimant's application for compensation was rejected. It consequently sought judicial review of this determination of the FCC, on the ground of illegality.

Ratio: The House of Lords held that the Commission, by misunderstanding the rules of the scheme that it had to apply, committed an error of law. The determination in the claimant's case was unlawful and therefore it had to be quashed. The House of Lords held this solution despite of an ouster clause, which did not prevent the claimant from challenging the decision under judicial review.

Application: This case is a traditional example of error of law where the application of a rule results on a wrongful interpretation. There is an error of law where it can be demonstrated that the public body misunderstood the intended meaning of a rule and subsequently applied it.

General principle: All errors that are decisive to a decision, in other words but for the error concerned the decision would have been different, are potentially reviewable by the courts. However, where the decision-maker is interpreting some special system of rules, courts will generally be reluctant to intervene.

R v Lord President of the Privy Council, ex parte Page [1993] 1 All ER 97

Facts: The claimant was made redundant by a decision to close the Philosophy department of a University. She sought judicial review against this decision. The question that arose was whether this decision was reviewable by the courts.

Ratio: The House of Lords held that decisions of University Visitors are subject to judicial review in that they exercise a public function. English law no longer draws a distinction between jurisdictional errors of law and non-jurisdictional errors of law. However, in the present case the decision-maker was interpreting some special system of rules, therefore the House of Lords decided not to declare it unlawful.

Application: In this case, even though it appears at first that the House of Lords extended the scope of the control over errors of law, it also laid down limitations on the types of errors that are not reviewable.

General principle: Where the power granted can be interpreted in a range of different ways, the courts will not necessarily declare the impugned decision unlawful just because they would have come to a different view that of the decision-maker.

R v Monopolies Commission ex p South Yorkshire Transport Ltd [1993] 1 All ER 289
Facts: A local Commission was provided with a power to intervene in trade regulation if the monopoly concerned an area involved which was sufficiently substantial to cause concern that it may operate against the public interest. In this case, a bus company took over another, giving it an effective monopoly within the region. The exact wording of the statute to be interpreted was "a substantial part of the United Kingdom".
Ratio: The House of Lords allowed the Appeal. It considered that the right construction of the phrase "a substantial part of the UK" involved not necessarily a large part, but rather a part of considerable importance and character. Lord Mustill noted that the wording of the statute was very imprecise and stated that in such situations the Court should not intervene unless the decision-maker's conclusion was irrational.
Application: It should be noted that courts will be reluctant to quash public law decisions and impose a particular interpretation where the wording of the statute was imprecise and could lead to a wide range of different interpretations.

Errors of appreciation of the facts

In principle, judges will not interfere with the appreciation of facts as interpreted by the decision maker. If a public body gets factual details wrong, courts are reluctant to impose their view as they are only experts of law and not experts of facts. In addition to this, the procedure of judicial review is not adapted to the investigation of disputed fact given that judges make a limited use of cross-examination. However, there are some exceptions for which some errors of facts will be reviewable by the courts.

Precedent facts

Also known "jurisdictional facts", are facts that are necessary in their existence for the public body to act. They have to be established before the public body can act, therefore they are a central component of the decision-making process.

General principle: In order to exercise the power to detain an illegal entrant, under statute, it should be established that the detainee illegally entered the country. The error on such a precedent fact is reviewable by the courts.

R v Secretary of State for the Home Department, ex parte Khawaja, [1984] HL 10 Feb 1983
Facts: The appellant was detained as an illegal immigrant under the Immigration Act 1971 which imposed that only "illegal entrant" could be detained. He claimed that there was an error of fact and that he did not enter the territory illegally.
Ratio: The House of Lord held that the determination of whether or not the appellant entered illegally the territory was a precedent fact which had to be established for the power to detain to arise in the first place. It noted that when reviewing the decision of the immigration officer, courts should go beyond asking only whether there was evidence on which the officer could have reached his decision, and look also at the sufficiency of that evidence. On a judicial review it was for the administrative authority to prove the facts upon which the decision it had reached had been made.
Application: This case is a traditional example of an error on a precedent fact which has a major influence in an individual's rights. It should be noted that these cases are quite rare because they imply an obvious error of facts which is potentially possible but not very frequent in practice

Facts which have no supporting evidence

Errors of facts traditionally include situations where a public body makes a decision regarding a fact for which there obviously no objective supporting evidence. In this area, one of landmark cases is **Coleen Properties v Minister of Health and Local Government [1971]** 1 WLR 433.

General principle: A decision based upon a supposition which is not supported by any evidence may be reviewed by the courts as an error of facts.

Secretary of State for Education v Tameside MBC, [1977] AC 1014

Facts: This case concerned a decision by the Secretary of State to prohibit the re-introduction of grammar schools. The Secretary of State argued that this would lead to educational chaos and undue disruption (because of the shortage of time in which to bring in the new policy). This decision was challenged under judicial review on the basis that the minister's assumption of chaos and disruption was not supported by any evidence.

Ratio: The House of Lords held that the decision of the Secretary of State was unlawful because it was based on a fact which was not supported by any evidence but was merely based upon a supposition. It considered that the Secretary of State had either misunderstood or was not informed as to the nature and effect of the professional educational advice available to the local education authority and had wrongly jumped to conclusions. As Lord Wilberforce stated: "If a judgment requires, before it can be made, the existence of some facts, then, although the evaluation of those facts is for the Secretary of State alone, the court must inquire whether those facts exist, and have been taken into account, whether the judgment has been made upon a proper self-direction as to those facts, and whether the judgment has not been made upon other facts which ought not to have been taken into account".

Application: It should be noted that the control of courts over these matters remains very exceptional. The courts' intervention will require a demonstration of the obviously wrongful nature of the error and its decisive impact on the decision.

Breaches of the ECHR

It should be noted that Section 6(1) of the Human Rights Act 1998 created a new head of incompatibility with human rights in judicial review proceedings under the ground of illegality. However, claims related to breaches of the right to a fair hearing will rather be argued under the ground of procedural impropriety. Public bodies are required to act in compliance with the European Convention on Human Rights. Accordingly, a public law decision that would infringe a Convention right is unlawful and should be declared null by the courts. In such situations, standing is established if the claimant proves to be a "victim" for the purposes of Section 7 of the HRA.

General principle: A public law decision which infringes a Convention right is unlawful by virtue of Section 6 of the Human Rights Act.

R (BBC) v Secretary of State for Justice [2012] EWHC 13 (Admin)

Facts: The claimant, the BBC, sought judicial review against the refusal from the Secretary of State to allow an interview with a prisoner. The claimant argued that this decision was unlawful for illegality as it violated its right under Article 10 of the Convention.

Ratio: The Court held that the decision to refuse the access to the prison was an illegitimate interference with the claimant's freedom of expression under Article 10 of the Convention. Accordingly, it was unlawful by virtue of Section 6 of the Human Rights Act.

Application: This case is an example of judicial review on the ground of illegality of a public law decision infringing the European Convention on Human Rights. Following the entry into force of the HRA in 1998, there had been numerous similar cases in the UK courts case law.

Summary

- Traditionally, the notion of grounds of judicial review refers to the legal arguments, generally accepted by common law, to challenge a public law decision. In practice, they will be invoked by the claimant seeking judicial review. Judicial review can be sought on different grounds.
- The Rule of law imposes on rulers to respect and act in compliance with law. The ground of illegality is the

perfect example to the most this idea. It ensures that the exercise of power is confined within the limits afforded by law.

- The doctrine of *ultra vires* refers to public law decisions actions exceeding powers conferred by law. For example, a police officer acts *ultra vires* when he arrests someone for a minor offence without having the power to do so.

- As a general constitutional rule, where a public body is empowered to take a decision, it should not delegate this power to another body. However, the delegation of power within central government, from ministers to civil servants within their departments is allowed, even if the law does not expressly authorise it.

- Public law discretion conferred by law to decision-makers should not be abused. Fettering discretion, taking irrelevant factors into account or ignoring relevant factors can affect the legality of a public law decision.

- A public law decision may be unlawful because its author took into account irrelevant factors. This irregularity may constitute an abuse of discretion.

- A decision maker acts illegally if he uses a power conferred to him by Parliament for a particular purpose pursuing a different objective.

- The courts review errors of law which derive from the misinterpretation or misunderstanding by a public body of its statutory powers to act. However, errors of law are not restricted to the mere determination of whether or not a public power existed (also known as questions of jurisdiction).

- In principle, judges will not interfere with the appreciation of facts as interpreted by the decision maker. However, there are some exceptions for which some errors of facts will be reviewable by the courts. For example, precedent facts have to be established before the public body can act, therefore they are a central component of the decision-making process. Errors of facts ALSO traditionally include situations where a public body makes a decision regarding a fact for which there obviously no objective supporting evidence.

- Section 6(1) of the Human Rights Act 1998 created a new head of incompatibility with human rights in judicial review proceedings under the ground of illegality.

Chapter 17 - Unreasonableness/Irrationality and Proportionality

Introduction to the ground of irrationality

In general, acts of Parliament do not state that the power or discretion conferred on a public body should be exercised rationally. However, courts have a ground of judicial review on the basis that Parliament never intended such a power to be used irrationally. Historically, it should be noted that irrationality has been presented as the most controversial ground of judicial review. This is mainly because the review of the reasonableness of a decision leads to the review of the decision itself, which infringes with the subsidiary principle. In addition to this, it has been argued that this also infringed the doctrine of the separation of powers as Parliament conferred a power to body of the executive and not to the judiciary. Nevertheless, the main safeguard against judicial activism and abuses is that, as it will be developed bellow, the courts have set a very high threshold for irrationality.

The traditional "Wednesbury test"

The broad idea is that everybody acts reasonably using their reason. Therefore, a decision-maker, by ascertaining and following the course which reason directs, cannot act unreasonably. The leading case concerning irrationality is **Associated Provincial Picture Houses Ltd v Wednesbury Corporation [1947]** 2 All ER 680, also known as the "Wednesbury test".

General principle: Public law decisions reviewable on the ground irrationality are unreasonable decisions that no reasonable authority could ever have come to it.

Associated Provincial Picture Houses Ltd v Wednesbury Corporation [1947] 2 All ER 680
Facts: The claimant, a company, was granted a licence by the Wednesbury Corporation to operate a cinema on condition that no children under 15, whether accompanied by an adult or not, were

admitted on Sundays. The claimant sought a declaration that Wednesbury's condition was unacceptable and outside the power of the Corporation to impose.

Ratio: The Court of Appeal dismissed the claim held that it could not intervene to overturn the decision of the defendant simply because the court disagreed with it. None of the traditional grounds of judicial review was arguable. On the particular ground of irrationality Lord Greene famously stated in this case stated that an irrational decision is "so unreasonable that no reasonable authority could ever have come to it". Accordingly, unreasonableness requires something overwhelming where a decision involved something that was so absurd that no sensible person could ever dream that it lay within the powers of the authority, such as, he suggested, dismissing a school teacher because she had red hair.

Application: It should be noted that Lord Greene's approach on the test for irrationality was heavily criticised in that it was argued that the standard was too high. The traditional "Wednesbury test" was subsequently amended at the end of the 20th century.

Modern conception of the "Wednesbury test"

Initially, the traditional "Wednesbury test", in the 1950's, referred to "unreasonableness". Nowadays, the term "irrationality" is preferred although unreasonableness is still accepted. In the words of Lord Diplock in the **GCHQ** case: *"It [irrationality] applies to a decision which is so outrageous in its defiance of logic or accepted moral standards that no sensible person who had applied his mind to the question to be decided could have arrived at it"*. The standard for irrationality has progressively been lowered. Lord Cooke, in **R v Chief Constable of Sussex, ex parte International Trader's Ferry [1999]** 2 AC 418, considered that the traditional test was too strict and its formulation was exaggerated, he suggested to replace it by the following question: Was the decision one that a reasonable authority could reach? Following these recent developments, it should however be noted that the application of this modern conception of the "Wednesbury test" has been marked by some inconsistencies.

Categories of irrational or unreasonable decisions

The traditional categories of irrational decisions are: decisions affected by material defects, oppressive decisions and arbitrary decisions. These categories, that will be studied in turn, have been theorised by De Smith & Jowell.

Material defects in the decision-making process

It should be noted here that the defects in the decision making process are not illegal but rather lead to the unreasonableness of the impugned decision. In such situations the boundary between irrationality and illegality may be difficult to draw.

General principle: A decision may be unreasonable where the decision-maker failed to give sufficient weight to a relevant factor.

R v Secretary of State for the Home Department, ex parte Cox [1993] Admin LR 17
Facts: The claimant, a prisoner convicted for murder, spent 12 years in prison before being released on licence. While at a pre-release hostel he was arrested, charged, and convicted of minor offences of dishonesty and being in possession of cannabis. His release order was cancelled by the Home Secretary and he was sent back to a prison. Because the claimant's case had already been examined by the Parole Board, a crucial factor in this decision was that sending his case back to the Parole Board would have led to another 2 years' imprisonment. He argued that the omission of this crucial factor made this decision unreasonable.
Ratio: The Court held that the decision was unreasonable because the Home Secretary had failed to give sufficient weight to the length of detention facing the claimant. It noted that implementing the impugned decision would have resulted on an imprisonment period substantially longer, far in excess of the tariff for the minor offences which he had committed.
Application: Here the distinction between irrationality and failure to give sufficient weight to a relevant factor and illegality for failure to take into account a relevant factor may be complex at first. However, one should bear in mind that an irrational decision

for failure to give sufficient weight to a circumstance is marked by the result or consequence that the entire decision is not just illegal but rather unreasonable, which sets a higher standard.

General principle: Example of irrational public law decisions include illogical decisions marked by a lack of comprehensible chain of reasoning.

R v Secretary of State for Environment, ex parte Fielder Estates (Canvey Ltd) (QBD) [1998] 3 PLR 62

Facts: A public inquiry was set up at the local level concerning a project to build houses in Canvey Island. It was expected to last for three days, the construction was about to start very soon. On the second day, when one of the objectors to the project came to present his conclusions, that the hearing had been closed by the Inspector on the previous day. The Secretary of State, without consultation, ordered a new inquiry to take place with a new Inspector. The Developers of the project, the claimants, sought judicial review objected because of the delays this would cause and argued that the conclusions of the objectors could be submitted in writing.

Ratio: The Court declared the Secretary of State's decision unlawful held that the decision was irrational and illogical as there was no logical reason why the objector's views could not have been considered in writing. It noted that the impugned decision lacked a comprehensible chain of reasoning.

Application: This case is a relevant illustration of an irrational decision which is deprived of logic. Here the standard is very high and the claimant has to demonstrate that the decision lacked a comprehensible chain of reasoning.

General principle: Refusing a request of adoption in the interest of the child where one of the potential parents has poor health conditions may reasonably be held and is thereby not irrational.

R v Secretary State for Health, ex parte Luff [1992] 1 FLR 59; [1991] Fam Law 472

Facts: A middle-age couple, the claimant, was refused a request to adopt Romanian orphans. When taking this decision the Secretary State for Health took into accounts two reports of public bodies:

one was stating that the couple was not suitable for adoption as the husband's health conditions were not good and the second that came to the opposite conclusion. The claimant sought judicial review of this decision arguing that it was irrational.

Ratio:, The Court found that the decision was not irrational as it considered the best interest of the child as having utmost importance and stressed the potential impact on the child on potential illness or death of one of their parents. Noteworthy, tit noted that this decision could be reasonably held.

Application: In such cases, judges will try to determine whether the decision was one that could be reasonably held. Even if judges do not agree with the decision, they will acknowledge that this decision was not completely irrational.

Oppressive decisions

Oppressive decisions are decisions which impose excessive hardship or unnecessarily infringe individual rights. Such decisions are unreasonable or irrational because they are immoral and result on unfairness that cannot be justified.

General principle: Oppressive decisions that result on the imposition of unfair penalties unreasonably punitive constitute irrational decisions.

Wheeler v Leicester City Council [1985] AC 1054

Facts: This case concerned a rugby team which was sanctioned; they were prevented to use a recreation ground for its matches, because of a unofficial tour played earlier in South Africa. This was during the apartheid regime. The claimant, the rugby club, argued that this oppressive decision was irrational.

Ratio: The House of Lords held that the ban had the effect of punishing the club unfairly. Although it was not established that the decision was illogical and immoral, it resulted on an unreasonable decision, according to the "Wednesbury test" as it had the effect of being unreasonably punitive.

Application: Oppressive decisions are decisions which impose a excessive hardship. Examples of such decisions include excessive punishment imposed as a result of a legal behaviour.

General principle: Oppressive decisions that result on the

infringement of individual rights and cannot be justified by any rational reasoning may constitute unreasonable decisions.

R v Secretary of State for the Home Department, ex parte Norney, [1995] 7 Admin LR 861

Facts: The claimants' cases, IRA prisoners serving discretionary life sentences, were refused to be referred to the Parole Board until their tariff had expired. They challenged this decision under judicial review as unreasonable and infringing their human rights.

Ratio: The Court held the decision unlawful because its implementation would have resulted on the claimants serving many months longer in detention than if referrals were made in advance. It considered that the decision was unreasonable given that it was not justified by compelling reasons. The Court also noted that such a decision infringed the rights of the claimants under Article 5(4) of the ECHR.

Application: The second category of oppressive decisions contains decisions that infringe individual rights and cannot, by any means, be justified by any rational reasoning.

Arbitrary decisions

The *rationale* of this category of decisions is the respect for the Rule of law. Decisions made by public bodies should be consistent and rules should be sufficiently certain. However, decisions that lead to inequality before the law, for example, can satisfy the "Wednesbury test" of unreasonableness.

General principle: Public law decisions that result on arbitrary inequality of treatment before the law may constitute unreasonable decisions.

R v Secretary of State for the Home Department, ex parte McCartney [1994] COD 528

Facts: The Home Secretary had set the tariff sentence for the claimant, who was serving discretionary life sentences for the attempted murder of a policeman. The claimant sought judicial review of this decision arguing that this resulted on inequality before the law as his tariff was set at a higher level than for others who had committed more serious crimes of a similar type.

Ratio: The Court of Appeal held the decision of Home

Secretary unreasonable under the Wednesbury principle as it resulted on an inequality before the law. It noted that the Home Secretary was inconsistent with the treatment of other similarly affected persons.

Application: The reasoning of this judgement is based on the fundamental importance of the respect for the Rule of law. Indeed, the Rule of law entitles judges to scrutinise and quash decisions of the executive affecting individuals that are arbitrary.

Degree of review

Here, the issue is to expose certain criteria in order to determine the degree to which courts will scrutinise the impugned decision when appreciating if it can be successfully challenged. This is also known as the intensity of review, which will depend on the type of decision but also the interests at stake. The question of the intensity of review of unreasonable decisions raise important issues related to the doctrine of the separation of powers.

As mentioned above, the Wednesbury had been set very high. However, it should be remembered that this threshold has been lowered. In addition to this, there a circumstances particular to specific cases that will justify a higher or a lower degree of review. These specific categories are mainly decisions that imply broad social and economic policy issues or infringing fundamental rights.

Decisions implying broad social and economic policy issues

As mentioned earlier, courts will generally be quite reluctant to review decisions which imply broad social and economic policy issues. The reason for this high degree of deference (and conversely low degree of review) is related to the fact that such questions touch upon the essence of politics and decision-making.

General principle: A low intensity of review is applied to cases involving issues depending essentially on political judgment.

Nottinghamshire County Council v Secretary of State for the Environment [1986] 1 AC 240

Facts: Local authorities sought judicial review to challenge the budget allocated to them by central government that they considered unfairly low. They claimed unreasonableness and irrationality of the decision under judicial review.

Ratio: The House of Lords refused to intervene in public financial administration which had been previously approved by the House of Commons. It recalled that a low intensity of review is applied to cases involving issues depending essentially on political judgment. In the words of Lord Scarman: "Unless and until a statute provides otherwise, or it is established that the Secretary of State has abused his power, these are matters of political judgment for him and for the House of Commons. They are not for the judges".

Application: As in many other instances, courts ae reluctant to intervene in questions of policies, especially when Parliament has previously approved the actions of the executive. This case has been heavily criticised and labelled by the doctrine as a "super Wednesbury" as setting a standard even higher.

General principle: The involvement of matters of broad social and economic policy issues does not automatically prevent the court from intervening on very obviously irrational decisions.

R v Secretary of State for the Home Department, ex parte Javed [2001] EWCA 789

Facts: The Secretary of State made a statutory instrument, which designated Pakistan as a country in which "in general there is no risk of persecution". It should be noted that Parliament had approved the statutory instrument by Resolution. As a result, all Pakistani asylum-seekers were denied a right of appeal against refusal of asylum. The claimant sought judicial review of this statutory instrument as resulting from an irrational decision as evidence established that Pakistan was not a safe country.

Ratio: The Court of Appeal held that the decision was irrational given the well-established and widespread information demonstrating that Pakistan was not a safe country. Accordingly, a public body could not reasonably hold this decision. It was therefore declared unlawful.

Application: It is important to note that this decision illustrates that although courts use a high degree of deference in cases involving policy issues, it is not absolute and the courts will still review decisions that are obviously irrational.

Decisions affecting fundamental rights

The intensity of the review depends on the interests at stake. As mentioned above, judges will apply a low degree of intensity where issues of policy are involved. However, where fundamental rights are at stake, they will rather apply a high degree of review. This is because the protection of fundamental rights is one of the core objectives of a democratic society. Since the 1980's, courts have progressively applied an increasing degree of intensity of decisions affecting human rights. Accordingly, judicial review became a way to comply with the UK's international obligations and avoid violations of the European Convention on Human Rights.

General principle: Courts apply a high degree of scrutiny to public law decisions affecting fundamental rights.

Bugdaycay v Secretary of State for the Home Department [1987] AC 854

Facts: The claimants, Pakistanis nationals, were members of a sect and victim of discrimination in Pakistan. They applied for political asylum in the UK and their applications were rejected by the Secretary of State for the Home Department on the basis that he considered they did not in fact face persecution if they were returned to Pakistan. They applied for judicial review on the grounds of Wednesbury unreasonableness.

Ratio: The House of Lords declared that the Court had jurisdiction to review this decision on the grounds of Wednesbury unreasonableness. In the present case, there was no such unreasonableness and the Secretary of State had not erred in his approach to the decision. However, the Court noted the importance of applying a strict scrutiny to public law decisions that affect human rights on the ground of irrationality. In this respect, Lord Bridge said that the courts were entitled: "to subject an administrative decision to the more rigorous examination, to ensure that it is in no way flawed, according to the gravity of the issue which the decision determines. The most fundamental of all human rights is the individual's right to life and when an administrative decision under challenge is said to be one which may put the applicant's

life at risk; the basis of the decision must surely call for the most anxious scrutiny".

Application: In tis case, the House of Lords emphasised that the scrutiny of the reasonableness of public law decisions affecting human rights is of utmost importance. This approach has subsequently resulted on a constant and progressive intervention of judges to protect individual rights in judicial review proceedings.

The adoption of the Human Rights Act 1998 has later reinforced this evolution on the development of judicial scrutiny in respect of decisions that affect fundamental rights.

The rise of proportionality

Definition

Recent developments of judicial review have illustrated the emergence of an additional ground: proportionality. As it was announced by Lord Diplock in 1984 in the **GCHQ case**:   "That is not to say that further development on a case by case basis may to in course of time add further grounds. I have in mind particularly the possible adoption in the future of the principle of proportionality".

The review of proportionality is concerned with the aim of a public law decision and the assessment of the means to achieve this objective. The means deployed should be no more than those necessary to achieve the legitimate aim. For example, if a minister of the crown, acting under an imaginary Confidentiality Act 2019 which protects governmental information related to national security and diplomatic interest (a legitimate aim), decides to prohibit all civil servants to go abroad on vacation in order to avoid disclosure, this measure will could hypothetically be reviewed by courts under the ground of proportionality.

The test of proportionality is not completely new. It was inspired by the European Court of Human Rights' case law and the examination of the proportionality of the interference to achieve a legitimate aim (see Chapter 10). The doctrine of proportionality as devised by the ECHR ensures that domestic courts have conducted a fair balance between pursuing a legitimate aim and protecting

Convention rights.

In the words of Fordham proportionality is an added value for UK administrative law: "its great virtue is a structured approach, under which the State must convincingly demonstrate that the response in question is appropriate and necessary to achieve a legitimate aim, strikes a proper balance and avoids imposing excessive burdens".

Proportionality and the HRA 1998

Before the Human Rights Act 1998 Act, this doctrine was rejected by domestic courts, preferring to use UK law standards.

General principle: Historically courts have been reluctant to recognize a free-standing ground of proportionality in UK administrative law.

R v Home Secretary, ex parte Brind [1991] 1 AC 696

Facts: In this case, directives of the Home Secretary prohibited the action of broadcasting speeches from members of a terrorist organisation of Northern Ireland. These decisions were challenged by journalists, the claimants, who argued that they were Wednesbury unreasonable and disproportionate. They sought judicial review of these directives.

Ratio: In the circumstances of the case, the House of Lords held that the contested decisions were not unreasonable. Interestingly, it refused to accept the second set of arguments based of disproportionality of the measure to achieve the legitimate aim. As Lord Ackner concluded: "Unless and until Parliament incorporates the convention [ie the ECHR] into domestic law (...) there appears to me to be at present no basis upon which the proportionality doctrine applied by the European Court can be followed by the Courts of this country".

Application: This case illustrates the reluctance of courts, at first, to incorporate a European legal concept into UK law, considering that national standards were preferable and sufficient. It should be noted that this approach has been significantly challenged and undermined in a number of subsequent cases.

Nowadays, Section 2 of the HRA enables UK courts to apply the doctrine of proportionality. As stated in Chapter 11, the HRA not only incorporated the European Convention but also the European Court's case law and main principles such as the doctrine of proportionality. It was later developed through the practice of judicial review and has arguably become an independent ground.

General principle: UK courts later accepted to apply the proportionality doctrine to protect individual rights restricted by inflexible interferences that appear to go beyond what was necessary for the purposes of pursuing a legitimate aim.

R (T) v Chief Constable of Greater Manchester [2013] EWCA Civ 25

Facts: This case concerned statutory provision imposing a blanket statutory scheme requiring disclosure of cautions held in the police national computer. The question asked to the Court was related to the compatibility of those provisions with Article 8 of the Convention (the right to respect for private and family life).

Ratio: The Court of Appeal held that the *rationale* for the additional level of disclosure (where employers are responsible for children or vulnerable adults) was reasonable. However, the scheme did not control disclosure of information by reference to whether the information is relevant for enabling the employer to assess the suitability of the individual for particular work. Accordingly, such a regime was disproportionate and went beyond legitimate aims of protecting employees and vulnerable individuals. Therefore, the impugned laws were incompatible with Article 8 of the Convention.

Application: As illustrated in this case, the passing of the HRA has resulted on a subsequent use of the doctrine of proportionality by British judges.

Proportionality and irrationality

For long, the European concept of proportionality was compared to irrationality in UK law. However, the distinction between these two different legal concepts has progressively been highlighted by the courts. The question here is to determine whether they can be treated nowadays as to separated grounds.

General principle: The tests of proportionality and irrationality are two different legal tests with regard to individual rights. Accordingly, it can be demonstrated that although rational, a public law decision is disproportionate.

R v Ministry of Defence, ex parte Smith [1996] QB 517 and **Smith and Grady v UK (2000)** 29 EHRR 493

Facts: In this case, the question was to know whether the ban on homosexuals to serve in the armed forces could be reviewed by the courts. Three gay men and a lesbian woman sought judicial review on the ground of irrationality. After having been dealt with at national level, the claimants petitioned the ECHR.

Ratio: The Court of Appeal did not feel entitled to declare the ban unlawful. Although it declared the justiciability of the matter under judicial review, it could not be said that the challenged policy was irrational.

At the European level, the ECHR held that there had been a violation of Article 8 of the Convention in connection with sexual life. It considered that the blanket policy resulted on an automatic interference into individuals' sexual orientation that could not be justified as being disproportionate.

Application: In the present case, it should be noted that the ban was later lifted by the European Court of Human Rights in its decision **Smith and Grady v UK (2000)** 29 EHRR 493. It is interesting to note the difference between the approach of UK courts and the approach of the European Court.

The importance of making a distinction between these two grounds of judicial review is that the proportionality test is much stricter than the irrationality test. Indeed it is easier for a public body to prove that a decision was rational by demonstrating that the action was not absurd, than it is to prove that a decision was proportionate which requires demonstrating that it was a balanced and necessary one.

Although UK courts recognised the independent existence of the ground of proportionality in judicial review of decisions affecting human rights, the second question is to determine whether it is also the case where no European Union or European Convention issue is raised in a given case.

This question remains very controversial. However, it seems that, for now, UK courts are not ready to acknowledge such a legal evolution. As Dyson LJ commented in **Association of British Civilian Internees – Far East Region v Secretary of State for Defence [2003]** 3 WLR 80: "the criteria of proportionality are more precise and sophisticated (…) the strictness of the Wednesbury test has been relaxed in recent years even in areas which have nothing to do with fundamental rights. The Wednesbury test is moving closer to proportionality and in some cases it is not possible to see any daylight between the two tests … we have difficulty in seeing what justification there now is for retaining the Wednesbury test. But we consider it is not for this court to perform its burial rites. The continuing existence of the Wednesbury test has been acknowledged by the House of Lords on more than one occasion".

Summary

- In general, acts of Parliament do not expressly state that the power or discretion conferred on a public body should be exercised rationally. However, courts have a developed this ground of judicial review on the basis that Parliament never intended such a power to be used irrationally.

- The main idea of reasonableness is that everybody acts reasonably using their reason. Public law decisions reviewable on the ground irrationality are unreasonable decisions that no reasonable authority could ever have come to it.

- The standard for irrationality as laid down by the traditional "Wednesbury test" has progressively been lowered.

- A decision may be affected by material defects where the decision-maker failed to give sufficient weight to a relevant factor. Example of irrational public law decisions include illogical decisions marked by a lack of comprehensible chain of reasoning.

- Oppressive decisions are decisions which impose excessive hardship or unnecessarily infringe individual rights. Such decisions are unreasonable or irrational because they are immoral and result on unfairness that cannot be justified.

- Public law decisions that result on arbitrary inequality of treatment before the law may also constitute unreasonable decisions.

- The various degrees of intensity of judicial review allows that there a circumstances particular to specific cases that will justify a higher or a lower degree of review. The intensity of the review in a given case depends on the interests at stake.

- Recent developments of judicial review have illustrated the emergence of an additional ground: proportionality. The review of proportionality is concerned with the aim of a public action and the assessment of the means to achieve this objective.

- Before the Human Rights Act 1998 Act, the proportionality doctrine was rejected by domestic courts, preferring to use UK law standards.

- Nowadays, Section 2 of the HRA enables UK courts to apply the doctrine of proportionality in cases where individual rights are at stake. The tests of proportionality and irrationality are two different legal tests with regard to individual rights. Accordingly, it can be demonstrated that although rational, a public law decision is disproportionate.

- For now, UK courts are not ready to acknowledge that proportionality is a free standing ground where there is no issue related to individual rights.

Chapter 18 – Procedural impropriety

Introduction to the ground of Procedural impropriety

Procedural impropriety is the third ground of judicial review identified by the traditional typology presented by Lord Diplock in the **CGHQ case**: "I have described the third head as "procedural impropriety" rather than failure to observe basic rules of natural justice or failure to act with the procedural fairness towards the person who will be affected by the decision. This is because susceptibility to judicial review under this head covers also failure by an administrative tribunal to observe procedural rules that are expressly laid down in the legislative instrument by which its jurisdiction is conferred, even when such failure does not involve any denial of natural justice".

A public law decision breaches the ground of procedural impropriety if it ignores either statutory requirements or common law requirements, also known as the duty to act fairly (formerly the principles of natural justice).

This duty to act fairly composed of the rule against bias (*nemo judex in causa sua*) and the right to a fair hearing (*audi alteram partem*). In the words of Lord Denning in **Kanda v Government of Malaya [1962]** AC 322: *"The rule against bias is one thing. The right to be heard is another. These two rules are the essential characteristics of what is often called natural justice. They are the twin pillars supporting it".*

Statutory requirements

Parliament can subject the decision-making process to procedural requirements laid down by statutory provisions. This part of procedural impropriety is closely related to the ground of illegality. However the main distinction between the two rests on the fact those statutory requirements in the context of procedural impropriety remain, by essence, mainly procedural: examples include a duty to consult a body before adopting a decision or a requirement of notification.

Historically, courts distinguished between mandatory requirements (an essential factor in the decision-making process) and directory statutory requirements (a less important factor whose breach results on minor defects). As a consequence, failure to comply with a mandatory requirement would invalidate the decision whereas the breach of a directory requirement would not.

General principle: The failure to comply with a statutory requirement to consult representative bodies, as an essential step in the decision-making process, generally invalidates the decision.

Agricultural, Horticultural and Forestry Industry Training Board v Aylesbury Mushrooms [1972] 1 WLR 290
Facts: In this case, Section 1(4) of the Industrial Training Act 1964 provided for prior consultation by the Ministry of Labour with "any organisation or association of organisations appearing to him to be representative of substantial numbers of employers engaging in the activities concerned". The Mushroom Growers' Association, the claimant, was not consulted although the Minister made clear before the decision that they were representative. The claimant sought judicial review of the decision to impose a levy by a 1966 Order on the ground of procedural impropriety.
Ratio: The Court held that the requirement to consult the Mushroom Growers' Association was mandatory under the Industrial Training Act 1964. It found that the Minister failed to comply with this statutory requirement and invalidated the decision.
Application: In this case, the Court stressed that a statutory requirement to consult representative bodies is a mandatory and important requirement. This judgement illustrates the traditional distinction historically applied by courts between mandatory and directory requirements.

General principle: The failure to comply with a statutory provision requiring to notify of the right to appeal a decision generally invalidates it.

E 1/ (OS Russia) v Secretary of State for the Home Department [2012] EWCA Civ 357
Facts: This case concerned a notice cancelling the claimant's

Indefinite Leave to Remain (I LR) in the United Kingdom. The claimant, a Russian national, sought judicial review of this decision invoking that it failed to comply with a statutory requirement to notify him of his right to appeal this decision.

Ratio: The Court of Appeal allowed the appeal and quashed the invalid notice. It noted that the importance of the compliance with the notification requirement justified that the decision was to be invalidated in case of breach. This was because this procedural guarantee had a major impact on the right to a fair hearing.

Application: In this case, the Court stresses the importance of the notification requirement as being part of the right to a fair hearing. It should be noted that this procedural requirement had been construed similarly in earlier cases such as **Agricultural, Horticultural and Forestry Industry Training Board v Kent [1970]** 1 All 340.

General principle: Courts look at the consequences of the non-compliance with the requirement and ask whether, in the light of those consequences, Parliament could have intended the outcome of that non-compliance to have been the invalidity of the decision.

R v Soneji [2006] UKHL 1 AC 340

Facts: In this case, the defendants were opposed confiscation orders. They sought judicial review on the basis that the orders were made more than six months after their sentence. The prosecutor later appealed arguing that the fact that the orders were not timely did not invalidate them.

Ratio: The House of Lords allowed the prosecutor's appeal and held that the Court of Appeal wrongly quashed the confiscation orders. Lord Steyn stated the following: "Having reviewed the issue in some detail I am in respectful agreement with the Australian High Court that the rigid mandatory and directory distinction, and its many artificial refinements, have outlived their usefulness. Instead (...) the emphasis ought to be on the consequences of non-compliance, and posing the question whether Parliament can fairly be taken to have intended total invalidity. That is how I would approach what is ultimately a question of statutory construction".

Application: In this case, the House of Lords adopted an approach based on Parliament's intention which is more flexible than the traditional mandatory/directory distinction. This approach was subsequently followed by the Supreme Court in **R v Guraj [2016] UKSC 65.**

It should also be noted that this case illustrates that generally the breach of statutory time limits does not tend to invalidate the decision. As Wade and Forsyth put it: "It has often been held that an act may be validly done after the expiry of a statutory time limit".

Level of the duty to act fairly

A public law decision may also breach the ground of procedural impropriety if it ignores common law requirements, also known as the duty to act fairly (formerly the principles of natural justice). This second set of rules has been replaced, along with the evolution of judicial review in UK law, by the notion of general duty to act fairly. Accordingly, in all cases, a decision-maker must act fairly or in accordance with the principles of "natural justice".

In this area of administrative law, it is important to note that the incorporation of the provisions and jurisprudential developments on Article 6 of the European Convention on Human Rights into UK law had a major impact. It now operates in combination with the common law duty to act fairly.

General principle: Historically, the principles of natural justice were only applied to judicial decisions and excluded in judicial review of administrative decisions.

Franklin v Minister of Town/Country Planning, [1948] AC 87
Facts: This case concerned an order by the minister to designate a new town. However, before this order, the Minister went on a visit to the town and made declarations in favour of the future order. This Order was eventually confirmed following objections and a public inquiry. However, the claimants sought judicial review of the order arguing that it was biased as the previous declarations illustrated a pre-conceived view. As a consequence, the minister had not acted fairly regarding the claimants' objections, in breach of the principles of natural justice.

Ratio: The House of Lords dismissed the claims and held that the decision had been purely administrative. It concluded that the principles of natural justice could only be applied to judicial decisions and not to administrative decisions. As long as the correct procedure had been followed with regard to the objections, it was not prepared to interfere.

Application: This case illustrates that in the first part of the 20th century, courts adopted a quite restrictive approach on the principles of natural justice. However, it has changed with later case-law developments.

General principle: Although courts later accepted that the principles of natural justice applied both to judicial and administrative decisions, it considered however that administrative decisions attracted a lower level of natural justice.

Ridge v Baldwin [1964] UKHL AC 40

Facts: In this case, the claimant, a Chief Constable of the police, had been dismissed for negligence by the Baldwin's committee in accordance with a statutory provision. He sought judicial review of this decision claiming that it was made without offering him an opportunity to defend his case.

Ratio: The House of Lords held that Baldwin's committee had violated the doctrine of natural justice which applied to administrative decisions and required a prior notice of the charge against the claimant and a proper opportunity of contesting it. It noted that the reason for the application of the principles of natural justice relied on the fact that the exercise of the statutory function in the present case affected the claimant's individual rights.

Application: This landmark case represents a turning point in the common law approach of procedural impropriety and is the starting point of subsequent development of the application of the doctrine of natural justice in administrative law.

Nowadays, the application of the duty to act fairly in judicial review of public law decisions constitutes a significant safeguard of the interests of individuals.

General principle: The appropriate level of fairness in a decision-making process depends on the character of the decision-making body, the kind of question it has to make and the statutory or other framework in which it operates.

Lloyd v McMahon [1987] AC 625

Facts: In this case, the district auditor issued a certificate under the 1982 Act surcharging the claimants, local councillors, in the sum of 106,103 pounds considering that it was the amount of a loss incurred by their wilful misconduct. The claimants sought judicial review of this decision invoking a breach of the duty to act fairly.

Ratio: The Court dismissed the claimants' case and held that an aggrieved objector to local government spending should pursue his rights under the Act and not by way of seeking judicial review. Lord Bridge clarified the test to be applied when appreciating the appropriate level of fairness: *"the so-called rules of natural justice are not engraved on tablets of stone. To use the phrase which better expresses the underlying concept, what the requirements of fairness demand when any body, domestic, administrative or judicial, has to make a decision which will affect the rights of individuals depends on the character of the decision-making body, the kind of question it has to make and the statutory or other framework in which it operates".*

Application: In this case, the Court laid down a modern version of the test to be applied when appreciating the appropriate level of fairness in the context of the decision adopted.

Accordingly, the application of the duty to act fairly, and the subsequent appropriate level of fairness required by the courts, may vary depending on the decision, its general context and the legal issues at stake.

In this respect, the appropriate level has been set very low in cases related to national security or emergency where public safety demands urgent actions (see, for example, **R v Secretary of State Transport, ex parte Pegasus Holdings Ltd. [1989] 2 All ER 481**).

Licence Applications

Courts have historically attributed a higher level of fairness to licence applications, making it clear that the applicant does have a right for their application to be fairly and properly considered. For instance in **R v Brighton Corporation, ex parte Thomas Tilling Ltd. (1916)** 85 LJKB 1552, Sankey J stated that: "Persons who are called upon to exercise the functions of granting licences for carriages and omnibuses are, to a great extent, exercising judicial functions; and though they are not bound by the strict rules of evidence and procedure observed in a court of law, they are bound to act judicially. It is their duty to hear and determine according to law, and they must bring to that task a fair and unbiased mind".

General principle: Courts make a distinction between forfeiture and application cases: where a licence is being taken away from a holder, a higher degree of fairness will generally be applied.

McInnes v Onslow-Fane [1978] 1 WLR 1520

Facts: In this case, the claimant held various licences from the British Boxing Board of Control. These licences were withdrawn. He applied several times for new licences that were all rejected. Applying for the sixth time, he requested an oral hearing. This request was refused and he subsequently sought judicial review on the ground of procedural impropriety.

Ratio: The Court held that there was no breach of fairness considering that in the claimant's application case, there was no obligation to inform the plaintiff of the basic reasons for the refusal of his application. It noted that the British Boxing Board of Control was simply obliged to act fairly in the general sense. The Court drew a distinction between forfeiture and application cases: in the former, where a licence is being taken away from a holder, he will usually be entitled to expect that this will not be done without a good reason, in the latter, however, notification of specific reasons of the decision would be impractical. Notification of charges and of adverse comments is only required by law, under certain circumstances, in forfeiture cases.

Application: This is a landmark case concerning the judicial review of licence applications and forfeitures. The Court drew a clear distinction which is crucial to determine the degree of fairness required.

Common law requirements: Right to be heard

The right to a fair hearing or the right to be heard is expressed by the legal maxim: *audi altem partem*, which literally means: "the other side must be heard". In other words, a person affected by a decision made by a public body should be given the opportunity to present arguments supporting his or her case.

The right of individuals to be informed of cases against them

The most elementary component of the right to be heard is the right of a person to have a notice of a case against them. In the absence of such a notice, the public body acts unfairly.

General principle: The absence of notice will only affect the decision's lawfulness if the claimant can demonstrate that his defence could potentially have changed the decision.

R v Chief Constable of North Wales Police, ex parte Thorpe [1998] 3 WLR 57 (CA)

Facts: In this case, the claimants were ordered by the police to evacuate a caravan park. They argued that this decision was unlawful as they were not informed of the case against them.

Ratio: The Court of Appeal admitted that the police case should have been disclosed to the claimants. However, it considered that this failure did not affect the order's lawfulness given that nothing from the claimant's arguments could have reasonably changed the police's decision.

Application: In this case, the Court of Appeal adopts a restrictive approach on the right of individuals to be informed of a case brought against them, excluding situations where the lack of notice that result on merely procedural defects.

The right to have sufficient time before the decision to prepare a defence

General principle: The duty to act fairly requires that parties should be given reasonable time to prepare their case.

R v Thames Magistrates, ex parte Polemis [1974] 1 WLR 1371

Facts: A ship's master was summoned to answer a charge under the Control of Pollution Act 1971 on the same day of the notice and was subsequently convicted. He sought judicial review and argued that his right to have sufficient time before the decision to prepare a defence had been violated.

Ratio: The Court quashed the claimant's conviction on the basis that natural justice required to give him an opportunity to prepare his defence. In the words of Lord Widgery CJ: "Nothing is clearer today than the breach of the rules of natural justice is said to occur if a party to proceedings, and more especially the defendant in a criminal case, is not given a reasonable chance to present his case (...) it necessary extends to a reasonable opportunity to prepare your case before you are called on to present it".

Application: This second limb of the right to be heard is the necessary corollary of the right to be informed. Indeed, your right to be informed of a case brought against you is only important if you are informed promptly, which gives you a reasonable opportunity to prepare your defence.

The right to make representations and the right to an oral hearing

The right of individuals to prepare cases against them logically implies that they should be heard, in oral or writing, in order to try to influence the decision before its adoption. The issue here is to determine whether representations in writing are sufficient or if it is necessary to organise an oral hearing.

However, it should be noted that there is no general right to make representations or to be provided with an oral hearing for every public law decision. The necessity to respect these procedural safeguards will depend on the interests at stake.

General principle: Life sentence prisoners should be provided with the opportunity to make written representations concerning the period they should serve before the review of their sentence.

R v Secretary of State for the Home Department, ex parte Doody [1993] 3 WLR 154

Facts: Four prisoners serving mandatory life sentences requested judicial review of the Home Secretary's refusal to release them after serving their minimum terms. They argued, *inter alia*, that they were not given the opportunity to make written representations.

Ratio: The House of Lords held that the Home Secretary was required to provide mandatory life sentence prisoners with the opportunity to make written representations concerning the period they should serve before the review of their sentence.

Application: In this case, the House of Lords acknowledged the claimants' right to make written representations. This solution can be explained by the seriousness of the interests at stake and the potentially dramatic consequences on the claimants' lives.

General principle: In order to determine whether oral hearings are required to meet the requisite standard of fairness, courts look at the subject matter and circumstances of the case, the nature of the decision to be made and the existence of substantive issues of fact that cannot be satisfactorily resolved on the available written evidence.

R v Army Board of the Defence Council, ex parte Anderson [1992] 1 QB 169

Facts: This case concerned claims of racial discrimination from a soldier to the Army Board. The board investigated the case but rejected the claimants' request for an oral hearing. He subsequently sought judicial review and claimed that he had a right to an oral hearing.

Ratio: The Court of Appeal quashed the decision, holding that the Board's inflexible policy never to hold oral hearings was unlawful. Taylor LJ stated that although there was no general right to an oral hearing, in order to determine whether oral hearings are required to meet the requisite standard of fairness, one had to look at the subject matter and circumstances of the case, the nature of the decision to be made and the existence of substantive issues of fact that cannot be satisfactorily resolved on the available written evidence. In this case, an oral hearing was required to meet the requisite standard of fairness.

Application: It should be noted that the test to determine whether a person has a right to an oral hearing is a contextual one which depends on the circumstances of a case and has to be assessed on a case-by case basis.

In the context of multi-stage procedures, it should be noted that the fairness of the procedure is assessed globally, regardless of the fact that the claimant feels that he was heard at the wrong moment in time regarding the adoption of the decision (see **Wiseman v Borneman [1971]** AC 297).

Witnesses

The refusal to call for witnesses or to cross-examine testimonies might also infringe the right to be heard (see **R v Hull Prison Board of Visitors, ex parte St Germain [1979]** 1 WLR 1401). However, there is no general duty to accept witnesses in all procedures. This possibility will depend on the circumstances of each case and the public body's appreciation of the necessity to organise a "legalistic" procedure.

The right to legal representation

If the right to be legally represented before a criminal Court cannot be denied, there is no general right to be assisted by a lawyer in other circumstances. Once again, the appreciation of the fairness of a procedure will be assessed on a case-by case basis. Needless to say, the risk of allowing legal representation before any public body is that IT may complicate and lengthen procedures. As Lord Denning MR famously stated in **Enderby Town Football Club Ltd v Football Association Ltd [1971]** 1 Ch 591: *"In many cases it may be a good thing for the proceedings of a domestic tribunal to be conducted informally without legal representation. Justice can often be done in them better by a good layman than by a bad lawyer"*.

General principle: When appreciating the right to legal representation, the seriousness of the charge, the likelihood that a point of law may arise, the ability of the person to conduct his own case and the need for a speedy process should be taken into account.

R v Secretary of State for the Home Department, ex parte Tarrant [1985] QB 251
Facts: This case concerned prisoners' right to be legally

represented. The Board of visitors rejected the request of two prisoners charged with mutiny. They challenged this decision under judicial review and claimed that they had a right to be legally represented.

Ratio: The Court held that the refusal to allow legal representation of the two prisoners was unlawful given their restricted ability to conduct their own case and the especially grave offence they were charged with. When appreciating the right to legal representation: the seriousness of the charge; the likelihood that a point of law may arise; the ability of the person to conduct his own case; and the need for a speedy process should be taken into account.

Application: In this case, the Court laid down several factors to be taken into consideration when determining whether or not a person has a right to legal representation. It should be noted that courts tend to afford a greater protection to prisoners given their restricted ability to conduct their own case from prison.

The duty to give reasons for a decision

The duty to give reasons was initially imposed on courts, such as for instance the Tribunals and Inquiries Act 1992 which applies to all tribunals listed in Schedule 1 to the Act. However, as J. Auburn puts it: *"there is a clear trend towards requiring public bodies to give reasons for their decisions"*. Lord Mustill, in **R v Secretary of State for the Home Department, ex parte Doody [1993]** 3 WLR 154, made clear that: *"The law does not at present recognise a general duty to give reasons for an administrative decision. Nevertheless, it is equally beyond question that such a duty may in appropriate circumstances be implied"*.

General principle: A public body may be imposed a duty to indicate the general areas of concern regarding a public law decision to the claimant so that they can prepare their defence and make representations before the decision.

R v Secretary of State for the Home Department, ex parte Al Fayed [1997] 1 All ER 228

Facts: The claimants applied for British nationality under the British Nationality Act 1981. Their applications were refused without providing them with any reason for this decision. They sought judicial review of this decision for failure to give reasons for an administrative decision.

Ratio: The Court of Appeal held that although Section 44 of the British Nationality Act 1981 expressly provided that there was no duty to give reasons, the Home Secretary still had to act fairly in arriving at a decision. Accordingly, the Home Secretary had a duty to indicate the general areas of concern regarding the refusal of British nationality to the claimants so that they could prepare their defence and make representations before the decision. Accordingly, the decision was quashed. As Lord Woolf MR stated: *"I appreciate that there is also anxiety as to the administrative burden involved in giving notice of areas of concern. Administrative convenience cannot justify unfairness but I would emphasise that my remarks are limited to cases where an applicant would be in real difficulty in doing himself justice unless the area of concern is identified by notice".*

Application: *This case illustrates* that although Parliament expressly excludes a duty to give reasons for specific administrative decisions, courts may interpret Parliament's will has to give it an effect that ensures that the decision-maker complies with the duty to act fairly.

Recent case-law developments have shown that common law is moving towards an evolution on the duty to give reasons. In the words of Elias LJ in **Oakley v South Cambridgeshire District Council [2017]** EWCA Civ 71: *"In view of this, it may be more accurate to say that the common law is moving to the position whilst there is no universal obligation to give reasons in all circumstances, in general they should be given unless there is a proper justification for not doing so".*

Common law requirements: The rule against bias

The rule against bias, also known as *nemo iudex in causa sua* literally means that: "No one should be a judge in their own cause". In other words, the decision-maker must be unbiased. In the contrary, the decision can be quashed and the decision-maker disqualified to adopt the said decision. The rule against bias is generally divided into two categories: decisions where there is direct interest and decisions where there is indirect interest.

Direct interest

A direct bias, such as a pecuniary interest on the part of the decision-maker, will invalidate a contested public law decision unless the very strong presumption applied in these cases can be rebutted. This type of bias is generally referred to as "automatic disqualification".

General principle: Where a decision-maker has a pecuniary interest in the outcome of a decision that he has to adopt, he is automatically disqualified.

Dimes v The Proprietors of the Grand Junction Canal (1852) 3 HL 759
Facts: The claimant's request to obstruct the Grand Junction Canal's land was rejected. It appeared that one of the decision-makers held shares in the company.
Ratio: The House of Lords held that the decision-maker was disqualified to take the decision given that he had direct pecuniary interest in the outcome of the decision. As Lord Campbell stated: "No one can suppose that Lord Cottenham could be, in the remotest degree, influenced by the interest that he had in this concern; but, My Lords, it is of the last importance that the maxim that no man is to be a judge in his own cause should be held sacred".
Application: This case provides with an example of direct pecuniary interest. Indeed, the fact that a decision-maker holds shares in a company or owns a property directly affected by the outcome of a decision infringes the rule that no one should be judge in their own cause. It should be noted that this rule applies to decisions of groups of individuals or committees, even where only one of their members has direct interest.

Indirect Interest

Where the interest is indirect, there is no automatic disqualification; the outcome of the case depends on the circumstances. Indirect interests are not necessarily financial or pecuniary.

General principle: The membership of a judge to an

organization who expressed views whose interests are at stake in a given case is not sufficient for disqualification as far as there is nothing apart from membership to link the judge with any of these views.

Helow v Secretary of State for the Home Department [2008] UKHL 62

Facts: The claimant was a Palestinian who applied for asylum in the UK. His application was rejected on appeal by Lady Cosgrove in the Scottish Court of Session. It was subsequently discovered that she was a member of the International Association of Jewish Lawyers and Jurists (IAJLJ). The claimant sought judicial review of this decision claiming that it was biased as Lady Cosgrove was a member of an "anti-Palestinian" organization. The President of the association had recently made statements illustrating this position.

Ratio: The House of Lords dismissed the claimant's Appeal considering that the decision was not biased. Lady Cosgrove could not be disqualified on the sole basis that she was member of the IAJLJ, as there was nothing apart from membership to link her with any of the views recently expressed by the President of the association. The House of Lords also noted that the IAJLJ had not intervened in the proceedings of the present case.

Application: In this case, the House of Lords applies a restrictive approach on indirect bias. It should be noted that the law Lords made here a major distinction with the case **Pinochet Ugarte** [2000] where Amnesty International had intervened during the proceedings.

Unauthorised Participation or Presence

General principle: The mere presence of an individual which has interest when the decision is taken, even if he does not actively participate, is sufficient to create an appearance of bias and leads to disqualification.

R v Hendon RDC, ex parte Chorley [1933] 2 KB 696

Facts: In this case, a district council had to decide on the authorisation to transform a garage into a restaurant. One of the councillors, which was also the estate agent acting for the owners, had attended the meeting although apparently taking no active part. The claimant, a neighbour who claimed to be affected by the decision, sought judicial review arguing that the decision was biased.

Ratio: The Court held that the mere fact that one of the councillors which had an interest attended a meeting which was decisive for the decision-making process created an appearance of bias. Accordingly, it quashed the decision and disqualified the councillor.

Application: In this case, the Court relied on the traditional test laid down by Lord Hope in **Porter v Magill [2001]** UKHL 67: "The question is whether the fair-minded and informed observer, having considered the facts, would conclude that there was a real possibility that the tribunal was biased".

View Formed in Advance/Pre-formed Opinion

General principle: The decision may be biased because a person had a view formed in advance because of their membership in different bodies involved in the decision-making process.

Hannam v Bradford City Council [1970] 2 All ER

Facts: The claimant, a school teacher, was dismissed by school governors. A council's committee approved the dismissal. The claimant sought judicial review of this decision arguing that some of the governors were also members of the committee and had therefore an opinion formed in advance when they approved the dismissal.

Ratio: The Court quashed the decision taking into consideration that three out of ten members of the committee (including the chairman) were also governors. Accordingly, the decision was biased and the governors were subsequently disqualified. As stated by Sachs LJ: "No man can be judge of his own cause. The governors did not, on donning their sub-committee hats, cease to be an integral part of the body whose action was being impugned, and it made no difference that they did not personally attend the governors' meeting".

Application: This type of indirect bias is also part of the broader category of appearance of bias: the claimant may conclude, after observing the presence of individuals in different bodies involved for the decision, that the entire decision-making process is biased.

Policy Bias

General principle: A decision-making process where a body announces a policy or a course of action and later hears objections is not as far as the body has genuinely considered the objections submitted.

Franklin v Minister of Town and Country Planning [1948] AC 87

Facts: In this case, a government department announced an intended policy, presenting a course of action and later heard objectors before adopting the decision. This decision was challenged by the claimant who claimed that the said government department had a view formed in advance and therefore the decision was biased.

Ratio: The House of Lords dismissed the claims and refused to quash the decision. It held that the only obligation on the part of the department in such a case was to genuinely consider objections submitted and if it had been done, the decision-making process was not biased.

Application: In this case, the House of Lords limited the scope of indirect bias on the ground of view formed in advance. There is no obligation for administrative bodies to refrain from announcing a view before hearing arguments of objectors. This would unreasonably complicate the administrative decision-making process.

Necessity

One of the rare exceptions to the application of the duty to act fairly is necessity. In some rare cases, it might justify an exemption from the duty to act fairly. For example, if only one person or body is empowered make a public law decision, then disqualification for bias is excluded in order to avoid an administrative blockage. The necessity rule will, then apply in cases where in its absence the proceedings or the decision-making process would not progress further. For instance, in **The Judges v AG for Saskatchewan, (1937)** 53 TLR 464, the Privy Council held that it was for the Court to decide whether or not the salaries of judges were liable to income tax, notwithstanding the apparent bias.

Summary

- Procedural impropriety is the third ground of judicial review identified by the traditional typology presented by Lord Diplock in the **CGHQ case**. It implies a breach of procedural fairness in the decision-making process.

- A public law decision breaches the ground of procedural impropriety if it ignores either statutory requirements or common law requirements, also known as the duty to act fairly (formerly the principles of natural justice).

- On the first hand, Parliament can subject the decision-making process to procedural requirements laid down by statutory provisions.

- Historically, courts distinguished between mandatory requirements and directory statutory requirements. Nowadays, courts look at the consequences of the non-compliance with statutory requirements and ask whether, in the light of those consequences, Parliament could have intended the outcome of that non-compliance to have been the invalidity of the decision.

- On the other hand, the duty to act fairly composed of the rule against bias (*nemo judex in causa sua*) and the right to a fair hearing (*audi alteram partem*).

- Historically, the principles of natural justice were only applied to judicial decisions and excluded in judicial review of administrative decisions. Nowadays, the application of the duty to act fairly in judicial review of public law decisions constitutes a significant safeguard of the interests of individuals.

- The right to a fair hearing or the right to be heard is expressed by the legal maxim: *audi altem partem*, which literally means: "the other side must be heard".

- This latter common law requirement includes the right of individuals to be informed of cases against them, the right to legal representation, the right to make representations and the right to an oral hearing, the right to have sufficient time before the decision to prepare a defence and the right of individuals to be informed of cases against them.

- The rule against bias, also known as *nemo iudex in causa sua*, literally means that: "No one should be a judge in their own cause".

- A direct bias, such as a pecuniary interest on the part of the decision-maker, will invalidate a contested public law decision unless the very strong presumption applied in these cases can be rebutted.

- Where the interest is indirect, there is no automatic disqualification; the outcome of the case depends on the circumstances. Indirect interests are not necessarily financial or pecuniary.

Chapter 19 – Legitimate Expectation

Introduction to the ground of legitimate expectation

Legitimate expectation relates to the concept that an expectation of either a procedure or a benefit may be protected in law. This expectation can arise from both an express representation or promise made by a public body or even an implicit representation illustrated by established past practice.

The doctrine of legitimate expectation has been long employed in EU Law. Historically, legitimate expectation emerged from procedural impropriety, as it was not one of the traditional grounds cited by Lord Diplock in the **CGHQ** case.

One of the first UK cases to mention legitimate expectation is **Schmidt v Secretary of State for Home Affairs, [1969]** 2 CH 149, where Lord Denning held that: "an administrative body may, in a proper case, be bound to give a person who is affected by their decision an opportunity of making representations. It all depends on whether he has some right or interest, or, I would add, some legitimate expectation, of which it would not be fair to deprive him without hearing what he has to say". Legitimate expectations can be divided into two categories: one is procedural and the other is substantive.

Procedural legitimate expectation

A procedural legitimate expectation will arise where a public body has promised or represented that a particular procedure will be followed before a decision is made or where there has been an established practice for the public body to use a particular procedure.

General principle: A procedural legitimate expectation may arise from an undertaking assuring a consultation of trade unions before the adoption of a decision.

Regina v Liverpool Corporation ex parte Liverpool Taxi Fleet Operators Association [1972] 2 QB 299

Facts: A local Council took the decision to increase the numbers of hackney cabs operating in the city, without consulting local trade unions and in breach of a previous undertaking that the numbers of hackney cabs would not be increased until the proposed legislation.

Ratio: The Court held that on account of this public representation, a legitimate expectation arose from the local council's undertaking. Accordingly, the Corporation could not depart from this undertaking. As stated by Sir Gordon Willmer: "It seems to me that in these very special circumstances, having regard to the history of how this matter had been dealt with in the past, and having regard especially to the giving of the undertaking, the Applicants are justified in regarding themselves as "aggrieved" by what I can only describe as unfair treatment on the part of Liverpool Corporation".

Application: This case is an example of procedural legitimate expectation which results from a promise of a local council. Once it is demonstrated that the expectation is legitimate, it is legally binding and the administration cannot depart from it.

Substantive legitimate expectation

Recently, the concept of legitimate expectation has been expanded by the courts to substantive expectations where a promise has led an individual to believe that they will receive a particular, tangible benefit. The question of substantive legitimate expectation has been raised for the first time in the case **R v Inland Revenue Commissioners, ex parte Preston [1985]** AC 835, although the House of Lords did not specifically mention this ground.

General principle: A clear and unambiguous promise to forgo tax by the competent public body may constitute a substantive legitimate expectation.

R v IRC, ex parte MFK Industries MFK Underwriting Agents Ltd [1990] 1 WLR 1545

Facts: In this case, the Inland Revenue Commission promised that it would forgo tax, which would otherwise have been payable. The claimant was later ordered to pay taxes. He sought judicial review of this decision.

Ratio: The Divisional Court held that the representation was binding because it constituted a legitimate expectation. It noted that the Inland Revenue Commission's statement was clear and unambiguous.
Application: This case illustrates that the benefit which is expected in substantive legitimate expectation may be a tax exemption for example. Although a benefit is peculiar by definition, courts have recognized other types of benefits.

Sources of legitimate expectation

As Lord Fraser stated in the **GCHQ** case: "Legitimate expectation may arise either from an express promise given on behalf of a public authority or from the existence of a regular practice which the claimant can reasonably expect to continue". These two types of sources of legitimate expectations will be examined in turn.

Express Promise or Specific Representation

In this first category, the promise or representation is expressly made by the public body. From this promise stems a presumption that the expectation is legitimate. The undertaking in the case **Regina v Liverpool Corporation ex parte Liverpool Taxi Fleet Operators Association [1972]** 2 QB 299 is a good example of a specific representation.

General principle: Where a public body promises to follow a certain procedure before reaching a certain decision, good administration requires that it should act fairly and implement its promise.

AG of Hong Kong v Ng Yuen Shiu [1983] 2 AC 629
Facts: In this case, the government of Hong Kong (a former British colony) announced a policy of automatic repatriation of Chinese nationals entering the territory illegally by Macau. After a public consultation, the government amended the procedure and accepted that each case would be examined on a case by case basis.
Ratio: The Privy Council held that the Hong Kong government was legally bound by the procedure that it initially promised as it gave rise to a legitimate expectation. It considered that as a

matter of principle where a public body promises to follow a certain procedure before reaching a certain decision, good administration requires that it should act fairly and implement its promise.

Application: This case illustrates that a specific representation may arise from a policy laid down by a public body. However, as this will be discussed further in details below, this policy, in order to create an expectation which is legitimate, has to satisfy the requirement of clarity, and may require knowledge and reliance.

Established Past Practice

An expectation may also arise from an established practice or settled course of conduct of a public body towards the claimant or a group to which he belongs.

General principle: A continuous acceptance of late loss relief claims for more than 20 years is an established past practice which creates a legitimate expectation.

R v IRC, ex parte Unilever plc [1996] STC 681

Facts: For more than 20 years the Inland Revenue Commission (IRC) accepted the claimant's loss relief claims, which were submitted over two years after the relevant accounting period. Suddenly it decided to reject these claims. The claimant sought judicial review of this decision for breach of a legitimate expectation.

Ratio: The Court of Appeal held that although there had been no specific representation that the IRC accepted late loss relief claims, there had been a clear and consistent pattern of conduct accepting them. The Court noted that the IRC suddenly changed its behaviour without warning the claimant.

Application: In this case, the Court of Appeal stressed the fact that the continuous implicit acceptance from a public body of a particular usage with a claimant may constitute established past practice for the purposes of legitimate expectation.

The definition of a legitimate expectation

An expectation is enforceable under judicial review only if is legitimate. The assessment of the legitimacy of an expectation takes into account several factors. It requires a detailed examination of the promise made or the established past practice (See **R v North and East Devon Health Authority, ex parte Coughlan, [2000] 2 WLR 622**).

Relevant factors for the assessment of legitimacy include: clarity, legality, knowledge and reliance. These criteria will be examined in turn.

Clarity

In order to assess the legitimacy of an expectation, one has to look, in the first place, at the clarity of promise, the representation or the past practice.

General principle: A legitimate promise is clear, unambiguous and devoid of relevant qualification.

R v IRC, ex parte MFK Underwriting Agents Ltd [1990] 1 WLR 1545

Facts: Before taking part into an investment opportunity, the claimant asked Inland Revenue Commission (IRC) about the future tax implications. The IRC stated that there would be no increase and later put taxes up. The claimant argued that this change of practice was contrary to a legitimate expectation.

Ratio: The Court dismissed the claims considering that the promise was not clear enough and thereby the expectation was not legitimate. It however stated that the IRC could not withdraw from a representation as it would cause substantial unfairness to the claimant; if the conditions for relying upon any such representation were fulfilled; and if holding the IRC to the representation did not prevent it from exercising its statutory duties. The Court stated that a claim to a legitimate expectation can be based only upon a promise which is clear, unambiguous and devoid of relevant qualification.

Application: This landmark case sets the traditional test which requires the promise to be clear enough in order to give rise to a legitimate expectation.

General principle: The fact that the claimant asked several times for very specific assurances is a relevant factor when

assessing the clarity of a promise.

R (Patel) v General Medical Council [2013] EWCA Civ 327
Facts: The appellant proposed an academic course to the General Medical Council for the study of "Primary Medical Qualification". He obtained a number of assurances that his proposed course would be accepted. It was later refused and he sought judicial review of this decision on the ground of legitimate expectation.
Ratio: The Court of Appeal held that the expectation was legitimate because the appellant asked for a number of very specific assurances. As Lord Jones LJ stated: "The fact that the appellant went back repeatedly in an attempt to obtain a clear answer to his question is also highly relevant as part of that context. First, it shows the importance he attached to the information he was legitimately seeking from the GMC. Secondly, it shows that he was trying his utmost to provide a clear statement of his intentions and to obtain a clear unequivocal response to his question".
Application: In this case, the Court of Appeal made it clear that the clarity test is an objective one which takes into account to particular context of each case.

General principle: An established past practice is also subjected to the requirement of clarity: it should be unambiguous, widespread and well-established.

R (Davies) v The Commissioners for Her Majesty's Revenue and Customs, [2011] UKSC 47
Facts: A group of tax payers considered that Her Majesty's Revenue and Customs had changed its practice, infringing a legitimate expectation stemming from IR20, a booklet designed to provide guidance in relation to residence and ordinary residence of individuals. The Court of Appeal held that the expectation was legitimate.
Ratio: The Supreme Court held that there was insufficient evidence as to establish that Her Majesty's Revenue and Customs had established a practice in respect of the claimant taxpayers. Lord Wilson held that an established past practice had to be "so unambiguous, so widespread, so well-established and so well recognised as to carry within it a commitment to a group of taxpayers including themselves of treatment in

accordance with it".

Application: In this case, the Supreme Court extended the scope of the test laid down in **R v IRC, ex parte MFK Underwriting Agents Ltd [1990]** 1 WLR 1545 to established past practices.

Legality

A representation, in order to be legitimate, should be legal. In other words, the promise should be within the powers of the body making it. In **R (Bibi) v Newham LBC, [2001]** 1 WLR 237, Schiemann LJ made clear that a representation, in order to be legitimate should: "lay within the powers of the authority both to make the representation and to fulfil it".

General principle: The promise is legal if its author, the public body, has the power to make and it fulfil it.

Rowland v Environment Agency [2003] EWCA Civ 1885
Facts: For several years, the Environment Agency treated a waterway adjoining a property owned by the claimant as being a private right of way. Suddenly, the agency re-considered the situation and declared that public navigation had always have applied over this waterway. The claimant sought judicial review of this decision.
Ratio: The Court of Appeal held that the Agency's practice did not give rise to an enforceable legitimate expectation. It considered that the Agency had no statutory power to extinguish the existing public right of navigation over the waterway, and so the claimant could not rely on past conduct to found a legitimate expectation.
Application: This case gave rise to academic debate. Some authors argued that this requirement can be unfair to individuals, as members of the public are generally unaware of the precise powers of public authorities.

General principle: A public body will not be bound by a representation of its agents where they acted outside their authority in making the representation.

South Buckinghamshire District Council v Flanagan [2002] EWCA Civ 690

Facts: In a dispute about the erection of temporary building, a solicitor which represented a local council reached a settlement with the other party and agreed to drop fines. The council acted in breach of this settlement arguing that the solicitor had not been given actual authority by the council to reach such a settlement.

Ratio: The Court held that the council was not bound by the representation made by its solicitor's actions because he was not given authority to reach such a settlement. Lord Justice Keene emphasised that "Unless the person making the representation has actual or ostensible authority to speak on behalf of the public body, there is no reason why the recipient of the representation should be allowed to hold the public body to the terms of the representation. He might subjectively have acquired the expectation, but it would not be a legitimate one, that is to say it would not be one to which he was entitled"

Application: Where an agent represents a public body, the approach is similar; one will have to look at the powers of representation in order to determine if the expectation was legitimate.

Knowledge

For long, knowledge was not considered to be one of the criteria for the assessment of the legitimacy of an expectation. This idea was illustrated in the case **R v Secretary of State for the Home Department, ex parte Ahmed and Patel** [1998] INLR 570 in which Hobhouse LJ stated that: "The principle of legitimate expectation is a wholly objective concept and is not based upon any actual state of knowledge of individual immigrants or would-be immigrants". However, this position was later overturned by the House of Lords.

General principle: A person cannot claim to have had an expectation founded on a representation or past practice if that person was not aware of this representation or past practice at the relevant time.

R v Ministry of Defence, ex parte Walker, [2000] 1 WLR 806
Facts: The claimant, a British soldier, had been injured during a peace keeping mission of the United Nations in Bosnia. He sought to claim compensation for his injury. Originally, in 1980 the

government had excluded from the compensation scheme injuries caused "by an enemy". It should be noted that none of the factions in the Bosnian war were enemies of the UK. However, a few months before the injury, a minister had announced in the House of Commons that injuries suffered during the Bosnian conflict would be not be compensated.

Ratio: The House of Lords held that the claimant could not claim to have had a legitimate expectation that he would be entitled to compensation in case of injury. It was not sufficient that, at the time he went to Bosnia, he believed that he would be entitled to compensation if he was injured. He had no knowledge of the original criteria of the compensation scheme.

Application: In this case, the House of Lords made it clear that knowledge was a criterion in the assessment of the legitimacy of the expectation. However this approach has been restricted by later cases.

As opposed to the "doctrine of knowledge", the administrative law principle of good administration, which is independent from the ground of legitimate expectation, requires that policies are applied consistently to all. Accordingly, a policy should be capable of generating a legitimate expectation, even when the person benefiting from it had not relied upon it at the time. In this respect, knowledge has not been required in cases such as **Lumba v Secretary of State for the Home Department [2011]** UKSC 12 taking into account that a policy adopted by a public authority must be consistently applied and can only be departed in the public interest.

Reliance

The question here is to determine whether a claimant is required to have relied upon the expectation for it to be legitimate. Courts have developed the concept of detrimental reliance which implies that the departure from a past practice, which was relied upon, gave rise to a loss for the claimant. As for the criterion of knowledge, reliance will not be required with the same strictness than it is for legality or clarity.

General principle: Reliance is not an essential requirement but rather a decisive factor to take into consideration when

determining whether an expectation was legitimate.

R v Secretary of State for Education and Employment, ex parte Begbie [2000] 1 WLR 1115

Facts: This case concerned a political statement made by a politician as to his intentions on a particular matter if elected. His statement was not respected after the election and it directly affected individuals, and more precisely the costs of a child's education. The claimant sought judicial review on the ground of legitimate expectation.

Ratio: The Court held that the expectation in this case was not legitimate. It noted that the claimant could not demonstrate that he had relied upon the promise. The Court upheld that although reliance was not a requirement for the legitimacy of the expectation, it should be taken into consideration. In the words of Peter Gibson LJ: "In my judgment it would be wrong to understate the significance of reliance in this area of the law. It is very much the exception, rather than the rule, that detrimental reliance will not be present when the Court finds unfairness in the defeating of a legitimate expectation"

Application: In this case, although the Court made it clear that reliance is not an essential requirement to legitimate expectation, the fact that the claimant had not relied upon the promise was a decisive factor in the assessment of the legitimacy of the expectation.

The approach in the case **Begbie** was later confirmed by Lord Hoffmann who took a similar approach in **R (Bancoult) v Secretary of State for Foreign and Commonwealth Affairs (No 2) [2009]** 1 AC 453: "It is not essential that the applicant should have relied upon the promise to his detriment, although this is a relevant consideration in deciding whether the adoption of a policy in conflict with the promise would be an abuse of power and such a change of policy may be justified in the public interest, particularly in the area of what Laws LJ called "the macro-political field".

Frustrating a legitimate expectation

The fact that an expectation is legitimate, according to the criteria and factors examined above, does not bind the courts to enforce it.

Indeed, in certain circumstances, courts will consider necessary to frustrate a legitimate expectation. In this respect, Lord Dyson made the following point in the case **Paponette and Others v Attorney General of Trinidad and Tobago [2010]** UKPC 32: "The critical question in this part of the case is whether there was a sufficient public interest to override the legitimate expectation to which the representations had given rise".

Procedural legitimate expectation

In the area of procedural legitimate expectation, courts will generally refrain from frustrating legitimate expectation (see, for example **Regina v Liverpool Corporation ex parte Liverpool Taxi Fleet Operators Association [1972]** 2 QB 299).

General principle: In principle, courts will generally refrain from frustrating procedural legitimate expectation. As an exception, courts will allow frustration when there are compelling public interest reasons.

R (Bhatt Murphy) v Independent Assessor, [2008] EWCA Civ 755

Facts: This case concerned the withdrawal by the Secretary of State of compensations schemes for victims of miscarriage of justice. The claimant challenged this decision under judicial review and argued that he relied on a legitimate expectation that the scheme would be maintained or that advance notice would be given and a consultation organised in case of change.

Ratio: The Court of Appeal held that no promise was made as to a consultation in case of change relating to the compensation schemes. In addition to this the claimant could not rely on the practice that the policy would be maintained as the result would be to judicialise the political process. They were compelling public interest reasons to frustrate the legitimate expectation.

Application: This case provides a good example of compelling public interest reasons that allow the frustration of a procedural legitimate expectation. For instance, examples include situations where enforcing a legitimate expectation would result on judicialising the political process.

Substantive legitimate expectation

Determining whether a substantive legitimate expectation can be legally frustrated is more problematic than for a procedural one. This is mainly because of judicial caution when courts intervene into public authorities' appreciation of their ability to change their policies. Accordingly, it raises concerns about the separation of powers in general.

The problematic here is that although it is demonstrated that an expectation is legitimate, courts cannot enforce it in all circumstances otherwise public authorities are stripped off their powers to make decisions and change policies.

General principle: A substantive legitimate expectation can be frustrated where enforcing it would result on restricting the public body's power so as to hamper, or even to prevent, changes of policy.

Re Findlay [1985] AC 318

Facts: In this case, the Home Secretary proposed a change of policy which provided that parole would be denied to certain classes of prisoners. The claimants, four prisoners, challenged this decision under judicial review and argued that they had a legitimate expectation since they had excellent prison records and were supposed to be granted parole the next year.

Ratio: The House of Lords unanimously rejected the claimants' arguments and allowed the frustration of their legitimate expectation. It noted that enforcing such a legitimate expectation would hamper or even prevent the Home Secretary from ever changing the policy. As Lord Scarman stated in this case: "It is said that the refusal to except them from the new policy was an unlawful act on the part of the Secretary of State in that his decision frustrated their expectation. But what was their legitimate expectation? Given the substance and purpose of the legislative provisions governing parole, the most that a convicted prisoner can legitimately expect is that his case will be examined individually in the light of whatever policy the Secretary of State sees fit to adopt provided always that the adopted policy is a lawful exercise of the discretion conferred upon him by the

statute. Any other view would entail the conclusion that the unfettered discretion conferred by the statute upon the minister can in some cases be restricted so as to hamper, or even to prevent, changes of policy".

Application: This case provides a good example of the frustration of a substantive legitimate expectation where the judiciary protects the executive's constitutional functions.

Sedley J in **R v Ministry of Agriculture, Fisheries and Foods, ex parte Hamble Fisheries (Offshore) Ltd [1995]** 1 All ER 714 presented a different approach considering that courts had a duty to protect expectations that outweigh a policy choice that threatens to frustrate them for reasons of fairness. On this point, important debates arose between the competing approaches of the frustration of legitimate expectations for compelling reasons and the duty of public authority to act fairly.

The Coughlan case

The **Coughlan** case is a landmark decision which had a major impact on the frustration of both procedural and substantive legitimate expectations. In **R v North and East Devon Health Authority, ex parte Coughlan, [2000]** 2 WLR 622, the Court of Appeal took a contextual approach based upon the particular circumstances and contexts of the legitimate expectation.

Lord Woolf , in the **Coughlan** case, identified two situations appearing before the courts:
- Where confronted with a procedural legitimate expectation, courts will require the procedure to be complied with, unless there is an overriding reason to depart from it. The adequacy of the reason will be assessed on the basis of fairness.
- Where confronted with a substantive legitimate expectation, courts will refrain from frustrating the expectation where this would be so unfair as to amount to an abuse of power.

General principle: In specific circumstances, the frustration of substantive legitimate expectations may be prevented where it would result on particularly unfair situation.

R v North and East Devon Health Authority, ex parte

Coughlan, [2000] 2 WLR 622

Facts: In this case, the claimant was left severely disabled after a car accident. She had been moved to a house for disabled people and she was promised that she could live there as long as she wanted. The house was later closed for financial reasons and she had to move and find a new place without assistance. She challenged this decision and argued that she relied upon a legitimate expectation.

Ratio: The Court of Appeal held that the health authority was bound by the promise and the decision to close the house was thereby unlawful. It considered that it was unfair for this public authority to resile from that promise. The Court also noted that the health authority did not make any effort to offer the claimant a suitable alternative to replace what was promised to her.

Application: It should be noted that in this case, the Court of Appeal particularly stressed the lack of effort from the health authority to offer the claimant an equivalent accommodation. Such an effort would certainly have justified the frustration of the legitimate expectation in the first house.

General principle: Decisions that lie within the "macro-political" field should attract a less intrusive approach by the courts whereas those lying outside that field a higher intensity of review.

R v Secretary of State for Education and Employment, ex parte Begbie [2000] 1 WLR 1115

Facts: This case concerned a political statement made by a politician as to his intentions on a particular matter if elected. The promise was not respected after the election and it directly affected individuals, and the costs of a child's education. The claimant sought judicial review on the ground of legitimate expectation.

Ratio: The Court held that the expectation in this case was not legitimate. It noted the claimant could not demonstrate that he had relied upon the promise. In the words of Law LJ: "In some cases a change of tack by a public authority, though unfair from the applicant's stance, may involve questions of general policy affecting the public at large or a significant section of it (...) here the judges may well be in no position to adjudicate save at most on a bare Wednesbury basis, without

themselves **donning the garb of policy-maker, which they cannot wear"**.

Application: In this case, the problematic is related to the doctrine of the separation of powers. As expressed several times in earlier chapters, Courts are generally reluctant to interfere with high-policy where the executive is constitutionally competent.

In **R (Nadarajah and Abdi) v Secretary of State for the Home Department, [2005]** EWCA Civ 1363 Laws LJ made a number of important *obiter* comments which argued for incorporation of the proportionality approach to review both procedural and substantive forms of legitimate expectation in high policy or macro-political contexts.

He stated the following: "Accordingly a public body's promise or practice as to future conduct may only be denied, and thus the standard I have expressed may only be departed from, in circumstances where to do so is the public body's legal duty or is otherwise, to use a now familiar vocabulary, a proportionate response (of which the court is the Judge, or the last judge) having regard to a legitimate aim pursued by the public body in the public interest. The principle that good administration requires public authorities to be held to their promises would be undermined if the law did not insist that any failure or refusal to comply is objectively justified as a proportionate measure in the circumstances".

Summary

- A procedural legitimate expectation will arise where a public body has promised or represented that a particular procedure will be followed before a decision is made or where there has been an established practice for the public body to use a particular procedure.

- Recently, the concept of legitimate expectation has been expanded by the courts to substantive expectations where a promise has led an individual to believe that they will receive a particular, tangible benefit.

- Legitimate expectation may arise either from an express promise given on behalf of a public authority or from the existence of a regular practice which the claimant can reasonably expect to continue.

- An expectation may also arise from an established practice or settled course of conduct of a public body towards the claimant or a group to which he belongs.

- An expectation is enforceable under judicial review only if is legitimate. It requires a detailed examination of the promise made or the established past practice.

- A legitimate promise is clear, unambiguous and devoid of relevant qualification.

- A representation, in order to be legitimate, should be legal. In other words, the promise should be within the powers of the body making it.

- A person cannot claim to have had an expectation founded on a representation or past practice if that person was not aware of this representation or past practice at the relevant time.

- Courts also tend to look at whether a claimant is required to have relied upon the expectation for it to be legitimate. Reliance is not an essential requirement but rather a decisive factor to take into consideration when determining whether an expectation was legitimate.

- The fact that an expectation is legitimate, according to the criteria and factors examined above, does not bind the courts to enforce it. Indeed, in certain circumstances, courts will consider necessary to frustrate a legitimate expectation.

- In the area of procedural legitimate expectation, courts will generally refrain from frustrating legitimate expectation.

- Determining whether a substantive legitimate expectation can be legally frustrated is more problematic than for a procedural one. The problematic here is that although it is demonstrated that an expectation is legitimate, courts cannot enforce it in all circumstances otherwise public authorities are stripped off their powers to make decision s and change policies.

- The Coughlan case is a landmark decision which had a major impact on the frustration of both procedural and substantive legitimate expectations. It provides namely that in specific circumstances, the frustration of substantive legitimate expectations may be prevented where it would result on particularly unfair situation.

Chapter 20 – Judicial Review Remedies

The different remedies available

A claimant establishing that a public body has breached one of the grounds of judicial review may obtain a remedy. The diagram bellow illustrates the procedural requirements for judicial review and its concrete outcome if courts consider necessary to grant remedies:

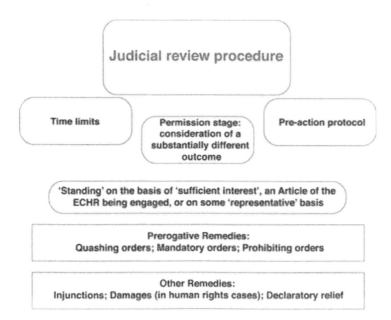

Traditionally, six remedies are available to the judge. These remedies stem from three different sources. Quashing orders, prohibiting orders and mandatory orders are generally referred to as prerogative orders. Injunctions and declarations are equitable remedies. In some cases, damages, a common law remedy, may also be ordered.

Quashing orders

Quashing orders are the most common remedy sought by claimants in judicial review, their effect is to quash or invalidate unlawful administrative decisions. They are formerly known as *certiorari*.

General principle: A Court may issue a quashing order to invalidate an unlawful public law decision.

R v Secretary for Health, ex parte United States Tobacco International Inc [1992] 1 QB 353
Facts: The claimant, a company, produced oral snuff and had a factory in the UK. The Secretary of State for Health suddenly decided to restrict the marketing of the product by adopting the Oral Snuff (Safety) Regulations 1989. The claimant sought judicial review of this decision arguing that the Secretary of State for Health failed to consult relevant economic actors.
Ratio: The Secretary of State had a duty to consult the company and had thereby acted unfairly in failing to disclose the committee's advice. The Court granted a quashing order of the Oral Snuff (Safety) Regulations 1989 on the ground that the claimant had not been given the opportunity to make representations before its adoption.
Application: This case provides a good example of a quashing order issued in a concrete legal dispute.

Prohibiting orders

Prohibiting orders are anticipatory in effect; they are issued to prevent unlawful action from being taken. To some extent, they are pre-emptive as they have the effect of preventing a public law body to act unlawfully.

General principle: A prohibiting order may be issued preventing a public body to reproduce future unlawful decisions.

Regina v Liverpool Corporation ex parte Liverpool Taxi Fleet Operators Association [1972] 2 QB 299
Facts: A local Council took the decision to increase the numbers of hackney cabs operating in the city, without consulting local trade unions and in breach of a previous undertaking that the numbers of hackney cabs would not be increased until the proposed legislation.

Ratio: The Court held that on account of this public representation, a legitimate expectation arose from the local council's undertaking. Accordingly, the Corporation could not depart from this undertaking. The Court thereby issued a prohibiting order preventing the local council from granting further taxi licences without first hearing the representations of interested parties.

Application: This case provides a good example of a prohibiting order issued in a concrete legal dispute.

Mandatory orders

Mandatory orders compel public authorities to take legally required acts. Mandatory orders are traditionally known as *mandamus*.

General principle: A mandatory order may be granted in order to compel a Minister to consider a complaint submitted to him according to the law.

Padfield v Minister of Agriculture [1968] 1 All ER 694

Facts: Under the Agricultural Marketing Act 1958 the minister had a power to refer complaints to a committee of investigation. The claimants made such a request and the minister decided to refuse because he believed he could be embarrassed by an unfavourable report. The claimants sought judicial review against this decision and argued that it was driven by an improper purpose.

Ratio: The House of Lords held that the impugned decision was unlawful because the minister's discretion was exercised for a wrongful or improper purpose. It noted that the said discretion was not unlimited and was conferred on him to promote the object and policy of Parliament's intention which was expressed through the Agricultural Marketing Act 1958. The House of Lords directed the Minister of Agriculture to consider the complaint submitted by the claimant according to the law.

Application: This case provides a good example of a mandatory order issued in a concrete legal dispute.

Injunctions

An injunction is an equitable remedy which compels a body to perform an act or restrain it from doing so. In this respect, it is similar to prohibiting and mandatory orders. Injunctions can be granted in ordinary proceedings and can also be interim measures. The fact that injunctions may be granted temporarily makes it a flexible remedy.

General principle: An interim injunction may be issued in order to prevent a public body from enforcing an act which is incompatible with EU law.

R (Factortame Ltd) v Secretary of State for Transport (Case C-213/89) 1990 ECR 1-2433

Facts: The case involved companies registered in the UK but mainly owned by Spanish nationals. The Merchant Shipping Act 1988 required a certain percentage of UK national ownership for the registration of a vessel. This provision expressly violated the "non-discrimination on nationality" principle of Article 12. The Divisional Court granted an interim relief suspending the operation of the impugned law. The House of Lords then made a reference to the ECJ arguing than nothing neither in the UK Constitution nor in EC Law permitted such interim. The question before the Court was the following one: does the incompatibility of an act of Parliament, enacted after accession to the Treaties and expressly introducing inconsistencies to EC Law, permits judges to suspend the legal effect of the domestic provision?

Ratio: The House of Lords firmly recalled that no Act of Parliament, even enacted after the accession Treaties, that would be inconsistent with EU Law, can be enforced by UK courts. In addition to this, national courts confronted with statutory legislation incompatible with EU Law are required to do everything necessary to set aside the impugned law. Accordingly, the House of Lords issued an interim injunction which prevented the Secretary of State from enforcing the Merchant Shipping Act 1988.

Application: This case provides a good example of an interim measure issued in a concrete legal dispute.

Declarations

A declaration is an equitable remedy which is non-coercive and can be disregarded without legal consequences. It is a formal statement of the law by the courts. Declarations can be issued on an interim basis.

General principle: A Court may decide to make a declaration that a public law decision is unlawful.

Equal Opportunities Commission and another v Secretary of State for Employment [1994] 1 All ER 910
Facts: The Equal Opportunities Commission sought a declaration that the Employment Protection Act 1978 was incompatible with EU law as it indirectly discriminated against women.
Ratio: The House of Lords accepted that the Equal Opportunities Commission had standing as a body acting in the public interest. It issued a declaration that provisions of the Employment Protection Act 1978 were contrary to European Community Law as they were discriminatory.
Application: This case provides a good example of a declaration issued in a concrete legal dispute.

Damages

Part 54 Civil Procedure Rules provides that a claim for judicial review might include a claim for damages in conjunction with another remedy. However, in order to obtain damages, the claimant will have to prove that the public body, in adopting the unlawful decision, has been negligent. For instance, a breach of individual rights as enshrined by the provisions of the European Convention on Human Rights can give rise to damages. Section 8 (1) of the HRA provides that: "In relation to any act (or proposed act) of a public authority which the court finds is (or would be) unlawful, it may grant such relief or remedy, or make such order, within its powers as it considers just and appropriate". This Section further allows any courts usually entitled to award damages to do so, and in the determination of damages they must follow the ECHR guideline laid down by article 41 of the Convention. It should be noted that in practice, awards of damages will be relatively modest.

The discretionary nature of remedies

Remedies in judicial review cases are discretionary. In other words, even though a public authority has been found to have acted unlawfully, courts may refuse to issue a remedy if this is in the public interest. In other words, in such cases, a Court can decide to provide no remedy at all or to order a different one than the one sought by the claimant. In their discretionary appreciation, judges may take into account the behaviour of the claimant but also the consequences of ordering a remedy, namely where it would result on an adverse effect on general administration, third parties or where the remedy would provide no tangible benefit in practice. The discretionary nature of remedies in judicial review can be contrasted with private law cases where a claimant is entitled to relief.

Where appropriate, a combination of remedies is possible. The typical example is a quashing order and a mandatory order, the unlawful decision is quashed and the public body is consequently ordered to make a new (lawful) decision.

The effectiveness of judicial review

Judicial review is a relatively new procedure in UK law. It is therefore an important topic for academic debate. The main question here is whether judicial review is effective to improve good administration and justice in general.

Factors which support judicial review effectiveness

It is undisputed that judicial review improves good administration as it forces public bodies to exercise their powers in accordance with the law as decision-makers are aware that courts may review their decisions. Accordingly, judicial review has a sort of pre-emptive effect. It should also be noted that judicial review gave rise to important frictions between the courts and the executive during the past decades. Arguably, it is a sign of healthy democracy as the executive is held to account.

In addition to this, judicial review has been significantly used to protect and improve the situation of human rights in the UK as historically human rights violations have mainly been committed by the state itself. This protection has been made possible by Section 6(1) of the Human Rights Act 1998 which created a new head of incompatibility with human rights in judicial review proceedings under the ground of illegality.

Factors which question judicial review effectiveness

First of all, it should be noted that historically, courts have confined themselves to questioning the decision-making process rather than the decision itself. Although this approach may establish procedural guarantees, the effectiveness of judicial review in providing the claimant with concrete remedies will, in some cases, is limited. This is because even though courts may quash public law decisions, they cannot replace these decisions in practice. Moreover, because of the discretionary nature of judicial review remedies, courts may decide to not provide any remedy at all, although the decision is unlawful.

In addition to this, the scope of judicial review is not absolute and some areas of decision-making such as national security are not reviewable by the courts. It should also be remembered that judicial review is a remedy of last resort, where there are no other remedies available.

Finally, the statistics of success of judicial review cases have been very controversial since December 2014 when the MOJ stated that "The proportion of all cases lodged found in favour of the claimant at a final hearing has reduced (...) to 1% in 2013 and has remained the same in 2014". However, the situation is not that dramatic. The 1% statistic refers to the proportion of cases lodged in the Administrative Court in 2013 and 2014 in which the claimant had a successful outcome at final hearing. It should however be noted that in 2013 less than 3% of cases lodged made it to a final hearing.

Yet more significantly, the MOJ's overview of the Civil Justice Statistics Quarterly paint a picture of relatively high rates of success in judicial review in favour of claimants, namely in cases that settled before a hearing.

Summary

- A claimant establishing that a public body has breached one of the grounds of judicial review may obtain a remedy.

- Quashing orders, prohibiting orders and mandatory orders are generally referred to as prerogative orders. Injunctions and declarations are equitable remedies. In some cases, damages, a common law remedy, may also be ordered.

- Quashing orders are the most common remedy sought by claimants in judicial review, their effect is to quash or invalidate unlawful administrative decisions. They are formerly known as *certiorari*.

- Prohibiting orders are anticipatory in effect; they are issued to prevent unlawful action from being taken.

- Mandatory orders compel public authorities to take legally required acts. Mandatory orders are traditionally known as *mandamus*.

- An injunction is an equitable remedy which compels a body to perform an act or restrain it from doing so. Injunctions can be granted in ordinary proceedings and can also be interim measures.

- A declaration is an equitable remedy which is non-coercive and can be disregarded without legal consequences. It is a formal statement of the law by the courts. Declarations can be issued on an interim basis.

- Part 54 Civil Procedure Rules provides that a claim for judicial review might include a claim for damages in conjunction with another remedy.

- Remedies in judicial review cases are discretionary. In other words, even though a public authority has been found to have acted unlawfully, courts may refuse to issue a remedy if this is in the public interest.

Printed in Great Britain
by Amazon

81549641R00203